DEC 03

DATE DUE

GAYLORD   PRINTED IN U.S.A.

Of Another World

ERIK ASCHENGREEN (DENMARK)

is Denmark's most highly respected dance critic and historian. In 1989 Aschengreen introduced
dance as an academic discipline at the University of Copenhagen where he was Associate Professor until he retired in 2000 at the age of 65. He has been a dance critic for the Danish newspaper
Berlingske Tidende since 1964, and a correspondent for the international magazines *Les Saisons de la
Danse*, Paris, *Balletto*, Milan, *Dance Magazine* and *Dance Chronicle*, New York. He has been a lecturer
of ballet history at the Royal Danish Ballet School and has lectured on Bournonville and dance all
over the world.

Aschengreen's works comprise: *Fra Trine Rar til Maria Stuart* (1961 – on the Danish actress
Johanne Luise Heiberg), *Engang den mest spillede* (1969 – on the French playwright Eugène Scribe),
Études (1970), *The Beautiful Danger* (1974)/*Farlige Sylfider* (1975), *Ballettens Digter* (1977), *Ballet-
bogen* (1982 (1992), with Ole Nørlyng), *Ballettens Børn* (1986, photos: Marianne Grøndahl), *Jean
Cocteau and the Dance* (1986, doctoral dissertation, University of Copenhagen) and *Der går dans,
Den Kongelige Ballet 1948-1998* (1998). Aschengreen has also been co-editor of *Perspektiv på
Bournonville* (1980) and the Bournonville website *www.bournonville.com* (2001).

Of Another World

Dancing between dream and reality

Festschrift presented to
Professor Emer. Erik Aschengreen

Edited by Monna Dithmer

MUSEUM TUSCULANUM PRESS
University of Copenhagen
2002

Of Another World

Festschrift presented to Professor Emer. Erik Aschengreen

©MUSEUM TUSCULANUM PRESS

Copy editor: Marianne Koch Nielsen

Editor of illustrations: Anne Merete Møller

English translation and revision: The Language Center, Copenhagen Business School, Joyce Kling; Gaye Kynoch; James Manley; Sophy Preston; Aline Storm

Cover design and composition: Veronique van der Neut

Cover photo: Ana Laguna in *Swan Lake*, Cullberg Ballet, 2000, Lesley Leslie-Spinks

Photo on the back of the cover: Lis Jeppesen in *Sylphide*, Royal Danish Ballet, 1989, David Amzallag.

ISBN 87 7289 682 5

Published with support from:

Augustinus Fonden

Den Berlingske Fond

Felix-Fonden

Konsul George Jorck og Hustru Emma Jorck's Fond

Landsdommer V. Gieses Legat

Nordea Danmark Fonden

Overretssagfører L. Zeuthens Mindelegat

Statsaut. El-Installatør Svend Viggo Berendt og hustru Aase Berendt, født Christoffersens Mindelegat

Museum Tusculanum Press
Njalsgade 92
DK-2300 Copenhagen S
www.mtp.dk

Acknowledgements

Of Another World has been prepared in honour of Professor Emeritus Erik Aschengreen, on the occasion of his retirement as head of Dance History and Aesthetics, University of Copenhagen.

The idea and planning of the festschrift was instigated by Inger Damsholt, Erik Aschengreen's successor at the Institute. Without her initiative and commitment this publication would not have been possible.

The publisher and editor would like to thank Majbrit Hjelmsbo, Gaye Kynoch, and Karen Vedel.

Museum Tusculanum Press gratefully acknowledges support from:

Augustinus Fonden

Den Berlingske Fond

Felix-Fonden

Konsul George Jorck og Hustru Emma Jorck's Fond

Landsdommer V. Gieses Legat

Nordea Danmark Fonden

Overretssagfører L. Zeuthens Mindelegat

Statsaut. El-Installatør Svend Viggo Berendt og
hustru Aase Berendt, født Christoffersens Mindelegat

Contents

Of Another World

Introduction

Monna Dithmer

> In ballet we rediscover the flight of dreams,
> the strange lightness that is given to us in sleep
> Jean Cocteau

The first ballet Erik Aschengreen ever saw at the Danish Royal Theatre, aged 13 and accompanied by his mother, was aptly entitled *Drømmebilleder (Dream Pictures)*.[1] As he writes in his most recent book, *Der går dans (And the Dance Goes On)*, he was struck by what Jean Cocteau called "le mal rouge et or", an affliction brought on by red and gold, a passion for the magic of theatre.[2] And a lifelong commitment has endured for this *coryphée* in the world of dance scholarship, be it in the form of reviews or books, teaching or research, for the benefit of dance not only in a Danish but an international context.

The fascination of *Dream Pictures* for Erik Aschengreen was the element of fantasy in this nostalgic Biedermeier divertissement created by the Danish choreographer Emilie Walbom in 1915. Here we have the Danish composer H.C. Lumbye sitting on a bench, peacefully falling asleep, when out of a dream spring seductive, merry figures such as Columbine and Harlequin and grotesque Polichinelle couples, while Lumbye himself waltzes off with his beloved Amélie, to the accompaniment of his own music. Such dreamlike figures and states of mind are at the heart of Erik Aschengreen's research – with Bournonville and romantic ballet as one main area and Jean Cocteau and Les Ballets Russes as the other. In both areas dance is seen fundamentally as an expression of a longing for another world. In *The Beautiful Danger* Aschengreen characterised the grand romantic yearning in ballet as a craving for that which lies beyond this world, that which cannot be grasped and which comes to expression in a man's love of a fairy-like being.[3] Similarly his doctoral dissertation, *Jean Cocteau and the Dance,* describes

Cocteau's ambition to express "le spectacle interieur" as a mythical, supra-individual universe, penetrating via the mirror of theatre into another world, one that is "plus vrai que le vrai".[4]

This is the spirit in which *Of Another World* is intended: a venture into the notion of dance as being of another world. Far from being an airy cliché, often used to locate ballet in a harmless, illusory world of fairy tale, the other world is seen to represent other dimensions of reality. In this respect it touches the very essense of dance as being an art of transformation and transcendence, dealing with the transfiguration of man, physically as well as spiritually.

The recurrence of the dream motif is indicative of the fundamental, transformative aspect of dance. Dream and sleep are an image of how dance transports us into a different state. This applies to Petipa's *The Sleeping Beauty*, the most famous sleeper of them all, to Balanchine's *La Sonnambula,* who can bring about a man's death through her seductive roaming, and to Pina Bausch's sleepwalkers in *Café Müller* as they blindly ramble around without so much as seeing the men surrounding them, lost in their pathos of yesterday. Or take Fokine's *Le Spectre de la rose* in which a young girl falls asleep only to be swept away by the soaring Spirit of the Rose. In Bournonville's *Sylphide* the dance centres on another dreamer, James asleep in his heavy chair, while the Sylphide bewitchingly encircles him – very much a real, live figure from the unreal world of dream.[5]

The heroines of classical ballet are even equipped with the ability to manifest themselves as a dreamlike spectre: Giselle as a live apparition in the moonstruck night, Aurora as a vision seen by Prince Désiré in the forest, or Odette who in a sudden revelation appears before the deluded Siegfried. Here, as in Bournonville's *A Folk Tale* – with Hilda realising in a dream where she actually belongs - dream is the province of truth. In the classical narrative manner Hilda's dream is securely inserted as a distinct inner reality within the more realistic framework of the story. Nevertheless, just like most classical ballets, it is basically a question of dream and reality constituting equivalent and to some extent merging realities, in which the world of dream is the most compelling, touching the essence of existence. Consider *The Nutcracker*, in which the nightmare and rapture of dream burst forth with such force that the actual story is swept aside. This is the main narrative route for the big ballets: to move from a more realistic world into the realm of the unreal.

Although these dreamlike states nearly all operate within the classical framework of ballet, this does not mean that ballet alone has an immediate connection to another reality. Similarly, it is not only dream that is indicative of another world; this is also emphasized by other extreme states of being "beside oneself" such as madness, grief, rage, spiritual rapture, hypnotic enchantment or passionate love. As Nikolaj Hübbe says later on in this book, "Dancing is living another reality – it's a dream, imagination made real (…) Dance and reality hold each other at bay."

Inner world

Although the concept of another world is a recurrent element in the discourse on dance, especially in connection with ballet, it is often used in a rather vague sense to refer to an illusory world or a supreme, otherwordly, spiritual realm. However, the notion of another world is more comprehensive than that.

On a basic level, not only dance but art as such *is* of another world, in that it has its own aesthetic and synaesthetic ways of perceiving, depicting and addressing the world. This is not to say that art is autonomous. The artistic approach, however is characterised by not merely representing one reality, but various dimensions of reality as a heightened, intensifed state af being. This does not necessarily mean a state beyond the real. According to the abstract Russian painter Victor Shklovsky, art de-familiarises things in order to bring us closer to life:

> Art exists that one may recover the sensation of life: it
> exists to make one feel things, to make the stone *stony*.
> (…) The technique of art is to make objects "unfamiliar",
> to make forms difficult, to increase the difficulty and length
> of perception.[6]

The painter Paul Klee adds, "Art does not reproduce the visible; it makes visible."[7] Dance has a particular access to making the invisible visible, just as other art forms have their specific approaches. Although the theatre of text is also based on the body, Western theatre with the speaking, psychologically oriented individual at the centre has always had greater difficulty in rising above everyday reality. Despite the fact that dance is the most physical of all art forms, it is basically an abstract idiom, intangible and transient, leading into a more ambiguous kind of reality, another approach to being human. The ambiguity of the the body's movement in space - physically concrete as well as abstract, with the added abstraction of time - makes dance oscillate between real and unreal, between the familiar and the unfamiliar. What is fascinating is that once a dancer steps on stage a live transformation takes place in front of the audience's eyes. Quite literally, a body is seen to become another, a recognisable being is transformed into more abstract matter and shape. As Rudolf Laban says:

> The dancer saturates his living self, his human body, with forces otherwise perceptible only separately from it and thus when he places his body before us, it appears in a transcended form.[8]

This is not just a question of the remoulding that occurs when the body is subjected to the demands of technique, but of a general transformation as the dancer works with stylized movements in the service of an abstract pattern, a rhythm, a pulsation of energies, an overall form and a more or less explicit narrative universe - depending on whether the dancer is inhabited by a character or dances a part of pure movement.

The *Gestaltung* of the human figure within the framework of a story is marked by the fact that dance is more akin to an inner than an outer reality, due to the abstract nature of dance. Quite literally, it is difficult to tell a specific, concise story in the stylized idiom of dance – as Balanchine's famous dictum states, "there are no mother-in-laws in ballet". Nor is there a yesterday and a tomorrow, no possibility to make exact differentiation between what is said and what is done. It is not a question of taking action in rationally progressive stories - even though the *ballet d'action* might seem to be trying to make it look like that - but of surrender to states of mind, emotions and sensations, situations and atmospheres. The stage is primarily expressive of an inner world, a place where a person is demonstratively part of a bigger whole, inextricably linked to other people like an inner shadow cabinet.

Ballet telling us about these men who go astray in the depth of the forest, only to meet women who in alliance with nature represent a superior force, can clearly be interpreted psychologically as an encounter with another side of oneself. You only reach home, your deeper self, having first gone astray – that is, surrendered to another power, more often than not passionate love. No wonder love, as the complete union between man and woman, is typically the grand theme in dance, with the pas de deux as the central metaphor for the harmonious interconnection between various dimensions of human life, principally the balance between body and soul. As the term "pas de deux" could be said to indicate (with a French pun): it is not two, but one. The ideal is that two persons move as one - on another level, as an image of a wholly integrated person.

It all infers that in the fluid, fleeting world of dance sharp demarcations between mind, soul and body, one individual and another, as well as between real and non-real, worldly and otherworldly, are not to be found. Identity and reality are at stake. This is the essence of the transformation in dance: whether it is in the shape of the ideal, godlike beings of classical ballet or the more everyday creatures of modern dance, the aim is to show man in a state that transgresses the limits of ordinary life or a certified reality.

The life of the immediate

In the history of dance the other world has appeared in different guises, most explicitly in the case af classical ballet. There seems to be a consensus in dance scholarship that dance is of another world only when it comes to ballet's sylphide-yearning, dreams of flight and fairy-tale stories involving both the ideal and its shadow - as presented in what Deborah Jowitt here calls "the dream-of-elusive-women scenario". In ballet, by tradition, we are out on the fringes of reality with man striving to be a godlike image of perfection, beauty, symmetrical harmony and immortal youth. The universe is vertically oriented, dualistically expanded between high and low, princes and peasants, between heavenly divinity and earth-bound, mortal imperfection - or even the baseness of a demonic underworld. Although Bournonville's ballets are set in a universe drenched in Biedermeier atmosphere and with recognisable everyday humanity – as Nikolaj Hübbe and Dinna Bjørn point out in their interviews – the point of fascination is precisely that such intense yearning, spiritual powers and magical forces of nature can emerge out of this context. The other world of ballet is a place of combat and reconciliation between high and low, between this world and another world.

What then, when we come to modern dance and its less ideal ideology, both in terms of the image of man and of reality? Ever since Isadora Duncan planted her bare feet on the turf, modern dance has been considered of *this* world, on a different footing with reality - and with an idiom which, in contrast to ballet, accentuates the disharmonious and non-ideal, the physically expressive and down-to-earth. It is a contrast between paradise and paradise lost, as Lena Hammergren discusses in her article. This distinction cannot be disputed, but it does not preclude that the other world of dance can manifest itself in different forms.[9] In modern dance the other world does not differentiate itself as a separate, supernatural sphere, it is woven into the whole in a more inscrutable manner. The modern universe is horizontally organised, as man is primarily in conflict with himself and his neighbour rather than with with godlike apparitions and base creatures. The other world can manifest itself through everyday, functional gestures or abstract, formalised movement.

When Aurora, in Mats Ek's modern version of *The Sleeping Beauty*, pricks herself, not on the spindle of the fairy tale, but on a syringe, the visual evocations are still of another world, although appearing in a drug-induced psychedelic mix of mass media dreams from lovesick soap operas, actions films or TV-shows with celebrity chefs. When William Forsythe mixes classical ballet with the release techniques of contemporary dance, or Merce Cunningham makes his own rigourous, abstract blend, the other world can be located in the mere abstraction of movement, no matter what style - as abstraction in itself can be said to point towards another world with its totally stylized art language.

Even though Pina Bausch's *Tanztheater* draws close to an everyday reality, looking for the authentic person behind the dancer, both music and costumes bear witness to the fact that this is also another world, a lost world of yesterday. Similarly, the everyday situations - through the distancing technique of montage - are expanded within a broader rhythmic and spacious structure and a context of mythical dimensions. In the Belgian-based choreographer Meg Stuart's work with the body as a piece af "damaged goods", it is the tremendously physical and anything-but-heroic flesh itself that in all its sensuousness provides access to another world. Even where post-modern dancers in trainers and tracksuits have demonstratively wanted to rub shoulders with everyday life, claiming that all movement was dance and that any body could be a dancing body, there has been a distancing, stylized element; for example, in the extreme, minimalist use of repetition, which pointed in a different, non-realistic direction.

The confrontational power of modern dance and modern ballet can thus be said not just to rely on turning the classical ideals topsyturvy, but on letting the other dimensions of reality appear even in the shape of the all-too-ordinary, as the incarnation of everyday life and the mysteries of the ordinary body - which eventually turns out to be just as extra-ordinary. In its modern versions the other world is obviously more of a *terrain vague* - difficult to pinpoint, being closely interwoven with the recognisably familiar or coined in purely abstract terms. However, it is all a matter of metaphors. Sweating bodies in crash collision can just as well serve to visualize another world as the classical paraphernalia of elusive women vanishing into thin air. It is basically a question of delving into the unknown, no matter if you try to capture it by calling it the shadow side of culture, the invisible, the collective unconscious or another world.

The crucial point is that dance has the potential of transporting you into a state of presence where you, ideally, get into contact with some sort of existential essence - as if the ordinary world opened in a sudden flash, with a subtle switch to a completely different vibration. It is "the life of the immediate", as Nikolaj Hübbe calls it. Suddenly you feel the extreme power and insight a body can possess, feel time and space expanding to reveal the reality of here and now as a plethora of different shades. The usual separation between inner and outer reality is dissolved.

In this respect ballet's flight is a direct expression of the feeling of freedom and movement beyond boundaries which we - quite physically - recognise from our own nocturnal dreams, and which is basically an experience of body and soul merging.

Here we touch upon the metaphysical notions of transcendence and spiritual reality connected to the idea of another world. Just as Noverre enjoined that dance should be "a mirror of the soul", so West-ern dance has been ascribed this privileged interface with our spiritual life ever since it was established as an art form.[10] However, it has always been a sort of mystery how the soul actually got into dance. With batterie and press-ups? How can the Western body, being ideologically separated from and subordinated to spiritual matter, suddenly dance hand in hand with the soul? In his ingenious essay on the nature of dance, *Über das Marionettentheater*, the romantic writer Heinrich von Kleist ponders upon this alluring mystery: how to follow "the path of the dancer's soul".[11] With a dancing marionette and a fencing bear as models, he conjures up the potential of dance to enter paradise through a backdoor. By surrendering to the abstract form, physical mechanics and sensuous intelligence of dance, beyond the control of individual, rational consciousness, there is a possibility of finding the path of the soul - this being a concord between body and soul, our outer and inner existence.

As a physical cognitive form in which you think with the body, feel with the thought and allow the spirit to flow, dance can ideally be said to represent a place beyond schism of outer and inner. Thus it constitutes a necessary cognitive position in contemporary culture, which in its external cultivation of the body is still a stranger to the insight the body accommodates, not least as the domicile of the soul. The words of the philosopher Walter Benjamin still hold true, claiming that the body, especially your own body, is "that most forgotten land".[12]

Excursions into paradise and paradise lost

Once you venture into the field of another world, the compass is wide – as is evident from the articles in this book, which in accordance with the broad scope proper to anthologies address widely different subject areas with more or less direct relation to the overall theme. With Bournonville as the figurehead, the first part of the book looks at the romantic Golden Age of ballet in which the other reality of dance is cultivated as a magical world of flighty women and men split between ideal and reality.

With reference to the inspiration Bournonville absorbed during his period of study in Paris, which was so critical to his work, Ivor Guest gives a picture of the French ballet tradition at the time through a portrait of the great mime Sophie Chevigny. Mime was considered to be equally important as the actual dance, whether in the elevated passion of tragedy or the down-to-earth vitality of comedy.

Based on Bournonville's complex friendship with Hans Christian Andersen, Ebbe Mørk's essay uncovers what lay hidden behind his upright, bourgeois image as respected artist and family man: an at times inordinate self-esteem and an impassioned temperament, as was evident, for example, in his mounting jealousy of Hans Christian Andersen's international fame, while he himself feared that his ballets would be consigned to oblivion.

John Christian Jørgensen investigates Bournonville's dilemma between the ideal of the critic as the happy interpreter for the people and his less ideal experience of the critic as "a deaf onlooker at a ball". His own ballets were, however, subject to a veritable storm of approval and a more perceptive treatment than from the dance critics of today who, according to Jørgensen, are more concerned with writing in an entertaining fashion than with the actual analysis of what they write about.

Ole Nørlyng finds the other world in the way Danish Golden Age art treated Italy as the essence of popular culture and passion, concentrated in the image of the carefree dancing Italian. As in Bournonville's ballets, dance in Wilhelm Marstrand's paintings appears as images of desire, in which the dynamics between man and woman have to be toned down so as not to jeopardise the sacrosanct harmony of the times.

In interview form Nikolaj Hübbe and Dinna Bjørn each give their view of Bournonville and the other world. Hübbe highlights the ballets' irresistible joy in dance as well as their more disquieting, psychological depths; it is a universe rich in nuance, just as the steps themselves can be both robust and earthbound whilst having a subtle precision in a light-footed flow. Bjørn considers the Bournonville ballets' unique range of human characterisation to be pivotal. There is an intimacy in the dance, something vulnerable and recognisable in the characters, as well as a direct approach to an inner world.

The second part of the book deals with modern dance since 1900 and that paradise lost in which dance lands on bare feet in a more earthbound, physical form, and comes to grips with another world that is no longer to be distinguished as a separate otherworldly realm. Monna Dithmer's reflections on the animal as a key existential theme in dance serve as a bridge between the classical and the modern. The animal represents other dimensions of human existence, both of a physical and spiritual kind, than our narrow, individual profiles can sustain. This is shown in the description of how the animal as a shadow-picture and an image of yearning has developed from the classical *Swan Lake* to Mats Ek's erotic swans and the distorted organic figures of butoh dance.

Lena Hammergren points out that one should not dismiss ballet at the turn of the 19th – 20th century as a degenerate form and mourn the loss of the classical ideal of beauty and 19th-century dance paradise. A new ballet aesthetic emerged, inspired by modern dance with its physicality, plasticity and rhythmic flow; a new dance euphoria took shape, more closely connected to a modern reality. The romantic dream of passionate heroes and ethereal female beings was, in Deborah Jowitt's analysis, subverted by Nijinsky's *Faune* with its taut modernist form, stylized nymph-hunt and demonstrative sexuality. Furthermore, the erotic tension between faun and nymph in Jerome Robbins's relaxed, subtle touch becomes a question of reflecting this relationship in dance's world of mirrors.

With regard to the other world as revealed in the intangible relationship between music and dance, Stephanie Jordan points out that rather than traditionally regarding dance's relationship to music in terms of symmetry or visualisation, it should be seen as a multi-level relationship between two voices. This can involve both separation and fusion, rupture and rapprochement. Inger Damsholt describes how attempts have been made to explain the relationship as a marriage between male and female. Prior to the 20th century, this involved seduction, attraction and desire, but it has since, in step with women's liberation, become a case of the battle between the sexes and equal rights, in that dance sought a more autonomous status.

Whichever direction the contributors have taken as a venture into the other world of dance, we have endeavoured to follow Erik Aschengreen's capacity for communication, which can best be summed up in Søren Kierkegaard's words, "to dance lightly in the service of thought."[13]

Notes

1. With regard to Danish titles and names we have retained the Danish letters æ, ø and å instead of ae, oe, and aa.

2. Erik Aschengreen, *Der går dans, Den Kongelige Ballet 1948-1998*, København, Gyldendal, 1998.

3. Erik Aschengreen, *The Beautiful Danger*, Dance Perspectives 58, New York, 1974 (*Farlige Sylfider*, Copenhagen, 1975).

4. Erik Aschengreen, *Jean Cocteau and the Dance*, Copenhagen, Gyldendal, 1986, p. 12.

5. In this publication Bournonville's *Sylfiden* (1836) is called *Sylphide* in order to differentiate it from its predecessor, Filippo Taglioni's *La Sylphide* (1832), as both choreography and music are different and the ballet has its own performance history.

6. Victor Shklovsky, "Art as Technique" in *Art in Theory 1900-1990*, Charles Harrison & Paul Wood, eds., Oxford, Blackwell Publishers, 1992, p. 277. The full statement runs as follows, "And art exists that one may recover the sensation of life: it exists to make one feel things, to make the stone *stony*. The purpose of art is to impart the sensation of things as they are perceived and not as they are known. The technique of art is to make objects "unfamiliar", to make forms difficult, to increase the difficulty and length of perception because the process of perception is an aesthetic end in itself and must be prolonged. *Art is a way of experiencing the artfulness of an object; the object is not important.*"

7. Paul Klee, *Über die moderne Kunst*, Berne-Bümplitz, Benteli, 1945.

8. Rudolf Laban, *A Life for Dance*, London, MacDonald & Evans Ltd., 1963, p. 179.

9. Lena Hammergren likewise emphasises that modern dance is expressive of a "paradise re-gained", but in a new form.

10. Jean-Georges Noverre, *Lettres sur la dance et les arts imitateurs* (1760), Paris, Lieutier, 1952.

11. Heinrich von Kleist, *Über das Marionettentheater*, Sämtliche Werke und Briefe, vol. III, Carl Hanser Verlag, 1982, p. 340.

12. Walter Benjamin, *Benjamin über Kafka: Texte, Briefzeugnisse, Aufzeichnungen*, ed. Hermann Schweppenhäuser, Frankfurt am Main, Suhrkamp, 1981.

13. Søren Kierkegaard, *Philosophiske Smuler*, Copenhagen, C.A. Reitzels Boghandel A/S, 1977, p. 5.

Sophie Chevigny

A forgotten genius of French pantomime

Ivor Guest

When the young August Bournonville made his first visit to Paris in the summer of 1820 he found the Opéra in temporary quarters. Three months before his arrival, in full Carnival season, the Duc de Berry, nephew of two kings and in line of succession to the throne, was assassinated outside the former opera house in the Rue Richelieu, which now stood empty and forlorn, and condemned to demolition. For the past month performances had been given in the restricted surroundings of the Salle Favart, once the home of the Opéra-Comique, just off the Boulevard des Italiens. Although it was to be no more than a temporary refuge, it would be the scene of Bournonville's introduction to French ballet.

On this visit Bournonville remained in Paris for nearly six months, during which, armed with his free pass, he saw ten of the ballets then in repertory: four by Gardel (*Le Jugement de Pâris*, *La Dansomanie*, *Paul et Virginie*, *La Servante justifiée*), four by Milon (*Le Carnaval de Venise*, *Nina*, *L'Epreuve villageoise*, *Clari*), one by Aumer (*Les Amours d'Antoine et de Cléopâtre*) and one by Didelot (*Flore et Zéphire*). He was very assiduous in his attendance, seeing *Clari* eleven times, *Pâris* eight times, *Flore et Zéphire* four times, and *La Servante justifiée* and *Les Pages du duc de Vendôme* five times each. It was a solid introduction to what the Paris ballet could offer to an ambitious young man at the very outset of his career. Later in his early years as Director of the Royal Danish Ballet, he was to reproduce four of these ballets in Copenhagen: *Les Pages du duc de Vendôme*, *Paul et Virginie*, *Nina* and *Les Noces de Gamache*, no doubt with varying degrees of adaptation.[1]

Despite restrictions of space, what Bournonville saw of the Paris repertory in 1820 was impressive enough, giving him a concentrated introduction not only to the art of choreography, but also to that of pantomime on which depended the element of narrative that was obligatory in the ballet of that time. At many of the performances he sat enrapt by the affecting silent acting of Emilie Bigottini in such rôles as Lia in *L'Enfant prodigue*, Nina and Clari, and the memory of those affecting interpretations remained with him to the end of his days. "She was," he would unhesitatingly declare in his memoirs, "the greatest female pantomimic soloist I have ever seen." [2] And how fortunate he was to see her, for by the time of his next visit to Paris she had retired. About the general standard of pantomime in French ballet, however, he was less enthusiastic. He found it strange that a nation that produced Talma, an actor unsurpassable for his mime, could produce only a few outstanding mimes in the ballet, in which the miming seemed to him weak, cold and indistinct. [3]

Bournonville's opinion on this subject was not all that different from that held by Carlo Blasis in the late 1820s, when writing his *Art of Dancing*. Noting that ballets of the quality of Gardel's *Enfant prodigue*, Milon's *Retour d'Ulysse* and *Nina*, and Aumer's *Amours d'Antoine et de Cléopâtre* had not been followed by others of equal weight, Blasis ascribed this to the defective nature of their pantomimic element - a criticism from which he was careful to exclude a few fine mimes, notably Vestris, Chevigny and Bigottini. [4] The root of the problem clearly lay in the lack of adequate training in this area for the company as a whole. Mime was not taught to the young pupils in the Opéra's École de Danse, although it may have occasionally been touched upon in the perfection class. Only Louis Milon, himself a fine mime whose wife was Bigottini's sister, seems to have taught mime seriously. Mime, it seems, was only taught when a dancer rose to soloist level; when Bournonville was engaged in 1826 after his Paris début, he found himself entitled to take not only dance classes from Vestris, but mime classes from Milon. [5] The earlier ballets Blasis cited were products of the extraordinary flowering of ballet that took place during the Revolution and Empire. Napoleon understood full well the propaganda value of ballet as a show-case of French culture, and the Opéra and its ballet were generously supported during his reign - much more so than under the Restoration. Pierre Gardel and his assistant, Louis Milon, were constantly replenishing the repertory with new works. In 1820, however, Gardel, with more than thirty years of service as principal ballet-master behind him, was beginning to reduce his load, concentrating on divertissements for the operas and leaving the production of new ballets to others. It was the end of an era, but at the same time ushering in an inter-regnum before the triumph of Romanticism a

Nina.
(La folle par amour.)

"La folle par amour." As one of Chevigny's exquisite colleagues in the French pantomimic ballet tradition, Emilia Bigottini intensified young Bournonville's understanding of pantomime as being no less important an element than dance (Bigottini in Louis Milon's *Nina*, 1818, cliché Bibliothèque nationale de France).

decade later, for he would remain in charge as chief ballet-master until his retirement in 1827.

Bournonville was fortunate to see some of the great ballet-pantomimes of Gardel and Milon before, in the natural course, they dropped out of the repertory to give way to works by other hands. But he came at a moment when a generation of eminent mimes was passing. While he was lucky enough to see Milon and Bigottini, he came too late to experience the art of several of the finest dancer-actors of the early 1800s, such as Jean Goyon, who was the first Dansomane, and Charles Beaupré. Nor did he see his old teacher, Vestris, perform, although he was privileged to watch him preparing for his old rôle of Domingo in *Paul et Virginie*, which he was to play at his benefit in 1825.

Sophie Chevigny he never saw perform either, although he may well have met her, for she was living quietly in Paris at that time, and the dance world was very closely knit. In his memoirs, however, he mentioned her briefly in his memories of Pierre Laurent, who for a short time (in 1791-2) had been assistant ballet-master at the Opéra when she was but a promising young soloist. It was presumably Laurent who told him how "Vestris together with Mlle Chevigny was forced to dance in the Choir before the High Altar of Notre Dame during the festival in honour of the Goddess of Reason."[6]

Sophie Chevigny was a mime with a great range, equally impressive in comedy as in drama, who left a gallery of unforgettable interpretations that sadly disappeared with the ballets in which they featured. Baptised Geneviève-Sophie Chevigny, she was born in Paris, the daughter of a master gilder, on May 12th, 1772. At the outset of her career she seems to have owed much to the man whose mistress she became, and who fathered her son, the architect Jacques Cellerier. Cellerier had designed the new Ambigu-Comique, and it was on that stage that her career began; for a brief spell Cellerier became joint Director of the Opéra, a post of which he was dispossessed by the Committee of Public Safety during the Revolution, escaping arrest only by the skin of his teeth. Chevigny was trained by Jean-Antoine Favre (later known as Favre-Guiardele), who no doubt brought her to the notice of Gardel. In 1790 she was engaged at the Opéra as a *double* (junior soloist), and four years later rose to the intermediate rank of *premier sujet remplacement* in the demi-caractère genre, understudying Marie Miller, the future Mme Gardel.

Her interpretative talent was soon recognised. Her first mime rôle, Mélide in Maximilien Gardel's *Premier Navigateur*, which she played in September 1791, earned her much praise for her expressive acting. In the turbulent years of the 1790s, she was one of a remarkably talented quartet of young ballerinas - the others were Clotilde, Emilie Collomb and Louise Chameroy - who perforce took second place to the uncrowned queen of the ballet, Marie Gardel, whose supremacy was cemented by her marriage to the chief ballet-master.

That Chevigny was the most interesting of the four was clearly the opinion of Noverre, who wrote of her:

> Her dancing is perfect, her execution lively and brilliant. The formation and linking of her steps are correct and well defined; she has strength and grace, and as a dancer combines all the qualities and charms that her art demands. But Nature has not been content with endowing her with grace, vigour and agility; it has been lavish with other gifts: a noble countenance framing two lovely eyes that can express anything at will; mobile features ideal for conveying any passion; gestures which are eloquent because they come from the soul and are perfectly performed whatever the meaning or emotion to be depicted. As an outstanding mime she is not to be overlooked. Her speech has no need for a tongue, for she can declaim without recourse to her voice.[7]

In 1801 Milon was the first to recognise her acting gifts, casting her as the innkeeper's daughter, Quitterie, in his hilarious comic ballet, *Les Noces de Gamache*. She made an immediate impression as the naive heroine, delighting the public as much by the irrepressible verve of her acting as by her dancing. Vestris, playing her young lover Basile, was still at the peak of his powers, and they were featured in two brilliant dances in the Spanish style. The first of these had an interesting history. A short time before, she, Gardel and Milon had dined with the Spanish ambassador, who had entertained them with a dance performed by a young relative. Both Gardel and Milon committed it to memory with the intention of one day using it, and it was Milon who first found the opportunity to present it on the stage.

In 1803 Chevigny had the misfortune to contract an illness that interrupted her career for two years. When she returned, it was found that she had put on weight, and she was consequently reclassified in the comique genre, much to the disgust of the *premier sujet* in possession, Emile Collomb. Mlle Collomb was naturally far from pleased at having to share her rank with another, and the bitterness this caused was to poison their relationship. The two-year interruption of her career had one beneficial result in that her fuller figure drew the attention of the ballet-masters to her pantomimic gifts, and the last eight years of her career were gloriously marked by three unforgettable characterisations that greatly extended the boundaries of silent action within the framework of a three-act work in which pantomime occupied at least as much of the playing time as the dance.

The first of these was an enchanting cameo in Milon's *Retour d'Ulysse* (1807), in which she played Ulysses' old nurse Eurycleia who, when he returns to Ithaca after being absent for twenty years, recognises him by a scar he bears on his foot. Chevigny's plumper figure was even an asset in such a part, as Noverre observed:

> Great talent is not to be measured by a person's height,
> nor by the circumference of the waist. And furthermore,
> she has lost none of the dexterity and facility that come
> from her excellent training.[8]

Milon's scenario spelt out the action of this scene in such vivid detail that one can well imagine the choreographer, who played Ulysses, and Chevigny holding the audience spell-bound by what the critic Geoffroy called "a masterpiece of its kind":[9]

> [Eurycleia], who has been scrutinising this old man and
> comparing him with the statue [of Ulysses], is struck by
> the resemblance. She fetches a stool, and invites him to sit
> down. Hardly is he seated when she offers him a foot-
> stool. She then notices a scar that he bears; she looks at it

"Great talent is not to be measured by the circumference of the waist," observed Noverre, having seen Sophie Chevigny perform the rôle of the old nurse, Eurycleia, in Milon's *Le Retour d'Ulysse*. Chevigny's plump figure even seemed to enhance her extraordinary pantomimic gifts (costume sketch of Ulysses and Eurycleia, 1807, cliché Bibliothèque nationale de France).

again, becomes disturbed and begins to tremble. This sign leaves her in no doubt as to his identity, and recognising her master, she falls at his feet.

Placing his hand over her mouth, Ulysses enjoins her to silence. Penelope, who has been wholly absorbed contemplating her husband's statue, then turns and bows to her guest before retiring to her apartment.

When the Queen has left, Eurycleia gives way to her emotions. Her heart is pounding so fast she can scarcely breathe; joy, tears, love and respect for her master, all combine to hold her in a state of frenzy.

Ulysses tries to calm the faithful servant's agitation. He bids her return to the Queen, swearing her to the strictest secrecy. Only with a great effort can Eurycleia bring herself to leave her master, but at last she obeys, and with her eyes fixed on him, breaks free to go to the Queen.[10]

Eurycleia was a rôle of secondary importance, but her next creation was one of the two principal rôles in Aumer's first ballet for the Opéra, *Les Amours d'Antoine et de Cléopâtre* (1808). The central theme was the struggle between two women, Cleopatra and Octavia, for the love of Marc Antony. The majestic Clotilde was the Egyptian queen, while Chevigny played Antony's wife who was also sister to Octavius, the victor in the great civil war and the future Emperor Augustus. The latter rôle, that of a betrayed wife and mother, was spread over all three acts. Her appearance in the first act, to find her husband already hopelessly bewitched by Cleopatra, was vividly described by the critic, Salgues:

Octavia has effected a reconciliation between her husband and Octavian, from whom she has obtained a guard of a thousand men; she can have expected nothing but gratitude. But the services of a wife are of little account when set against the charms of a mistress. And those of

Cleopatra have already triumphed. However, Antony's better nature has not been entirely subjugated. Antony cannot look on his children without being moved; he clasps them in his arms, and is on the point of lavishing similar caresses on his wife when he restrains himself for fear of compromising himself. Octavia, astonished by such coldness, at once suspects the reason. She asks to speak to her husband in private, and Cleopatra retires, knowing that she will prevail in this struggle.

In the presence of her husband, Octavia uses every argument of conjugal and parental love: she bursts into floods of tears, clutches her children to her bosom, presents them again to their father, begging him to show feelings that are worthy of him. The faithless husband is troubled. His children kneel before him, and he is almost persuaded when Cleopatra reappears. Now victory is no longer in the balance. Antony, ensnared by a stronger will, follows his love and abandons Octavia. The unfortunate princess faints on the steps of the temple.[11]

In the second act she appeared disguised as a bacchante to keep a watch over Antony during a fête given in his honour on Cleopatra's barge and in the last act she made her appearance in an effort to comfort the mortally wounded Antony after his defeat by Octavian. Following his death and the suicide of Cleopatra, the latter's palace bursts into flames at the dead queen's order, and in a dramatic climax, Octavia braves the flames to rescue Antony's children.

Geoffroy was amazed by such a multi-faceted performance. "Her face," he wrote, "mirrors faithfully all the passions that successively pass across her features with incredible rapidity. Tenderness, jealousy, spite, hatred, scorn could not have been more realistically or more energetically expressed. All one can say about the admirable way in which she played the rôle of Octavia is that she created it." [12] And seven months later, he paid her an even warmer tribute. "Nature seems to have fashioned her to be playful and to give sensual pleasure," he observed, "so how can she excel in a pathetic rôle? Hers is a very rare talent, which is equally at home in tragedy and in comedy, and rare also because it is difficult enough to find dancers distinguished in just one of these genres."[13]

Next it was Gardel's turn to make use of those precious gifts. *Persée et Andromède* (1810) was staged as part of the festivities attendant on Napoleon's marriage to Marie-Louise - perhaps the Emperor's grandest hour when, save for the worrisome English who had obtained a foothold in the Iberian peninsular, French hegemony in Europe seemed virtually assured. Costing an unprecedented 80,000 fr., it was the most lavish spectacle ever to have been produced at the Opéra. Chevigny's rôle was Cassiopeia, and her great scene came in the last act at the moment when the Tritons carry off her daughter, Andromeda, to offer her to the dreaded sea-monster. Gardel had worked out her scene to the finest details, but it still needed her genius to achieve its shattering effect:

> Cassiopeia tries to defend [Andromeda]. Despair, tears, prayers make up for her flagging strength; she pleads to take her daughter's place, or at least to accompany her, but all to no avail. Several Tritons from across the water have already borne Andromeda away, while others hold back her unfortunate mother. At last her strength fails her, and she falls, as if lifeless, to the ground. In this cruel situation the Tritons abandon her.
>
> Cassiopeia comes to her senses and opens her eyes. It is as if she is waking from a dream, with no recollection of what has occurred. Why is she lying on the ground, alone, and so weak? Thoughts such as these, as her gestures reveal, flash through her mind. At last she rises to her feet, stretching out her arms as if seeking help.
>
> At this moment sounds of rejoicing are heard, and Perseus appears, surrounded by an immense crowd bearing him in triumph. Everyone around him carries a palm or a laurel wreath which are offered to him as they dance; they press around him admiringly, the whole scene ex-

pressing the joy and gratitude they feel for the hero. This only adds to the poor queen's delirium, and she stands as if affixed. Noticing her, Perseus quells the crowd's enthusiasm. He hastens towards her and throws himself at her feet. Utterly distraught, Cassiopeia looks about her with unseeing eyes, as if unaware of the crowd, even of Perseus. She puts a hand to her forehead, then turns her head involuntarily towards the distant shore where Andromeda is seen being carried off by the Tritons. Quick as lightning, Perseus flies in pursuit, followed by the crowd. This reaction restores Cassiopeia's memory of her distress. With loosened hair, and a wild look in her eyes, she walks towards the palace, crying and calling for help, her gestures revealing the disorder of her mind.

The disturbance brings on several personages of the court. The king himself arrives. The effect on him of his wife's madness is beyond description. Cassiopeia points frantically to his daughter in the distance. For a moment he is overcome by despair but paternal love gives him added strength and he sets off after her, followed by the queen and the court.[14]

Two years later, in 1812, when Napoleon was gathering his forces for his invasion of Russia, Gardel used her in his next major creation, *L'Enfant prodigue*, in the rôle of the prodigal son's mother. It was altogether a gentler characterisation, but not without its moment of drama when, after the boy has left his native village, she decides on an impulse to follow him, only to be rescued and brought back after being caught in a sandstorm. In this ballet she was partnered by Milon as the father. The main interest of the ballet, however, lay in the second act, in which she did not appear. It was set in the wicked city of Memphis, but the gentler ambiance of the village was nonetheless effective. Geoffroy had reservations about the ballet itself, finding the character of the prodigal son "odious" and the father "too weak", but he felt that Chevigny "brought such energy and truth to the depiction of a loving mother's alarm, sorrow and joy."[15]

In the following year, 1813, she sustained a serious injury to her knee. Realising that she would not be able to dance again, she was anxious to continue solely in the capacity of a mime, but for this there were no precedents and the Opéra refused to listen to her plea and she was placed on the retirement list at the end of June 1814.

Chevigny's retirement was a cause of great concern to Gardel, who appreciated far better than his masters the importance of maintaining the standards of pantomime. Several years after her retirement he pleaded that her unrivalled understanding of pantomime be exploited by engaging her as a teacher:

> As a pantomime actress, Mlle Chevigny has not been surpassed in the rôles she has played, nor probably will she be for a long time. No one else has rendered with such perfection all the emotions required in the ballets *Ulysse*, *Cléopâtre*, *L'Enfant prodigue*, *Persée*, etc., etc. In a vocation that by its very nature is circumscribed, she has developed such a wide range of expression and effect that she has virtually no equal. As a model, she would be of the greatest use to young dancers with a leaning towards pantomime. Would it not be possible in the interests of the Opéra to make an arrangement with her by which she would return to the Opéra on suitable terms solely to play pantomime rôles allotted to her by the *maîtres des ballets* in agreement with the administration? In this way the public would not be deprived of the talent of this artiste, whose loss would be singularly felt in all her rôles; and at the same time her example and the advice she would agree to give to the young persons who seek it would form an excellent school of pantomime. [16]

Sadly this appeal fell on stony ground.

A forgotten role-model in the art of pantomime. "As a pantomime actress, Mlle Chevigny has not been surpassed in the roles she has played (...) As a model, she would be of the greatest use to young dancers," Pierre Gardel, ballet master at the Opéra (n. d., cliché Bibliothèque nationale de France).

Little information has survived concerning Chevigny's retirement. Being Parisienne by birth, she probably spent the rest of her days in that city. It frequently happened that a retired dancer would emerge to participate in a benefit performance of a colleague, and during her retirement Chevigny seems to have done so only once, appearing as one of two farmer's wives in *La Dansomanie* at her friend Mme Branchu's benefit on February 27th, 1826. From the meagre records of the Opéra's pensions, she appears to have died some time in the 1840s; the exact date has not come to light, nor is it known where she was buried. But her contribution to her art, although until now undeservedly neglected, is well recorded and must place her securely as one of the most eminent of mimes in a period of ballet history when pantomime was no less important an element than dance.

Notes

1. *Hertugen af Vendômes Pager*, September 3rd, 1830; *Paul og Virginie*, October 29th, 1830; *Nina,* September 30th, 1834; *Don Quixote ved Camachos Bryllup*, February 24th, 1837.

2. August Bournonville, *Mit Theaterliv*, vol. I, Copenhagen, 1848, p. 29.

3. August Bournonville, ibid., p. 23.

4. Carlo Blasis, *The Art of Dancing*, London, 1830, p. 200.

5. August Bournonville, *Lettres à la maison de son enfance,* Copenhagen, 1970, vol. I, p. 118.

6. August Bournonville, *Mit Theaterliv*, vol. III, iii, Copenhagen 1878, p. 230.

7. Jean-Georges Noverre, *Lettres sur les arts imitateurs*, Paris and The Hague, 1807, vol. II, pp. 160-161.

8. Ibid.

9. *Journal de l'Empire*, March 10th, 1807.

10. Louis-Jean Milon, *Le Retour d'Ulysse* (programme), Paris 1807, Act III, scenes vii-viii, pp. 30-31.

11. *Courrier de l'Europe*, March 9th, 1808.

12. *Journal de l'Empire*, March 9th, 1808.

13. *Journal de l'Empire*, October 10th, 1808.

14. Pierre Gardel, *Persée et Andromède* (programme), Paris, 1810, Act III, scenes vi-ix, pp. 26-28.

15. *Journal de l'Empire*, May 7th, 1812.

16. Archives Nationales de France, AJ[13] 80, O[3] 1665. Gardel to the Council of the Opéra, undated but submitted in 1821.

The Golden Child and the Proletarian

August Bournonville and Hans Christian Andersen – a friendship in the Golden Age

Ebbe Mørk

On the September morning in 1819 when Hans Christian Andersen arrived from Odense and saw Copenhagen for the first time from the hill in Frederiksberg, his future friend, August, son of the ballet master Antoine Bournonville, was probably already at the barre in the rehearsal room practising his exquisite steps. It was, as Andersen wrote in his journal, "the self-same day that the theatre season started".[1] The two fourteen-year-olds came from such different parts of the country and society, and brought with them such different cultural baggage that it is impossible at first to imagine that they would form a lifelong friendship. One was a golden child, the other a lonely proletarian who, on seeing all the towers and spires that he had so desperately longed for, burst into tears "and felt that I now had nobody except God in heaven".[2] This was depressingly true.

Young August, on the other hand, was a highly-stimulated, budding artist who had been carefully nurtured and who already had professional experience of the stage that they both strove to conquer, but which Andersen had only stepped onto as a hankering, ambitious amateur in the provinces. August was schooled in languages and music. Hans Christian had problems with writing and knew nothing of how to read music, let alone the social rules in the capital's world of culture and artists. Intellectually and socially there was a huge abyss separating them and this was only bridged because both became creating artists at the same time, and felt such great mutual respect for each other's work that it led to frequent and fruitful exchanges. Their characters were as different as their backgrounds.

Bournonville became a soloist with experience from the international stage in dance, a ballet master, family patriarch, a good, unquestioning Christian, and in his writings he reveals at times a somewhat pompous self-esteem. Behind this facade, Bournonville was a passionate admirer and desirer of the fairer sex. He wished to do more than just dance with his ballerina and first Sylphide, Lucile Grahn, who left the Royal Danish Ballet after their violent disagreements. In later genealogical studies a child was discovered, the result of an earlier extra-marital affair in Paris.

Andersen was less bound by bourgeois virtue but was frightened off by woman-kind except as a romantic notion. Close contact was, as far as is known, never established. He was neurotically self-absorbed, but also modest and despite his faith he rejected Christianity's principal dogma. Just like his father in Odense, who was well-read in biblical matters, he was an outright rationalist who regarded Christ as "a person like us, but a very exceptional person".[3] He regarded his talent, however, as a gift from God.

Both the creator of fairytales and the creator of the ballet were extremely vain individuals, and it was, in fact, this very vanity that produced cracks in the friendship during the closing years of their lives, when Andersen was world famous and Bournonville, in despondent moments, envisioned his own possible obscurity.

38

Tortuous road to Mount Parnassus

Andersen's first encounter with the world of ballet was, according to his own description, somewhat grotesque. Back in Odense he had persuaded his patron, the printer and publisher Iversen, to write him a letter of introduction to Anna Margrethe Schall, the now forty-four year old solo ballerina of the Royal Ballet Company. Many years later, Bournonville drew an extremely unflattering portrait of Schall, both as an artist and as a person, since her numerous love affairs contributed more to the *chronique scandaleuse* of the time than to the artistic achievements of dance. The actress Julie Sødring is hardly friendlier to Madam Schall whom she presents as a comic character, fat and chattering with a great deal of decoration in her hair. She was not, however, without influence as she was very close, in all senses of the word, to Prime Minister Kaas, but she was unable to assist Andersen when he turned up at her house in Bredgade with Iversen's letter

The alluring Sylphide. In spite of Bournonville's respectable persona as Royal ballet master and family patriarch, he wanted to do more than just dance with his first Sylphide, Lucile Grahn (painting by Edvard Lehmann, 1831, The Theatre Museum, Copenhagen).

in his pocket. We recognise the performance from *Levnedsbogen* (*The First Autobiography*) and *Mit eget Eventyr uden Digtning* (*The True Story of My Life*):

> Before ringing the doorbell, I fell to my knees outside the door and prayed to God that here I might find help and protection.[4]

> She gazed at me for some time and, as she later told me, thought I was a little crazy, for when she asked me if I had any theatrical talent, I offered to act a scene from Anine's role in Cendrillon. This role had made a great impression on me but I had seen it only twice on the stage in Odense; I had never read it nor learnt a single one of its melodies. I improvised both text and music and in order to better perform the dance scene with the tambourine (What would it mean to be truly rich?), I placed my shoes in a corner and danced in my stockinged feet. She was unable, naturally, to build up my hopes! I wept, told her of my passionate love of the theatre, I would gladly run errands for her, make do with anything, however simple, if only she would help me. She offered me one meal per week (which I never took advantage of). "I will ask Bournonville (Antoine, ed.) if you can join the ballet" were her parting words before I weepingly took my leave. [5]

Andersen continued his house-to-house appeal, from Professor Rahbeck in Bakke-huset to theatre director Count Holstein. Andersen actually entered employment at the theatre and even appeared on stage as an extra in the ballet *Nina* with Madam Schall in the leading role. He had no contact with Antoine Bournonville. In *The First Autobiography* he writes, "I went directly to see director Bournonville, but he had left for Paris with his young son."[6] Thus, it is not Bournonville but the less shielded Carl Dahlén who comes to take care of Andersen's first steps. It is

Dahlén whom Andersen later uses as a model for the naive and chatty magistrate in the story *Portnøglen* (*The Gate Key*).

It is not insignificant that it is in *The First Autobiography* that Andersen notes that Bournonville is away. Andersen was twenty-seven when he wrote it, but the manuscript lay hidden and forgotten until Professor Hans Brix found it in 1926 in the Royal Library in Copenhagen. It had no title, so Brix christened it *Levnedsbogen* (*The First Autobiography*). In the official autobiography *The True Story of My Life* (1855) Andersen makes no mention of his disappointment at not having performed for Antoine Bournonville. If one chooses to believe *The First Autobiography*, August Bournonville is guilty of a serious distortion of memory concerning Andersen's entry into the world of ballet. Bournonville knew nothing of *The First Autobiography* when he published the fourth volume of his memoirs *Reiseminder, Reflexioner og Biografiske Skitser* (*Travel Memories, Reflections and Biographical Sketches*) in 1878, three years after Andersen's death and one year before his own passing away. Here, in his portrait sketch of Andersen, he tells of a scene strikingly similar to that which Andersen himself claims to have taken place in Madam Schall's home. August Bournonville writes:

> He came to my parents' house and was introduced to my father as a hopeful candidate for the ballet. His gangling figure and jerky movements did not, however, seem suited to dance. My father asked whether he would not prefer recitation, at which the young chap asked permission to recite one of his own poems. I do not remember what it was about, but this much is certain - I recognised immediately that here was genius, and rather than us finding him ridiculous, it struck me that it was he who found us comical.[7]

If this account is true, it is incredible that Andersen himself did not remember and describe it.

No one knows when Bournonville and Andersen first met. In the first volume of *Mit Teaterliv (My Theatre Life)*, Bournonville describes his home-coming from Paris and he spends much time on Carl Dahlén's neglect of the ballet:

> The soloist Dahlén who, despite being ten years younger than my father, had long since retired "behind the dance," had, in my father's absence, acted as the ballet master and accepted a mass of pupils. These he trained to be cupids and trolls in the ballet *Armida* which he was preparing to put on the stage.[8]

In this context, written many years after the events themselves, Bournonville naturally notes that two of Dahlén's pupils in this performance were, or became, Johanne Luise Heiberg, the great prima donna of the century, and Hans Christian Andersen. There was among the trolls "no one more conspicuous than a young fellow who was recently arrived from Odense and whose debut was to be in the finale of the last act where he stumbled headfirst through a cliff wall."[9] There is not a word here about Andersen's visit to the Bournonville residence.

In 1824 Bournonville returned to Paris and his career as a star began. He was fêted by the bigwigs of the dance world and by Rossini himself, who encouraged him to become an opera singer. Meanwhile, Andersen was being plagued at home in Slagelse Grammar School by the sadistic headmaster Meisling. The two did not come into contact with each other until Bournonville's return home in 1829 to take over the leadership of the Royal Ballet and to guide it to its most flourishing period. Bournonville discovered Andersen, as he later wrote, "on his way to climb the Danish Mount Parnassus"[10] - notably, not as a dancer but as a writer. They approached an equality of status and there was already a professional contact between the writer and the ballet master in 1832 during the staging of I. P. E. Hartmann's *Ravnen (The Raven)* with the libretto by Andersen.

Whether an awkward proletarian or a world-wide succes, Hans Christian Andersen remained a loyal friend to Bournonville. August seemed more concerned with keeping the upper hand (Andersen painted by Elisabeth Jerichau Baumann, 1869, The Royal Library, Portmann's Collection, Copenhagen).

To the Italy of the dreams

Next time it was Andersen who travelled abroad, to Italy. He returned home with *Improvisatoren* (*The Improvisatore*), which was published in 1835. This contained a chapter about *Blomsterfesten* (*The Flower Festival*), a title that Bournonville used many years later - in 1858 - although the plot of the story is quite different, an unlikely tale from Alexandre Dumas' *Impressions de Voyages*. Bournonville was so taken with *The Improvisatore* that he compared it to Madam de Staël's *Corinna* that had been published ten years earlier. Italy was for Andersen "the land of my longing and happiness". It was the land of dreams for Bournonville. Inspired by Andersen and the painters, he composed Italian ballets, *Pontemolle* and *Festen i Albano* (*The Festival in Albano*) - long before he experienced the country firsthand. *The Festival in Albano* led to a touch of controversy between the two as Andersen recounted in a letter to the authoress Henriette Hanck:

> I met him in the street the other day and thanked him for *The Festival in Albano.* When he asked if I had been quite satisfied, I replied that there was something or another that wasn't quite Italian - at which he went berserk! He assured me that next time he would gladly include buffoons in his newest work; that he was no grand signor but merely a bayadere! - "You are a fool!" I thought.[11]

Oil was soon poured on troubled waters, however, with mutual assurances of loyal friendship.

It was the *Toreadoren* (*The Toreador*) scandal in 1841 that sent Bournonville on a trip to Italy. The hot-headed ballet master and solo dancer had interrupted the performance when he was greeted by boos and whistles in protest against his break with Lucile Grahn. Turning to King Christian VIII who sat in the Royal Box, he asked, "What is Your Majesty's command?" "Carry on," answered the King. Piqued by having been drawn into a public scandal, the King ordered Bournonville sent on unpaid leave. He set off for Italy and returned with his programme for *Napoli eller Fiskeren og hans Brud* (*Napoli or The Fisherman and his Bride*). If one reads the libretto, which is Bournonville's best, the inspiration from Andersen is obvious. The work also became Andersen's favourite ballet. He was as delighted by *Napoli* as Bournonville had been about *The Improvisatore*, and the day after the performance he wrote to his friend:

> It must please you to know that I am full of that which you have given us; I am saturated by it and I must tell you, even though I am fond of you. I have understood you. You are SOMETHING. Yes, your mimed poems, had they not only been intended for Denmark, would be European. I love with all my heart that which God manifests in you!... Every word flows from the heart: God will bless and laud you! You are a true poet - and I put much into this short word... first now have I fully realised what we have in you. In my thoughts I press you to my breast![12]

The writer also declared his enthusiasm for *Napoli* and Bournonville publicly. In the daily newspaper *Fædrelandet* he wrote:

> Yes, you have felt and seen, understood just right,
> And in perfect harmony shown us the whole
> Yes, it is Naples and the life of the street !
> Thank-you for this fresh, sweet-smelling bouquet.[13]

Andersen's admiration, together with that of Oehlenschläger, the Danish poet, was partly responsible for the fulfilment of Bournonville's most burning ambition. He is the Poet of Ballet, a spirit of such rank and calibre as the best in the literature of the day. Andersen had the opportunity to emphasise this in the last years of their friendship when he, despite protests from literary circles, nominated Bournonville for the Anckerske Scholarship.

A hot-headed temperament. Bournonville as the fiery Alonzo in *The Toreador*. The ballet resulted in a case of lese-majesty, and Bournonville, being persona non grata, fled to Italy on unpaid leave (drawing by Edvard Lehmann, 1847, The Theatre Museum, Copenhagen).

Enamoured with a nightingale

Andersen was welcomed into the home of the Bournonville family, which became one of his many homes and one of the places where he read his new works aloud. In the portrait sketch mentioned earlier, Bournonville writes that Andersen had a "peculiar" way of reading aloud, and it is clear that he preferred to read Andersen than to be read to by him. There were plenty of opportunities for the former for the Bournonville family were well provided with all Andersen's work, always beautifully dedicated to the members of the family.

> The purpose of these preparatory readings was probably more to give the author breathing space than to hear the opinions of the audience. Of such tips and objections that dared be raised amid the delighted applause - well, no notice was taken.[14]

The sketch is not without acerbity.

The home of the ballet master was open and hospitable for many of the celebrities of the day from the dramatic, literary and visual arts. Andersen met them all; also Jenny Lind. He had first tried to pay his respects in 1840 when they were both staying at the Hotel du Nord in Copenhagen. She was twenty, he was thirty-five years old. She found him affected and foolish, but three years later the Swedish nightingale visited Copenhagen once more and moved in with the Bournonville family. She was friendly with Bournonville's wife Helene who was Swedish. Jenny Lind had not yet sung outside Sweden and she was terrified of meeting Danish audiences and of standing on a stage which was dominated by Johanne Luise Heiberg. She had seen Madam Heiberg and was just as fascinated as frightened. Andersen was called upon to make use of his powers of persuasion. Bournonville told Andersen that Jenny Lind was in town:

> that she remembered me kindly, that she had read my writings, that it would please her to see me, he asked me to accompany him to see her and then, with him, to win her over to give guest performances at the Royal Theatre.[15]

Andersen wrote this on Sunday, 3rd September. The following day and, again, on Wednesday, 13th September, Jenny Lind performed as a guest at the theatre, both times in *Robert le Diable*, and on Saturday, 16th September she gave a concert at the Hotel d'Angleterre with arias and Swedish songs. The mutual efforts required both courage and confidence, and Jenny Lind's success was an undeniable step on the road to world fame. On the evening of her debut, a party is held at the home of the Bournonvilles and Andersen writes in his diary, "... a toast to her and to me; in love".[16]

Andersen is now swept into a numbing love affair. He read Jenny his fairy tales *Den grimme ælling* (*The Ugly Duckling*) and *Englen* (*The Angel*). On 16th September he wrote, ".. in the evening at the Bournonvilles'; Jenny and I familiar".[17] On 18th September, "Visited her; read others' poems, thought about proposing." On 19th September, ".. sent her my portrait, wrote ballads. In the evening at the Nielsens' (the actor N. P. Nielsen and his wife, ed.) where she was serenaded by 300 students; I love her, came home at half-past one o' clock and wrote letters." On 20th September, "Out to Toldboden this morning at half-past four, to say goodbye to Jenny. Gave her a letter which she understood. I love!"[18] Bournonville was quite right that Andersen was strongly affected.

It is often claimed that the Swedish nightingale, as Jenny Lind was called, was the inspiration for Andersen's Chinese fairy-tale *The Nightingale*. There is, however, nothing in the text that supports this notion.

Friendship and rivalry

Andersen and Bournonville became close and used the address "thou," something that Andersen set great store by but which he never achieved in his relationship to the, otherwise just as close, Collin family who belonged to the uppermost echelons of society and who had helped Andersen from the very beginning. The composer I. P. E. Hartmann also uses "thou" in his extensive correspondence with Andersen. The friendship between Andersen and Bournonville develops, and Andersen is never miserly with his praise. In the previously mentioned portrait sketch from 1878, Bournonville writes:

Our relationship was at all times friendly and honest. I saw in him a strange phenomenon, admired his genius, and understood – through my own dispositions – his feverish craving for fame – an aspect called by so many vanity! – he could also become enthused by others' deserts, he was so pleased by my work, that is, when my works brought pleasure, but slunk away from me when luck failed. I shamed him and sent him a poem of consolation when his little play *Fuglen i Pæretræet* (*The Bird in the Peartree*) failed at the Royal Theatre.

Another time he was met by nemesis when, during a visit to Oehlenschläger, his host met him, enthusing about a book that he had just read; Andersen thought that this praise concerned his newly published *Ahasverus*, and was considerably disappointed when it was no more nor less than my *My Theatre Life* whose little eccentricities had caused so much amusement.[19]

Does one detect a hint of jealousy? The poem that Bournonville refers to is a lyrical disaster that hardly would have comforted Andersen. It includes the following:

Do not be ungrateful for your fate,
You have received much from its hand
For the poet will never lose the game
He cannot die, all his works are spirit.[20]

In this connection it may be interesting to mention yet another poem in the friends' correspondence. In 1845 Andersen had been ill. He writes in his diary:

Some days later, 5th April, I was invited by the ballet master Bournonville to a party in the morning at the

ballet school to celebrate my recovery. I was received with
the following song, performed by Mistress Egense (later
Liebe):

Wherever you may lead us
to the ice of the North, or the southern reach,
your words are song, your dance is speech.[21]

Andersen had written the song himself.

Shared pain

Friendship is often stimulated more strongly by common enemies than by mutual
friends. Bournonville and Andersen had both mutual friends and common enemies.
The relationship to the Heibergs, the great actress and her writer husband Johan
Ludvig Heiberg, who was the leading aesthete of the day and who was director of
the Royal Theatre from 1849 - 1856, was, as far as Andersen was concerned, at
best ambivalent but for Bournonville later directly hostile. Heiberg was worried
that Bournonville's central position and artistic reputation at the Royal Theatre
posed a threat to his own position. He was grossly critical of the ballet master and,
in fact, had him removed from the post of stage director in 1849. Heiberg had
absolutely no understanding of the merits of the musical theatre as opposed to
drama. In 1855 it became too much for Bournonville. He left the theatre in order
to become ballet master in Vienna, where he also came to work as opera director.
He was resolute in his conviction that he would never return.

It was Andersen who kept his friend informed of the situation in Copenhagen
while Bournonville was in Vienna. Prior to the departure, Andersen was so
pessimistic that he believed that now, "it is over with the ballet." [22] On 20th
December 1855 he wrote, "The Royal Theatre is still on its way down and all the
newspapers are attacking Heiberg and talking about the harm he is doing as
director."[23] On 12th February 1856, "There is a spiritual sickness within the Royal Theatre that the few sound limbs cannot overcome."[24]

Bournonville did, however, return for a short time, but only to take off again, this time to Stockholm where he was stage manager and director from 1861 to 1864.

Only one occasion arose for a collaboration of sorts between Bournonville and Andersen. This was when, in 1871, the ballet master found the inspiration for *Et Eventyr i Billeder* (*A Fairy Tale in Pictures*) in the tale of *Den standhaftige Tinsoldat* (*The Steadfast Tin Soldier*). The ballet was not, however, a success. In Andersen's diary throughout the 1870s are noted on many Sundays "Visit from Bournonville," but he rarely goes into detail about their conversation. On 22nd February 1873, however, the two friends were back together facing one of their old sore points, the Heibergs:

> Visit from Bournonville who talked much about Heiberg and his wife – that they judged talent according to sympathy or antipathy, frequently opposed the clever when these were not to their taste or had no need of them (Jenny Lind, I remember, was no favourite of Heiberg's). He told of their characteristic traits, their stubbornness and how he had teased them.[25]

Johan Ludvig Heiberg died in 1860.

The golden child deposed by the proletarian

Andersen's autumn was more harmonious than Bournonville's. Andersen had gained great fame while Bournonville feared for the future of his life's work. When he left the theatre in 1877 he noted with scepticism:

> I did not delude myself as to their future fate, like the compositions of my famous predecessors they would disappear as the original cast aged and retired, and other new works came to replace them.[26]

Bournonville's world-wide fame lay far, far in the future, but the ballets themselves survived even the dawning naturalism. In the same week of November 1879 when Bournonville was buried, the Royal Theatre presented the world premiere of Ibsen's *A Doll's House*, and his last ballerina, Betty Hennings, played the part of Nora. Valborg Borchsenius, who later became a key person in the conservation of the Bournonville repertoire, was one of the children in the performance.

In January 1874, Andersen had the opportunity to bear witness to his admiration of Bournonville. The ballet master - as the poet of ballet - had applied for the Anckerske Scholarship, a literary award. Andersen's diary on 26th January contains the entry:

> Visited today by Paludan Müller who brought with him the applications for the Anckerske Scholarship. He would stand shoulder to shoulder with me if I voted for Bournonville, but asked me to consider inquiring at the Ministry of Culture whether there was anything in the conditions of the fund to prevent this. I don't think we should ask, when in truth we recognise Bournonville as a scenic author who has offered the audience poetic works. There is nothing to ask about, he is among the poets, he has the right to apply and is considered by some to be the most significant of this year's applicants.[27]

Andersen submitted Bournonville's application to the Ministry for the Church and Education:

> My work as ballet master of the Royal Theatre affords a peculiar form of scenic writing that, in respect to tragedy and to comedy, is recognised by both our own countrymen and by foreigners as containing thought, poetry and invention. This does not only express itself through composition and staging, but also through the written work. In all fairness I believe that I ought to be counted

52

"I did not delude myself as to their future fate." On leaving the Royal Theatre in 1877, Bournonville strongly feared that his ballets would sink into oblivion (caricature from *Corsaren*, 1852, The Royal Library, Copenhagen).

as being among the original writers for the Danish stage and, as such, regarded as a qualified candidate for the travel grants awarded to Danish writers by the Anckerske Scholarship Fund.[28]

With the exception of Sophus Schandorph, the other candidates were rather inferior Danish writers so, despite a certain amount of opposition that Andersen strongly rejected, the scholarship was awarded to Bournonville.

Bournonville was not so generous when Andersen's - and his own - 70th birthday approached. The nation wished to honour Andersen; a committee was formed to raise money to erect a statue of the writer in Kongens Have. Mrs Melchior, of Andersen's other "close" family (in whose house he died in 1875), told him of the project and he was genuinely delighted, "I sat until late in the evening thinking of how wonderfully God had guided and helped me forward in the world."[29] The pleasure was short-lived - only until Bournonville's next Sunday visit. Andersen's entry for Sunday, 14th December 1874 says:

> I was interrupted in my luncheon by Bournonville who visited and told me the plot of his new ballet about Valdemar and Absalon (*Arcona*, ed.). I was interested and I am sure that, with Hartmann's music, it will bring great pleasure. Bournonville then talked about my statue saying that the idea was a beautiful gesture. I had many enthusiastic friends but also enemies, and now came a large section of the public who did not comprehend my significance. He was afraid if the statue were erected during my lifetime, that it would occasion the expression of opinions that would cause me so much vexation as to outweigh the pleasure of seeing the statue erected! There is certainly a lot of truth in this statement; it made a painful impression on me, and the good mood I was in this morning turned frosty. Did not receive an invitation to dinner from Mrs Melchior today.[30]

A disappointed Andersen who had just gained for his friend a much-honoured award.

The following day Mrs Melchior visited Nyhavn, and Andersen sadly recounted the story of Bournonville's visit. He notes in his diary:

> She became very angry with Bournonville! Is he mad?! Is it envy? She then told me something that she had kept to herself. She had visited Bournonville and asked if he would be involved since he represented the theatre and was a close friend. He had refused and had objected to the whole business as being too out of the ordinary. He said that if one wished to establish a Pantheon for the outstanding men of Denmark then he would willingly be involved and would grant me one of the first places – but never in my life would he erect a statue of me alone! This was the man's opinion and it had to be respected, but that he storms up to me, standing as I do outside the whole thing, and gives vent to his vexation is almost an affront, mildly expressed an example of tactlessness, of lack of consideration towards a sick man. Dinner at Henriques'.[31]

Bournonville emphasised – also in the portrait sketch – his principle that one shall not "apotheosize a person while he is alive".

Andersen was composed enough to ask his friend how he would have reacted if the memorial had been dedicated to him. To this the ballet master answered that he would feel like a ghost, having a monument raised before his death. Bournonville had not been so categorical earlier. In 1842 he had happily posed for a bust by Andreas Kolberg that can be seen today in the Theatre Museum and, in 1868, he agreed to sit for Theobald Stein - this bust was displayed at the Charlottenborg exhibition the following year. The original was in plaster of Paris but a "secret admirer" gave 400 Rigsdaler to finance a version in marble. The "secret admirer" was Helene Bournonville who donated the bust to the theatre - four years after Bournonville's death.

Those in Andersen's circle felt very bitter towards Bournonville. But this was not the only difficulty. On his last birthday, Andersen was informed that the fund-raising was complete and that the sculptor August Saabye had been asked to create the work of art. When Andersen saw Saabye's sketches he was furious. He wrote in the diary, 29th May:

> Visit from Saabye whose sketches for my statue I cannot abide. They remind me of old Socrates and young Alcibiades. I could not say this to him, but I refused to sit or even to talk with him. I am becoming more and more upset.[32]

Saabye wanted to depict Andersen reading aloud to a child, but Andersen did not want to be a "children's writer" and he could not stand "that tall boy lying in my lap". Andersen got the child removed and the final product, first exhibited after the writer's death, shows him on his own, with a book in his hand, reading for an invisible audience.

Bournonville did not see Andersen in bronze either, but he yielded a little at the end of his portrait sketch:

> The project received lively support from all classes of the nation and, as I had willingly lent my support to the cause, I look forward to seeing the statue in the gardens of Rosenborg Castle surrounded by the youth who have so avidly read Andersen's tales.[33]

Bournonville did not get his statue, nor the world-wide fame of his friend, but even so, a life after death that he had not dared to hope for.

The honoured Poet of Ballet could not bear the thought of a statue being erected for his friend and rival (Bournonville painted by Carl Bloch, 1876, The Royal Theatre, Copenhagen).

Notes

1. H.Topsøe-Jensen, ed., *H.C.Andersens Levnedsbog (The First Autobiography)*, 1971 (1962), Copenhagen, Schønberg, p. 50f.

2. Ibid., p. 51.

3. H.Topsøe-Jensen, ed., *Mit eget Eventyr uden Digtning (The True Story of My Life)*, 1942, Nyt Nordisk Forlag, p. 19.

4. *Levnedsbogen*, p. 54f.

5. *Mit eget Eventyr uden Digtning*, p. 32.

6. *Levnedsbogen*, p. 66.

7. August Bournonville, *Mit Theaterliv (My Theatre Life)*, III, 3, 1878, Copenhagen, p. 249ff.

8. Ibid., III, 2, 1877, p. 48.

9. Ibid., III, 2, 1877, p. 48.

10. Ibid., III, 3, 1878, p. 250.

11. Svend Larsen, ed., *H.C. Andersens Brevveksling med Henriette Hanck 1830-46*, II, 1946, Copenhagen, p. 393.

12. C. St. A. Bille and Nikolaj Bøgh, eds., *Breve fra H.C. Andersen*, II, 1878, Copenhagen, p. 61.

13. English translation in prose of the Danish poem *Til August Bournonville (To August Bournonville)* in the newspaper *Fædrelandet*, Nr. 833, 6677, 30.3.1842, in *Samlede Skrifter*, 2. ed., XII, 1879, Copenhagen, p. 285. See illustration on page 75.

14. *Mit Theaterliv*, III, 3, 1878, p. 251.

15. *Mit eget Eventyr uden Digtning*, p. 134f.

16. Helga Vang Lauridsen and Kirsten Weber, eds., *H.C. Andersens Almanakker*, 1990, p. 109.

17. Ibid., p. 109.

18. Ibid., p. 110.

19. *Mit Theaterliv*, III, 3, 1878, p. 252.

20. *Mit Theaterliv*, I, 1848, p. 245, *Digterens Træ* is the title of the poem.

21. According to Bournonville researcher Allan Fredericia in connection with the exhibition

Salute to Bournonville at the Royal Museum of Fine Arts, 1979, Copenhagen.

22. *Breve fra H.C. Andersen*, II, p. 332f.

23. Ibid., p. 332f.

24. Ibid., p. 341f.

25. Kåre Olsen and H. Topsøe-Jensen, eds., *H. C. Andersens Dagbøger*, XII, 1975, X, p. 33f.

26. Svend Kragh-Jacobsen and Torben Krogh, *Den Kongelige Danske Ballet*, 1952, Copenhagen, p. 338.

27. *H.C. Andersens Dagbøger*, p. 207. Incidentally, the date should be January 27. Andersen has misdated the note and writes incorrectly January 26.

28. Ibid., pp. 207-208.

29. Ibid., p. 368.

30. Ibid., p. 372f. Incidentally, the date should be December 13. Andersen has misdated the note and writes incorrectly December 14.

31. Ibid., p. 373.

32. Ibid., p. 453f.

33. *Mit Theaterliv*, III, 3, 1878, p. 253.

60

Bournonville's Dilemma

Dance criticism between harmony and disharmony

John Christian Jørgensen

In the introduction to his Bournonville essays in *Ballettens digter* (*The Poet of Ballet*), Erik Aschengreen tells how, during a visit to New York at New Year 1976-77, he had the opportunity to experience Hector Zaraspe's dance lessons at the Juillard school.[1] Before the more difficult step combinations were to start, *il maestro* clapped his hands to summon attention and to present the guest of the day, Mr. Aschengreen from Copenhagen. "Mr. Aschengreen is a critic," he said, with a rapturous smile, "and critics are by definition our enemies. But they are necessary enemies because they help us to become as perfect and complete in our art as is possible."[2] "Zaraspe displayed a beautiful understanding of the fact that we work for the same cause, even if it is each from our own side of the stage," Erik Aschengreen comments in his recollections.

The image of the ballet critic as a necessary enemy is one of several mediating characters in the schism between the non-verbal art form that is built up on stage, and the verbal criticism that displays itself in the columns of newspapers and magazines. The more the art of dancing is based upon harmony and joy, the more depressing and destructive any verbal reservations must seem. For August Bournonville (1805-79), who, in his choreographic credo, put emphasis on dance as a "fine art" that "strives for an ideal", "elevates the mind" and evokes "joy", any such criticism must have been a burden.[3]

At a late stage in his life, in 1870, Bournonville expressed some thought-provoking observations about the nature of the critic and his tasks in an essay "Om Critik" ("On Criticism").[4] This is not a crystal-clear, theoretical piece of writing with sharp distinctions and systematic consistency, but the inner contradictions of the writing reveal something of a prominent ballet master's attitude towards criticism in general and ballet criticism in particular, and it thereby touches upon the general dilemma of dance criticism. Bournonville, who himself had roots in the harmonious, provincial, middle-class Biedermeier culture, was forced in the early days of Naturalism to accept the concept of the necessity of criticism.

These thoughts were, however, not entirely new. In Denmark they had been drafted a hundred years earlier, by the philologist and man of letters Jacob Baden in *Den kritiske Journal* (1768-79) and his young pupil, the law student and theatre enthusiast Peder Rosenstand-Goiske in *Den dramatiske Journal* (1771-73). But with critics such as Clement Petersen and Georg Brandes the critical stance became markedly accentuated from the 1860s. It was around 1870 that criticism emerged as a new mentality in Denmark.

It was in this cultural climate that Bournonville took stock of his situation. The article was not a personal attack (he does not mention a single critic by name) but was instead a fundamental declaration of belief.

The gardener with the hoe

Quite in keeping with the classic tradition of the self-awareness of criticism Bournonville writes:

> The critic steps forward, lecturing, supported by knowledge and demonstrating the errors which ought to be avoided so that what is good can be given full justice. So it appears, to the utmost degree, charitable that the choking weeds are hacked away, that talent is prevented from being led astray, and that the so often seen tendencies to self adulation and arrogance among those who are gifted are dampened.

Bournonville's ideal critic makes himself in the image of Our Holy Father who having planted a Garden of Eden, thereafter gets rid of a few weeds. This picture of the critic as the good, steadfast gardener is a constant figure in the history of criticism, and appears also in the history of dance criticism. When the young ballet critic Henrik Lundgren (1948-90) in 1989, i.e. about a century after Bournonville, was invited to deliver the introductory speech for Erik Aschengreen's first students in "Dance History and Aesthetics" at the University of Copenhagen, he structured his lecture around the image of the gardener, hacking away with his hoe "trying to prevent there being too many spreading weeds and making sure that the things that need light and air also have the space they require."[5]

For Bournonville there was obviously a vast difference between ideal and reality, for, when you disregard his opening prayer about the good gardener and his obligatory closing prayer, "Rather a bad criticism than none at all", then he has many observations about critics who have misunderstood their purpose. There are those who "are led by the party doctrine or by evil passions"; those who "run the errands of the polemic"; the conceited "know-it-alls"; people who under the motto *Nil admiratur,* turn their noses up at everything; critics who want to support art that fits their own theories; academically weak critics; prejudiced nationalists who only want to acknowledge the home grown traditions, and those who, as Bournonville says, "write advertisements on demand". There are also some whose demands are so high that no man's efforts can live up to them, and then of course the archetype: the unrecognised genius who has had his works turned down, and avenges himself on other artists through his reviews. Finally, there are the reporters, who have to deliver an evaluation to the papers quickly and, therefore, do not take the necessary time to become familiar with the work of art in question, which only happens at the second or third visit to the theatre, according to Bournonville. This is truly a rich caricature album of critics, apparently drawn from experience and grouped according to the different areas of the arts.

The type of critic who reviews permanent works of art such as paintings, statues, books and major musical compositions does, according to Bournonville, the least harm. This is because no matter how much a writer, for example, is persecuted and abused, his writings, if they are of real worth, will survive after his death and bear witness to his genius. It is quite a different case with those critics who are concerned with fleeting impressions and with the moods and illusion of the stage. If they see it as their duty "to expose the hidden faults and flaws", then

Caught between the ideal and the deaf onlooker. Bournonville adhered to the idea of the critic as the happy interpreter for the people, but at the same time he was concerned that this critic turned out to be "a deaf onlooker at a ball" (n. d., The Royal Library, Copenhagen).

the enjoyment is diminished and with it the participation of the audience. The courage of the performers fails and, what is of further importance in this day and age; the production, on which time, money and effort has been spent, becomes dead capital.

With these exhortations not to discourage the audience, the performers and the theatre director, Bournonville has given his ideal critic so many other things to consider that it may be rather difficult to remain focused, so that he can wield the hoe with any precision. In other words, it takes more than ordinary good will to get Bournonville's theory concerning criticism to hang together with his practical demands.

Interpreter or counsellor

Things go from bad to worse when Bournonville, at the end of his essay, comes to the ballet critic. There seems to be an irreparable conflict between the method of the critic and that of the ballet. Bournonville says,

> in order to understand the nature of the spirit of the ballet, apart from a clear good will, a good measure of imagination is required. Above all, with a light and open mind, one will more easily realise that *the critic*, whose duty it is not to let himself get carried away, will only begrudgingly acknowledge this type of performance as a worthy object for serious treatment. The critic finds himself like a deaf onlooker at a ball where everyone swings around in whirling circles while he himself, propped up against a door post, views the scene as a magnificent madhouse.

Bournonville expands upon the disparity between the nature of ballet and the nature of criticism, further, by reminding the art-history-educated critic that the art of pantomime especially blossoms in periods of decay; by letting the philosopher remember that people only dance when drunk; by letting the music-lover be outraged over the richness of melodies that is wasted on jumps and arm-waving; by letting the critic of drama search for that which is legitimate - the word, and by letting the, basically enthusiastic, ballet reporter rush home to his newspaper and write advice on what should be shortened, which, if followed, would reduce the ballets to zero.

The ballet master admits that it would be hypocritical if he declared himself insensitive to praise and to censure. A motivated applause has been an encouragement to him, and he has never objected to criticism, as long as it has been honest, he says. In his emphasis on honesty we see something that resembles a return to the image of the gardener who dares to cut through.

Based on what he tells us, Bournonville seems to have been able to use some small tips and bits of advice from those ballet reviews that are basically positive. He expresses his use of criticism in the following way:

> Without consulting it (the criticism) during the creation of my compositions or taking its opinions as a guide for my artistic work, I have attentively sought out and used every hint that possibly could be of use to me, no matter from whom and from which source it came. On the other hand having learnt from experience, I have kept from reading those papers whose antipathies are familiar to me and whose criticism could be summed up in just one word, "Don't!"

Bournonville gives no concrete examples of how he used criticism, or even the names of the critics whose reviews he has considered useful. Concerning the critic's relation to the audience (which he for a while has placed in parenthesis), Bournonville explains, based on his proposals, that one can see that criticism "is not always the interpreter and organ of public opinion" but rather that it functions as its counsellor and imposes oppressive restraints on its expression.

I.

Bournonvilles eneſte Feil.

(Vide „Mit Theaterliv".)

„Jeg veed meget vel, at jeg har een Feil, og det er: at naar jeg gjør en Pirouette, saa kaſter jeg Hovedet for meget tilvenſtre."

The self-confident ballet master never objected to "honest criticism", especially when it came from himself. "Bournonville's only flaw," the caricature says, quoting from his memoirs *My Theatre Life*, "I know very well that I have one flaw: When doing a pirouette, I throw my head too much to the left" (the satirical journal *Corsaren,* no. 381, 1848, The Royal Library, Copenhagen).

This is where Bournonville introduces a new basic viewpoint regarding criticism. Now, the critic must no longer be the great gardener but the interpreter of public opinion. It is difficult to see how these two roles are to be combined. Doesn't the image of the gardener fit better with being the counsellor for public opinion? In short, Bournonville cannot make what he believes in theory match the experience he has acquired in practice. Regretfully he is too fond of harmony to juxtapose these contradictions. The great ballet master dances around the problems.

Never be a critic

One might think that Bournonville, after bad experiences with reviews by ignorant ballet critics of the physical and musical art forms which lack dialogue, would request a criticism based on ballet professionalism; but no. "Nor," he writes, "do I believe that you have to be a practitioner to pass fair judgement on a work of art." Now we return to the gardener perspective and away from being the interpreter of public opinion, "far too often we come up against the greatest talents that are completely blinded by egoism and bias." The logic in this argument is debatable. It seems as though Bournonville is saying that because some experts have set aside their professionalism, then expertise generally is unnecessary. If Bournonville had been capable of distinguishing between necessary and sufficient qualifications, he would have seen the flaw in his reasoning. He could have said that professional qualifications are necessary but not sufficient.

Generally speaking, logic is not Bournonville's forte in this piece of critical theorising. He personally has too much at stake. The essay falls to pieces as it progresses. Bournonville maintains the importance of criticism, he refers to it as "this meaningful vocation" and expresses understanding for the difficult position of the critic, because he "even with the best intentions" cannot help "but offend, yes even insult, the 'person', who is always behind the 'Issue'." However, Bournonville concurrently attributes irreconcilable roles to the critic – not least to the ballet critic, who now looks as though he must perform as a gardener without a hoe.

In the context of the history of criticism Bournonville is otherwise known for his razor sharp dictum on criticism, "Never be a critic, for it hardens the heart and makes it observe with coldness that which is created in warmth". This is written in his memoirs *Mit Teaterliv* (*My Theatre Life*).[6] The problem with this eloquently formulated statement is simply that it is placed in a chapter with good advice to the retiring ballet master. The quote continues with a challenge to spend efforts on guiding the young, and should the ballet master eventually want to write, then to write about the art form in which he himself has shone.

"Never be a critic" is hence not meant as a piece of general career advice on Bournonville's part. Nor is it a rejection of the importance of criticism. This, incidentally, has not kept the critic Frederik Schyberg from using the sentence as an opening to his history of criticism in the theatre,[7] where it is said that the words are typical of "the temperamental ballet master" and, further, that they "express the Danish theatre circle's general opinion about criticism." Schyberg's use of the quotation is tendentious. By making some adjustments he creates a sentence that is grist to his mill. At the same time, he has reduced Bournonville's concept of criticism to a violated artist's "No Thank-you".

As we have seen, Bournonville had his problems with criticism – not least a problem with achieving a correlation between his ideal of critical justice and the desire for a critique of the ballet that is positively disposed, out of consideration for the audience, the artists and the business or institution. But since Bournonville, even if rather equivocally, presents this dilemma, he appears much more thoughtful and interesting than Schyberg's adjusted dictum is trying to make him appear.

Emotionally Bournonville had a patriotic, romantic idea about the critic as the fortunate people's happy interpreter. Thinking more rationally, however, he realised the necessity of the critical critic. In all fairness, it should be added that Bournonville was not alone in his instinctive animosity towards the criticism of his time. Hans Christian Andersen felt persecuted by newspaper criticism throughout his entire life. Even the contemplative Søren Kierkegaard detested critics, "a critic to me is as disgusting as a rogue barber that comes running with his dirty water, used for all his customers, and with his clammy hands slaps me in the face".[8]

Bournonville's difficulties should be understood historically in a mental and institutional context. The Biedermeier poet of ballet writes his essay in a new critical time whose spirit, however, only partially intrudes into his own art form. In his book *The Poet of Ballet* Erik Aschengreen writes, "Ballets were a part of the

70

„Jeg har indtil dette Øieblik forsvaret min Post som første Solodandser." (Pag. 52.)

"I have up to this moment defended my post as the leading principal dancer." Bournonville challenged any criticism that did not live op to his harmonious ideal of the gardener with a hoe (the satirical journal *Corsaren*, 1848, The Royal Library, Copenhagen).

world of the audience and the theatre was conservative despite all modern trends in the wider cultural life."[9] Aschengreen's assertion can be confirmed by looking at the enthusiasm with which the young, critical Georg Brandes saluted the Bournonville ballet, *Et Folkesagn* (*A Folk Tale*), for its rich beauty and national significance. [10] When the great critic made himself comfortable in his seat in the Royal Theatre, he felt he was at home in the cosiness of the family.

Contemporary reaction to *Napoli*

A reading of Bournonville's work "On Criticism" very easily gives the mistaken impression that the ballet master had been pursued by petty criticism throughout his life. This was far from the truth. Bournonville was celebrated as being one of the most important cultural personages of his time. Before Brandes, the poet-critic Meïr Goldschmidt characterised Bournonville as "a genius" on stage and "great in all aspects of his art".[11] It is self-evident that not all of Bournonville's ballets were received with a flood of praise, but the most significant pieces were the object of veritable acclaim by the critics. When the ballet *Napoli* had its premiere in 1842, the leading Danish critic of the epoch, Johan Ludvig Heiberg, wrote that "our National Theatre is in possession of an artist who, in his field, is undoubtedly the premier in the world"[12] – much higher praise than this is hardly possible.

What the critics from Heiberg to Goldschmidt and to Brandes highlighted about Bournonville was his ability, in the words of Heiberg, to let the art of mime speak directly to the soul through the eye. They all highlighted the simplicity and that which was intuitively understandable in Bournonville's themes, the master's ability to make all words superfluous.

In his review of *Napoli* in the journal *Intelligensblade* Heiberg produced an 8-9 pages theoretical article in which the concepts of the genre of mime in the ballet were developed. Heiberg also discussed Bournonville's masterly abilities in realising this genre, and he refers to the "unanimous recognition which has been credited to this fine work". Just as the form of this review is typical of Heiberg, it is rare to read such a review in the ballet criticism of our time. While some would say that it should be so, others would lament the loss of academic ambition.

James
i Sylphiden.

"A genius," according to one contemporary reviewer. Both as dancer and choreographer, the ballet master met with acclaim and a perceptive critique. Bournonville's critical dilemma was therefore not the consequence of him having been the victim of petty criticism (costume drawing by Christian Bruun of Bournonville as James in *Sylphide*, 1836, The Theatre Museum, Copenhagen).

The premiere of *Napoli* took place at the Royal Theatre on Tuesday 29th March 1842. The following day news of the ballet was on the front page of the major newspapers. *Dagen*, a conservative, mainly Copenhagen newspaper, with a circulation of around 1000, gave the ballet a more-than-four-column, front-page review (about 1200 words) on Wednesday 30th March. Custom had it that the reviewer was anonymous, and he spared nothing in his use of superlatives, "Everything in *Napoli* is new, immensely rich, vivacious, realistically enchanting." However, this praise was presented in a theoretical framework not unlike that of Johan Ludvig Heiberg. The reviewer highlighted Bournonville's ability to enthral and thereby captivate the eye. He praised his sense for making the portrayal of everyday life his main task, "The story line of a ballet ought to be simple and easy to comprehend". The use of space was described as opulent by the standards of the day and provided the reviewer with the opportunity to comment on the individual dancer's performance and the importance of the decorations. To consider the ballet as *Gesamtkunst* is not at all new in ballet criticism. In *Dagen's* review was included what we would today refer to as report items with, among other things, information about how difficult it had been to get seats, and about the lucrative sale of tickets that took place outside the theatre.

Berlingske Tidende, a conservative newspaper, privileged by the state, with a circulation of over 2000, also reviewed *Napoli* on its front-page as its top story of the day (30th March). The review covered two long columns, about 1300 words, which roughly corresponds to a feature article in the current editions of the same newspaper. The anonymous critic - judging from the style to be the chief editor Mendel Levin Nathanson - appraised *Napoli* to be "a perfect work of art". He recounted the story line in detail and repeatedly pointed out how much pleasure the piece had brought to the audience. The music and the scenography created "a harmony so beautiful that it produced the most enthusiastic atmosphere throughout the theatre". The reviewer's only objection concerned the performance, criticising "the female staff" for failing to show "merriment and happiness". Finally, with a comment directed towards the theatre director, the reviewer complained that the ballet (as was the tradition in the 19th century) was performed as *Nachspiel* to a play (*Kvækeren og Danserinden (The Qaker and The Dancer)* by Scribe). The reviewer was of the opinion that *Napoli* could stand alone and "easily fill out the performance time". In due time he was, of course, proved to be right.

Fædrelandet, an opposition, liberal newspaper with a circulation of about 1500 also had *Napoli* as the top story of the day. The newspaper was still primarily a political organ and, instead of giving a review of the ballet, presented a poem "To August Bournonville":

> Yes, you have felt and seen, understood just right,
> And in perfect harmony shown us the whole
> Yes, it is Naples and the life of the street !
> Thank-you for this fresh, sweet-smelling bouquet.

Although this was possibly not great poetry, it was well-meaning and had great effect. The poem was signed Hans Christian Andersen.

The reception of *Napoli* bears witness to Bournonville's high status in a small cultural environment, in which the Royal Theatre was the absolute centre. The reviews ranged from pure lyrical applause (Hans Christian Andersen), to journalistic documentation and aesthetic analysis (*Dagen* and *Berlingske*), and finally to academic discourse (Heiberg).

Specialisation

While ballet reviews in Bournonville's century were, primarily, the work of literary and theatre critics - Heiberg, Goldschmidt, Clemens Petersen, Georg and Edvard Brandes - in the 1900s we have a ballet criticism written by actual ballet specialists. According to the article on ballet criticism in *Den Store Danske Encyklopædi (The Great Danish Encyclopaedia)*, a further specialisation occurs at the end of the 20th century in the form of critics of classical ballet and critics of various new dance forms. [13]

This specialisation is an expression of a general critical-historical trend. Paradoxically, the reviewers' most important medium, the daily newspaper, has undergone a process of homogenisation or standardisation. Throughout the century, newspapers have targeted the same readership with a greater and greater expanse

Til
August Bournonville.

———

Ja, Du har følt og seet, forstaaet ret,
Og i en deilig Samklang Alt gjengivet!
Ja, det er Napoli og Folkelivet!
Tak for Din friske, duftende Bouqvet!

H. C. Andersen.

Never be a critic – a poet is to be preferred. Following the premiere of *Napoli* in 1842, the newspaper *Fædrelandet* carried a sweet-scented tribute in the form of a poem signed Hans Christian Andersen: "Thank-you for this fresh, sweet-smelling bouquet." see p. 45 and 74; Yes, you have felt... (1842, The Royal Library, Copenhagen).

of increasingly specialised material. This may seem positive: the specialist critic has the opportunity to write for a highly-motivated, special readership. But, at some time a breaking point is reached, when the newspapers lack the money or the space for such specialised subject matter.

As we know, the standardisation of newspapers is the result of the keen competition in the market. Suddenly, a newspaper may lack the funds necessary to live up to its ambitions. In this situation it is tempting for the editors to give up the most specialised material i.e. that which has the fewest readers. In other words, one specialises in order to attract more readers, then one loses the job because the material has become over-specialised. This trend, and the risks associated with it, can be seen throughout the world. The best insurance, both for the material and for the job, is presumably still to write for as many readers as possible - in a professionally responsible manner. But, for the individual writer, this may pose a dilemma.

Napoli in the press, anno 1998

How do critics tackle this modern dilemma: popular universality versus professional specialisation? To what extent are critics still facing Bournonville's dilemma: critical reviews versus consideration for the business? In order to elucidate these questions and the issue of what has happened to dance criticism since Bournonville, I have selected three typical reviews of The Royal Theatre's production of *Napoli* in May 1998: Erik Aschengreen's in *Berlingske Tidende* (conservative newspaper, circulation approx. 150,000), Monna Dithmer's in *Politiken* (socially liberal newspaper, circulation approx. 140,000) and Charlotte Christensen's in *Information* (non-partisan, circulation approx. 20,000).[14]

We notice that female critics have made in-roads into ballet criticism. The only female critic at the time of Bournonville, Athalia Schwartz, was forced to use a pseudonym. Prejudice against female critics was so strong that the echoes can still be heard in Frederik Schyberg's *Dansk Teaterkritik (Danish Theatre Criticism)* in 1937, "Female theatre critics have quite rightly never been held in high esteem" (p. 260). We notice too that the newspapers for which the critics are writing are no longer aimed at an educated elite of a couple of thousand, but at a readership that is counted in hundreds of thousands. The reviews have, therefore, been moved off the front page and into the cultural section of the newspaper. They have generally become shorter, but since, in this particular case, we are dealing not only with the nation's most famous ballet writer, but also the ballet regarded by many as his most important work, the critics have been permitted to use quite a lot of column space (around 1000 words).

In the comprehensive newspapers of today, the articles compete for the reader's attention. The ballet reviews must also make a visual impact with their layout and illustrations. *Berlingske* sent its best sketch artist to the theatre along with the critic, so that one has a pictorial interpretation of the dancers' interpretation of their roles. *Information* has a stage photo of the dancers in the leading roles as its major illustration. In *Politiken* the text had to manage on its own - as it did in 1842.

In contrast to the critics of the 1800s, the modern critic does not have to defend ballet as an art form. The physicality and sensuality that seemed provocative in the age of Biedermeier values, seem very tame compared to other parts of the entertainment industry. Now critics can get directly to the point: observation and evaluation of the idea, choreography, the plot/action, the direction and interpretation, the dance performances and interpretation of the roles, scenography, lighting and musical composition.

These elements appear to differing extents in the reviews. The review in *Politiken*, however, ignores the musical performance altogether, although this is substantially made up for in a later review of the ballet's second and third casts.[15]

The division of ballet journalism into several types and styles - interviews, reports, reviews, re-reviews - is very typical of the modern newspaper, in its attempt to capture the attention of the busy reader with shorter texts. Thus, a new version of *Napoli* also gives rise to more general, concluding comments in the Danish press. Bournonville occasions ballet criticism in its most extensive form - and criticism that lives up to the ballet master's own demands on the critic, that is to see the same performance several times in order to be able to do more than note the grace of the ballerinas and the impressive set design, to have time to immerse oneself in the composition as a whole.

To a much higher degree than in the 1800s, the critic of today must write his observations and evaluations so that they form a stylistically coherent and rhetorically convincing composition - a newspaper item that can be read for its own sake. In 1842 many people read the entire newspaper and a majority of the readers went to the theatre themselves. This is no longer the case.

The extent to which each of the three critics was successful in capturing the attention of the readers is worth studying and discussing. Here I am interested in the ways in which the coherency is achieved as these lead directly on to Bournonville's dilemma. All three critics operate on the assumption of a more or less implicit understanding of the real Bournonville and the genuine Bournonville tradition. All three express the opinion that the Royal Theatre finds itself in a critical situation with reference to this tradition.

Erik Aschengreen expresses this mildly in his introduction and conclusion, "When the ballet performs a new production of *Napoli*, we believe that the Danish ballet tradition is still alive."

> It is in the style of Bournonville with its beauty, warmth and harmony that the Royal Danish Ballet must find its national identity. This is the only way forward, and this production of *Napoli* leads us to believe that the way still exists. May they dance further along this way.

These friendly and encouraging words hide an extremely demanding message. For this critic, the Danish ballet tradition - not only in the past, but also in the future - is identical to the Bournonville tradition.

Charlotte Christensen openly discusses the "leadership crisis at the Royal Ballet" and the fear "that Bournonville will find it as difficult as the stork to survive in Denmark". Contrary to Aschengreen, she does not think that the new version of *Napoli* is the way forward. Whereas Aschengreen sees progress in relation to the previous production in 1992, Charlotte Christensen thinks that in certain respects - the portrayal of Neapolitan life and the character studies - the latest production is inferior to the previous one. The two critics disagree about the concrete details and they have quite different views, for example, on the quality of the directing, Monna Dithmer is in partial agreement with the other two. She criticises "the

Dead or alive? "When the Ballet performs a new production of *Napoli*, we believe that the Danish ballet tradition is still alive," Erik Aschengreen (1998, Caroline Cavallo as Teresina and Aage Thordal Christensen as Golfo, Royal Danish Ballet. Photo: Martin Mydtskov Rønne).

show mentality and loss of tradition that is currently spreading through the Ballet" (The Royal Danish Ballet). As becomes very clear in her conclusion, Dithmer seeks a greater depth and seriousness in the interpretation, in accordance with her understanding of Bournonville's written intentions. She believes that his intentions have become distorted by "the increasingly light-hearted direction" that performances have taken in the course of the century.

The three critics are not in complete agreement. They disagree violently on certain points, but they are in agreement in their high estimation of Bournonville and in their criticism of the way his legacy is managed on the Royal stage. They all refer back to what they each regard as the proper Bournonville tradition. It is through this process of reference that they suspend what I have called Bournonville's dilemma in ballet criticism; they provide criticism but at the same time they show appropriate consideration. Their criticism is directed towards the current management of these traditions of the theatre, but they still show consideration with respect to Bournonville and, to some extent, the dancers. Referring back to the image of the gardener, the critics wield the hoe amongst the management of the Royal Theatre, but they put the hoe away as they approach Bournonville himself. It can be said that this example is uniquely felicitous: the critics solve the dilemma of the grand old poet of the ballet by drawing on his help.

This solution would, however, be valid in any context in which one defends a certain type of art against its bad management. One genre against an author. One author against a publisher. One actor against a director etc. In all such situations it is possible to be critical and considerate at the same time. In practice, Bournonville's dilemma is seen to be able to be resolved in ways in which the old master could not or would not have imagined.

You have to use your body

How then do these critics tackle the dilemma which arises from the modern competitive situation - academic specialisation versus popular appeal ? Do they write academically for the specialists or do they popularise using a basis of professional information? In all three cases it is clearly the latter. The relatively large number of words that the critics have at their disposal undoubtedly means that some newspaper readers, skimming over the columns, will skip such a long review, thinking that this must only be for the specially interested. On the other hand, the large amount of space allows the inclusion of explanatory material for those new to area.

Charlotte Christensen in fact uses the first half of the review to talk about Bournonville and the problems that are associated with carrying forward his ballet tradition. This is reminiscent of an introduction to an essay, and it is not until after this introduction that she gets down to considering the performance itself, with her evaluation made from the viewpoint of whether there is still life and vitality in the Bournonville tradition. The pattern is recognised as that of an academic thesis in which one first presents the premises. Erik Aschengreen, in the manner of a trained journalist, gets straight to the point, it being a new production, and he makes a clear evaluation. Monna Dithmer's variation in her opening lines lies somewhere between the previous two. Following a brief reference to it being a new production, she takes the reader back through the history of the ballet in order to interpret the central themes of the piece. Thereafter follows her assessment of this production.

Technical ballet terms appear in the reviews. When, for example, Dithmer says of a person that he "springs onto the stage and divides the throng of people with a heaven-bound jeté", the context makes it understandable that the technical term refers to a certain type of jump. When Charlotte Christensen writes about one of the dancers that "despite her splendid height, she always has ballon", this can also be understood from the context. The term "ballon", meaning "airiness", is also used outside of ballet circles. Neither does one need to go to the ballet in order to experience someone dance the "tarantella" referred to by the reviewer. It is a little more difficult though when Aschengreen writes that "The Balabile in the first act had a fine rhythm even though some of the very young need to become more confident." Some readers who are not ballet buffs might guess from the context that it must be about some kind of group dance. The terminology is nevertheless limited and does not hinder future reading.

Regarding the medium in which the three Bournonville critics write, the texts do not appear particularly technically intricate. Monna Dithmer's piece is the most complex, as well as being the most inventive, including: "the national sunshine smile", "Amsterdam treaty on the horizon", "dead clever macaroni seller", "Andy Capp" and "all that lemonade makes for jerky limbs and twitchy faces". Charlotte Christensen's review is written with the tempo of classic-academic prose. Aschen-green shows off his dancing journalistic style. Each of the newspapers has a tradition for its own style. Energetic and striking reviewers are able to influence and develop this style.

The Bournonville reception of our time will lead on to a discussion of the repertoire. This is due in part to the ballets already being well known - there is no need for detailed descriptions of the story lines, although the new reader must always be given the possibility to catch up - and partly because the Royal Danish Ballet is so strongly influenced by the Bournonville tradition. Modern ballet criticism is otherwise not so concerned with the discussion as with the experience. The dance performances are seen as being able to free themselves from language, which luckily fits in with what is to be found on the cultural pages of the reviews of rock. Expressions such as "moon-walk", "headspin", "show off", "sex machine" and "showbiz" are not foreign to the modern Danish dance critic. [16] Is this opening-up of language to a new audience also a closing-off of the old? Is this whipping-up of the language a last attempt by the dance critics to survive or merely their last desperate dance before we go home?

In this connection one could also raise the question as to whether dance criticism, having had difficulties after the 19th century in accepting the physical, now, at the end of the 20th century, has literally speaking developed such a "body" of language that there is almost no place for the intellect and the spirit?[17] "You have to use your body," says the flea in Hans Christian Andersen's fairy tale *Springfyrene* (*The Jumper*). Are the ballet critics of today like characters in this tale? Is the mediating strategy of the ballet critics now based on (regardless of the quality of the performance) the dazzling, energetic style of writing? To answer these questions would demand more space and more specific documentation than I have at my disposal.

When Mr. Aschengreen used his body

August Bournonville's *Napoli* plays a quite special role in Erik Aschengreen's ballet life: he performed in it. When the Royal Danish Ballet gave a guest performance on the stage of the Bolshoi Ballet in Moscow in 1973, Mr. Aschengreen was asked to take the role of the lemonade-drinking English tourist in the third act. After the performance, he was presented with violets by the ballet master's wife and received thanks from the leading soloists in the corps de ballet. "One should not attempt to repeat such a success," remarked Erik Aschengreen.[18] One should stick to one's metier, and Erik Aschengreen's is ballet criticism.

Having said this, I owe the reader an explanation. I am not a ballet critic. My background is in literature and I have worked with literary cirticism, both historical and contemporary.[19] In connection with this, I have written about reviews of cultural topics, a few lines about ballet and dance criticism in a cultural-journalistic textbook, and an essay-like portrait of Erik Aschengreen as a ballet critic in a book about cultural critics in Denmark.[20] My steps move in a critical-historical direction. In relation to the criticism of ballet, I stand in the wings as an interested, metacritical observer.

Notes

1. Erik Aschengreen, *Ballettens digter. 3 Bournonville-essays,* Copenhagen, Rhodos 1977.

2. Op. cit. p. 13.

3. August Bournonville, "Choreographisk Troesbekjendelse", 1865, photographic reproduction in Aschengreen op. cit. pp. 10-11.

4. August Bournonville, "Om Critik" in *August Bournonville, Efterladte Skrifter,* ed. Charlotte Bournonville, Copenhagen, André Schous Forlag, 1891. The following Bournonville quotations stem from this essay.

5. Henrik Lundgren, "Det kan se brutalt ud, når gartneren svinger lugejernet" in Henrik Lundgren, *Mellem Dans og Drøm,* eds. Marie-Louise Kjølbye and Anne McClymont, Copenhagen, Spektrum, 1993.

6. August Bournonville's memoirs, *Mit Theaterliv,* publ. in three vol. in 1848, 1865 and 1877-78. These works are reprinted in two vol. by Niels Birger Wamberg, Copenhagen, Thaning & Appel, 1979. The quotation "Never be a critic, as it hardens the heart and makes it observe with coldness that which is created in warmth" is to be found in this edition vol. 1, p. 227.

7. Frederik Schyberg, *Dansk teaterkritik indtil 1914,* Copenhagen, Gyldendal, 1937. Schyberg quotes Bournonville's dictum p. 7.

8. Niels Thulstrup, ed., *Søren Kierkegaards Papirer,* 2nd enlarged edition, Copenhagen, 1968, vol. IV A, p. 167.

9. Op. cit. Aschengreen, 1977.

10. Georg Brandes, *Kritiker og Portraiter,* Copenhagen, Gyldendal, 1870, see especially p. 194.

11. Meïr Goldschmidt, *Nord og Syd,* vol. 1, Copenhagen, 1848, pp. 76-77.

12. Johan Ludvig Heiberg, "Balletten Napoli", in *Intelligensblade,* 1842, No. 4, printed p. 271 ff. in Johan Ludvig Heiberg, *Prosaiske Skrifter,* vol. 7, Copenhagen, C. A. Reitzels Forlag, 1861.

13. Anne Flindt (now: Middelboe) Christensen, "Balletkritik", in *Den Store Danske Encyklopædi,* vol. 2, Copenhagen, Gyldendal, 1995. About the history of the Danish ballet critics, see same author's *Dansen med ordet. Dansk balletkritik - set gennem fem balletanmeldere 1771-1862 ,* master's dissertation from the Institute of Nordic Philology, University of Copenhagen, 1991, unpubl., summarised in "Jagten på anmeldelserne", in *Dansk Dansehistorisk Arkivs Årsskrift,* Copenhagen, 1992.

14. Erik Aschengreen, "Sol over Napoli", *Berlingske Tidende* 18.5.98, Monna Dithmer, "Uanede

dybder", *Politiken* 18.5.98, Charlotte Christensen, "Den italienske dansedrøm", *Information* 18.5.98.

15. *Politiken* 27.5.98.

16. Expressions found in the following reviews of a Brazilian dance performance in Copenhagen, Vibeke Wern, "Farvestrålende dans", *Berlingske Tidende* 11.7.98, Lise Garsdal, "Brasilianere i hårdtpumpet erotisk dans", *Politiken* 11.7.98, Anne Middelboe Christensen, "VM-sejr til Brasilien", *Information* 11.7.98.

17. See Flindt Christensen, op. cit., 1992.

18. Op. cit. Aschengreen, 1977, p. 15.

19. John Chr. Jørgensen, *Det danske anmelderis historie. Den litterære anmeldelses opståen og udvikling 1720-1906*, Copenhagen, Fisker & Schou, 1994 (English summary: "The History of Literary Reviewing in Denmark" pp. 314-19); *Dagbladskritikeren. Essays om at skrive, redigere og analysere boganmeldelser*, Fisker & Schou, Copenhagen, 1994; *Sprogblomster i spinatbedet. En bog om kritikersproget,* Copenhagen, Fremad, 1999.

20. John Chr. Jørgensen, *Kultur i avisen. En grundbog i kulturjournalistik*, Copenhagen, Gyldendal, 1991; *Kulturanmeldere i Danmark*, Copenhagen, Fremad, 1991.

The Finishing Touch

The saltarello as a pictorial motif

Ole Nørlyng

The art of the Danish Golden Age has its icons; works of art of such beauty, such illustrative power and such richness of meaning that they reach beyond the actual canvas and its motif. Their content is so comprehensive that they have created terminology and have become ingrained concepts. They bring, so to speak, a message of another world. Such an icon is the Golden Age's visual manifestation of the lifestyle of the South, a representation of the Italian *dolce far niente* attitude to life as painted by Wilhelm Marstrand and captured on the stage by the Italian ballets of August Bournonville. In both cases, the portrayal culminates in the rendering of the archetypal, carefree, dancing Italian. Here we find a whole epoch's image of the country with its "entourage of the romantics ... the gold of the oranges, the purple of the grapes," where "beauty, joy and song melt the Nordic Life" (Schack Staffeldt, 1800).

Viewed against the background of life in modern Italy, we are tempted nowadays to regard this image of *joie de vivre* in its most untroubled and pure form as an elaborate romantic myth. The picture of the Italian as carefree and dancing was cemented in the works of innumerable artists in the first half of the19th century. Artists who, during visits to the southern sun, painted visual proof after visual proof of this abundant vitality. A picture that stands in sharp contrast to the life lived in Italian cities today. It is not, however, merely an empty, romantic myth – not, at least, if one ventures far enough into the countryside. I dare to make this claim having been with a crowd of happy pensioners in Sicily, on the way back from a coach excursion to Mount Etna. The group could not resist dancing in the aisle of the bus to the tune of the loudspeakers' harmonica and tambourine, whistling and singing, making sparks fly, "Da da da di di, da da da di di, da da da di di."

Old women of enormous girth and gentlemen with greying temples and heavy stomachs moved heel-toe, heel-toe to the somewhat repetitive, bubbling semi-quavers of the tune, while their hands swayed to right and left, interrupted by four sharp, rhythmic claps. Since floor space in a coach is, naturally, rather limited, the variations introduced by movements of the hands and arms played the most important role. One can, it seems, dance the tarantella equally well sitting down while tapping out the rhythm on one's newly acquired bingo prizes. Even an extremely pessimistic retired radiotelegraphist, who believed that Garibaldi was the worst disaster ever to befall Italy and that Sicily, in a few years, would be just like Africa, joined the drumming on the boxed-set of bed linen that he had won a few hours earlier. Oh yes, it still happens. It is not just a dream.

When travelling, the distance to the reality back home is increased considerably and, at the same time, one is receptive to a whole range of other - new - realities. The busy reality of everyday life loses its significance while this new openness blossoms. We hope to encounter just a little of whatever it is that could change our lives. Thus, a tarantella, with its joy and erotic undertones, danced en route through the lava flows, can be an incredibly powerful experience - as if of another world.

Dance as a pictorial motif

Subjective experience is one thing, the image of the dancing Italian as a fixed pictorial motif is something different. Is it at all possible in a picture to capture and convey any of the spirit outlined in the introduction? What picture of the dance is conveyed by pictorial art?

Dance is the body in more or less codified movements in time and space, to some form of rhythmic or musical accompaniment. The nature of dance is essentially ephemeral. Pictorial art - in its traditional form - is static and silent. Therefore, only a small part of that which dance involves can be conveyed in a picture. From the standpoint of the history of dance, this is an obvious limitation. Seen from an art historian's perspective, this in no way precludes the potential for other significance.

Terra incognita. The dancing Italian became an icon for the Danish Golden Age as the representation of another world, a life not merely imbued with *dolce far niente* but with the unhampered play of passion (W. Marstrand, *Romerske Borgere forsamlede til Lystighed i et Osteri* (*Roman Citizens Assembled for Entertainment at an Osteria*), sketch, 1838, the Art Museum of Funen).

In a crucial article, "Iconography and Dance Research", Tilman Seebass attempts to define some general guidelines concerning just what a picture is able to do when dance is the motif.[1] Dance iconography, which Seebass describes as "terra incognita", assumes a loosely definable position somewhere between choreology and art history. Its research deals with the pictorial representation of dance. Its subject matter is not dance as such, but the visual work of art that exists in its own right. Dance as a pictorial motif has, therefore, little to do with the historical documentation of dance. When dance is the motif of a picture, an independent interpretation of the dance has taken place; an interpretation by the artist who has created the picture. Of course, the picture conveys information about the dance, but it contains and conveys much more than that alone. Representations of the dance are, therefore, often linked together with elements of, for example, symbolism and allegory. Dance as a pictorial motif reaches deep into such universal concerns as eroticism, death, ritual etc. and thus the representation of dance becomes a metaphor for something more than the physical act of dancing itself. In my consideration of dance as a pictorial motif, dance as a metaphor is juxtaposed to its historical documentation.

Die Welt wird Traum

The image of the dancing Italian is extremely old and has proved itself to be very durable. If one is unsure where to begin then Goethe is always a good proposition. From 1786 to 1788, Goethe lived in Italy; a sojourn described in his *Italienische Reise*, first published in 1816-1817 and 1829. Even though Goethe was well-prepared and knew what he wanted to achieve, it was a sabbatical during which he allowed himself to relax in the life that surrounded him. In his *Italienische Reise* and *Römische Elegien*, Italy - its art, its people and its customs - was canonised as the epitome of pure poetry and lack of affectation. Italy was perceived as the true homeland of art and life. "Rome is a world," proclaimed Goethe, and as Per Øhrgaard writes in his extensive work on the German author, he abandoned himself to Rome as to "the true reality - in art, in life, in nature, in love, and in roughly that order".[2]

90

Not least for the Northern European, Italy became an expression for the basic philosophy of, in the words of the poet Novalis, "Die Welt wird Traum, der Traum wird Welt."[3] Italy came to exert a tremendous appeal - not merely as the place for carefree leisure, but as the place where one could experience a closer and more genuine relationship between nature and culture, between the worlds of passion and of civilisation.

The portrayal of Italian life was really formed in the 1700s at the same time as pre-Romanticism. The first steps in the direction of an iconography of everyday life had already been taken. The Spanish Neapolitan painter Juseppe de Ribera's carefree pictures of children - for example *The Beggar*, known as *The Clubfoot* from 1642 in the Louvre; or Bartolomé Esteban Murillo's melon-eating beggar children - are examples of a new representation of reality in the form of genre scenes that emerged in the paintings of the 1600s.[4]

In the 1700s the genre expanded, in part due to the influence of the French philosopher Rousseau and his ideas of a return to nature. Numerous motifs from everyday life are incorporated into the portrayal of Italian life. In these paintings from the 1700s, it can sometimes be difficult to distinguish between pictorial convention, artistic imagination and a more accurate realism.[5] The vedute paintings of the 1600s, not least under the influence of the realism of Dutch painting, increased the pressure for a more accurate portrayal of reality, also in Italian painting. During the 1700s remarkable progress had been made in, for example, the scenes from Neapolitan life as experienced by travellers on the grand tour.

From a Danish point of view, the painting by Filippo Falciatore (documented as working in Naples from 1728-1768) *Scena di Vita Popolare al Largo di Castello* is very illustrative. Here we see the scenery that nearly one hundred years later is reproduced in the first act of Bournonville's ballet *Napoli*. The picturesque perception, as opposed to undisguised reality, was firmly established and with it the pictorial mode of expression. But neither of these, in the 1700s, had reached the cold climes of the North. Goethe, therefore, described Italy as "rich in form" and Germany as "non-descript".[6]

In the same way that the smoking cone of Vesuvius and the fun and games of Pulcinella became fixed components in the portrayal of Neapolitan life, the tarantella-dancing shepherds, peasants and gradually even citizens appeared in the picturesque description of the Italian people.

An important name in the construction of these fixed visual conventions in the portrayal of the Italian and the Italian way of life is that of the artist Pietro Fabris. He worked in Naples from 1763 to 1779, i.e. before Goethe's visit to the city. Fabris has been called "the English painter" because he had many well-established contacts with the English nobility visiting Naples, and his Italian genre scenes were exhibited in London. His *Gita a Baia* is an interesting painting - in addition to the typical Neapolitan fisherman, we see a well-dressed couple dancing. Even more interesting for our subject matter is his *Scampagnata con ballo di popolani*. The painting depicts young couples dancing the tarantella, an ox-cart ready for a trip and the arch of the open city gates - all elements later brought to life on stage in the third act of Bournonville's *Napoli*. Elements which display the innate connection for Italians of nature and culture, of the uninhibited and the controlled.

These considerations of the image of the Italian in the Golden Age serve merely to demonstrate that the artists of the Golden Age did not invent the picturesque representation of Italy. To a considerable extent it was the Italians themselves who created this image - slowly but surely throughout the 1700s. The image found its powerful expression, however, in the works of Goethe and other travellers. It already existed when Marstrand and Bournonville created their Italian works, but this does not mean that they did not bring their own characteristic nuances to the descriptions. There is more discussiona of this point later.[7]

The painter on his travels

With the dawning of Romanticism, the classic grand tour gained a renewed, in fact an overwhelming, significance. As we know, painters had for generations travelled to Italy, the homeland of art, sun and wine. But, whereas in the 1600s and for most of the 1700s one knew precisely what was to be visited, learned and digested - the purpose of the trip was decided in advance - now the sensitive traveller left openings to allow for the unpredictable in this new setting in a foreign land. It was one thing to seek learning, another to allow the mind to be inspired to bear fruit.

For centuries travellers to Italy had studied the ruins of the ancient world, Raphael and the wonderful fruits of the high Renaissance, as well as the great schools of the Baroque. The place was Rome, the eternal city. Of course, one also simply lived; eating, drinking and partying with other artists. It is characteristic that, although the Danish painter Nicolai Abildgaard and the Swedish sculptor Sergel both observed the life and people of Rome during their stay in the 1770s, the artistic legacy of the trip, as far as Abildgaard is concerned, is the manifesto work *Den sårede Filoktet* (*The Wounded Philoctetes*) inspired by Raphael, Titian and Michelangelo.[8]

The life of the people was not yet regarded as relevant for Danish artists. As Christian Molbech has expressed it, the irresistible influence of Italy was probably felt but not, as yet, the relevance of presenting a picture of a life that could drive people to fits of frenzied joy and delight.[9]

When Eckersberg returned home in 1816 after three years in Italy, he had, like his teacher Abildgaard, completed his training as a historical painter. He waited, as Abildgaard had done before him, for the great project - the decoration of Christiansborg Palace. In contrast to his predecessor, though, Eckersberg's head was full of more than just antiquities and Raphaels when he came home. One result of this was a great number of Roman views. It was not the life of Rome that had motivated this Nordic artist, but even so, it was a part of the real Rome that gave rise to these works. The views were painted *con amore* under the influence of the nature and art of the city. Most of them were hung in the "yellow room", as it was known, of Charlottenborg - the ceremonial room of the professorial residence.[10]

It was here that the paintings were seen by the young painters of the day and they were instrumental in awakening the longing for Italy felt by these young people. Classical architecture with its genius for geometry, perspective and plasticity. Light and shade, the clear blue sky and the views. But one thing was not seen in Eckersberg's yellow room: the life of the people.

Whether they were Constantin Hansen, Jørgen Roed, Martinus Rørbye or Christen Købke, the young painters on the grand tour of Italy visited the places and the motifs that they knew from the yellow room when they felt the pangs of home-sickness during the long sojourn. They repeated, developed and varied the views that Eckersberg had painted as a kind of basic picture. Eckersberg seldom used figures to ornament his landscapes and to give a sense of popular life. One sees a little to-ing and fro-ing in his masterful picture *Foran Santa Maria i Aracoeli* (*The Marble Steps Leading to the Church of Santa Maria in Aracoeli in Rome*), and in the motif of the Franciscan monastery next to the church of Santa Maria in Aracoeli one glimpses a Roman couple with tambourines in the cobbled quadrangle. Otherwise, however there are no people, at least none who would distract from the essential, the grand, immortal architecture.

Eckersberg was, primarily, a historical painter; the portrayals of people that are found in his works concern their heroic past, and are thus idealisations. The person is usually depicted in relative tranquillity or, when the situation demands a dramatic and dynamic portrayal, the pictures are characterised by Classicism's use of even earlier techniques. In his portrayal of people, Eckersberg is far from spontaneous in his approach.

If dance, or any form of physically-demanding movement, was something only marginally touched upon in Eckersberg's work, then the same is true of many of his pupils. This is obvious when we are talking about painters who choose architecture and landscape as their motifs; in the same way that portrait painters do not depict rapid movements, the ephemeral or that which accentuates the moment. Købke, Rørbye, Roed, Lundbye, Skovgaard, Constantin Hansen etc. do not choose energetic movement as their motif. When they do, as can be seen, for example, in Constantin Hansen's *Oplæser på Molen i Napoli* (*A Recitation of Orlando furioso at the Molo, Naples*), they choose to depict the expressive and meaningful gesture, the characteristic pose or posture. The painters mentioned rarely attempt to capture any violent and spontaneous movement. It is as if the pictorial art of the Golden Age, continuing the traditions of Thorvaldsen and Eckersberg, holds back from transgressing the potential of the medium of static pictures.

Wilhelm Marstrand

The painter Wilhelm Marstrand (1810-1873) is the great exception in this respect. He, as no one else, was able to convey a sense of movement and this gives his work a very special character. At the age of twenty, Marstrand exhibited the painting *Et Uheld på Kilderejsen* (*The Journey to the Miraculous Spring*), a surprisingly aggressive picture of a group driving by coach, where the wild galloping of the horses looks as if it will all end in disaster. That the young Marstrand really was capable of capturing characteristic movements and specific body-language can be seen in the painting *Beskænkede forlader Kælderen* (*Drinkers Leaving the Cellar Bar*) from 1834. This is a unique portrayal of drunken seamen, sent staggering into the street. In *En Auktionsscene* (*An Auction Scene*), painted in 1836 while he was studying under Eckersberg, Marstrand tackles the numerous, complicated and interactive movements of a crowd.

Movement, from the overall flow and total rhythm of a scene to individual and idiosyncratic body-language recorded in the tiniest detail, is the fundamental theme of Marstrand's art. As a historical painter, a depicter of genres and, to some extent, as a portrait painter, his art is built on the qualities that he developed, in part, through the study of nature - people in motion - and, in part, through the study of the stage, the theatre which he loved. He wanted to tell stories in his art. He wanted to capture everyday life. So he turned away from the allegory as a narrative form and Classicism with its stiff expressive poses as a form of representation. Instead he used the vital body-language and idiosyncratic gestures of the protagonists to construct the dramatic narrative. *Joie de vivre*, humour and noisy fun were important elements in Marstrand's universe. As such, historical tales of heroism, ancient architecture and Arcadian landscapes meant little to him, and when he did depict a heroic episode, such as Christian IV at *Trefoldigheden* (*The Trinity*), he attempts above all else to create as lifelike and as living a portrayal as possible.

In 1836 Marstrand set off on the classic journey to Italy and was away until 1841. "I am looking forward immeasurably to this flight into the world," wrote Marstrand on his departure. His choice of words is interesting: a flight into the world seen as a basic urge, in sharp contrast to the security offered by the ties of home. Rome was the actual destination, but on the way he made good use of visits to the important artistic centres of activity in Berlin, Dresden, Nuremberg and Munich. He was, as Gitte Valentiner writes in her monograph, a very focused 25-year-old who wanted to reach the top of his profession. While the powers-that-be at the Academy in Copenhagen would only reluctantly look beyond their four walls, Marstrand was aware of the new things that were happening everywhere.

He wanted an academic career as a historical painter, he also regarded genre painting as second-rate, but this very conflict between the traditional and the new brought forth not only insecurity and aggression, but also conditions that could bear fruit; "if there is anything original in me, then it will certainly be allowed to express itself as much as it wants," wrote Marstrand.[11]

Thanks to Marstrand's letters home, we are well-informed about the artist's journey and his thoughts. The following quotations tell us about his stay in Italy. He was overwhelmed by Rome:

> I have seen much, almost too much; one is so full of ideas
> that one takes the place of the other before the soul has
> had time to work them through.[12]

> One is as free as a bird in the sky and need not consult
> the bailiff as to how much one may enjoy oneself.[13]

Marstrand's opinions of the Italians as compared to the Scandinavians are familiar, "…all Scandinavians are cold, serious and calculating and they do not seem to enjoy life in full as Italians do." Marstrand thought that life at home in Denmark was cosy, "although tea is a poor substitute for grape juice." He studied carefully in order to learn how to express "the life and joy that is characteristic of an Italian party." He added, "Nothing pleases me more than to see a quick, carefree and courageous state of mind in others." Marstrand took note of the dance, and in his opinion, the saltarello was, "the finishing touch".

It is quite apparent that Italy appealed to the inner being of the young Danish artist. *Joie de vivre*, the wine, the sensuality, and, yes, the girls and the eroticism also played a part. But an encounter with the South was not without danger. Cholera, for example, made Marstrand think again. He gives an account of an English tourist who was murdered because the local people believed that he carried the disease, "This rough, fanatical and cruel people are only stripped of morality in this way because of their shameful clergy." Danish artists experienced the darker side of Italy, too. But this was not the source of inspiration. This was not what people wished to see, and it could not be sold at home in Frederik VI's Copenhagen. No, Marstrand knew exactly what he wanted:

> I hope to be there at the wine harvest in the month of October - to wallow in Nature's abundances. If the harvest is good, then people are full of ecstatic joy, and this I really want to see.[14]

Citizens of Rome

The first result of his stay in Rome was *En Fængselsscene i Rom* (*A Prison Scene in Rome*), 1837. It was an idealised portrayal of prisoners behind bars who are nevertheless having a fine time, playing cards with two peasants sitting outside the walls. Next Marstrand painted *St. Antoniusfesten i Rom* (*The Feast of St. Anthony in Rome*), a huge canvas that was exhibited at Charlottenborg in 1839. The motif here is a portrayal of popular life on the Day of St. Anthony, 17 January, with a priest standing outside the little church of San Antonio Abbate, sprinkling Holy Water as a blessing on all the animals brought before him by the people of Rome. Purely in terms of movement, this picture would be noteworthy. A dog jumping up, a donkey kicking backwards and, not least, the difficulties encountered by the driver of the donkey cart as he tries to get his vehicle moving. The driver energetically whips the braying donkey, but the cart will not move. The reason for this is simple: the left wheel of the cart is stuck against the stone step at the entrance to the church. A subtle and, for Marstrand, a typically humorous situation where the rituals of the bizarre Catholic feast - with its implications of heavenly intervention - are juxtaposed to something as prosaic as a wheel driven into a step.

The two imposing works from Rome which followed are masterpieces in which dance appears as a basic theme in the portrayal of the people of the city and their way of life. First, Marstrand painted *Romerske Borgere forsamlede til Lystig-*

The meeting of opposites. A saltarello-dancing couple with forceful jumps and seductively flourished apron, surrounded by their absolute counter-image: dark-suited, reclining Danish gentlemen (W. Marstrand, *Roman Citizens Assembled for Entertainment at an Osteria*, 1839, Nivaagaard Collection).

hed i et Osteri (*Roman Citizens Assembled for Entertainment at an Osteria*), 1838–39, and afterwards *Lystighed uden for Roms Mure paa en Oktoberaften* (*October Festival Evening outside the Walls of Rome*), 1839.

As inspiration for the former painting, Marstrand was probably familiar with a similar scene painted by Dietrich Wilhelm Lindau of Dresden in 1827, as this painting was exhibited in Copenhagen in the 1830s. The painting shows the interior of an osteria where the Danish contingent with Thorvaldsen at its head are seated at a table to the right while a young, dancing couple dominates the centre and left of the picture. We encounter not only the spontaneous, life- and dance-loving Italians in their saltarello, but also their counter-image in the seated, dark-suited foreigners. The picture clearly illustrates the contrast between the colourful and dynamic world of the Italians, and the dark and static existence of the visitors from the North.[15]

Let us look at Marstrand's picture of the osteria that he presented to his patron Court Vintner Waagepetersen and which now hangs in the Nivaagaard Collection. The Court Vintner wished to appear in the picture together with his companions but, whereas the commissioner of the work in Lindau's case wished to be prominent, Waagepetersen wanted modestly just to be part of the group of Danish artists in the background – a group that includes Sonne, Roed, Blunck and Constantin Hansen. The group is merely an aside serving to underscore the all-dominating role of the main motif – the saltarello-dancing couple. The focus is, as it were, shifted from the contrast between the black and the colourful, the static and the moving, to a comprehensive and detailed portrayal of dance and enjoyment.

In the earliest known sketch for this work, the group of black-suited men are sitting beneath a pergola of vines in the background (see p. 107). In the sketch which is hanging in the Art Museum of Funen, the artist has placed a Roman woman in front of the seated gentlemen, and has added a sentimental little motif of a child reaching towards one of the men, either to beg or perhaps to receive a morsel from his plate (see p. 89). In the finished painting, the Roman serving-woman has disappeared, but the child is still apparent (see p. 98). So much for the commissioner, the Danish artists and the background group of black-suited gentlemen.

Pinelli and Richter

From the beginning of his stay in Rome, Marstrand had known that life in that city was central to his area of interest. Long before the trip itself, Marstrand had worked with Italian life as a pictorial motif, at least as far as this was possible in Copenhagen. This meant, primarily, idyllic scenes of the city on the Tiber, its inhabitants dancing, having fun and enjoying life in their characteristic way. Copenhagen society was aware that the citizens of Rome danced the saltarello. In the flourishing salon milieu surrounding Frederikke Brun and her adored daughter Ida Brun, the saltarello had been played and most likely danced at Sophienholm, thanks to numerous visits to the Italian city.[16]

Thorvaldsen's Museum houses an important collection of drawings and graphic works by Bartolomeo Pinelli. Here we find illustrations for *Don Quixote* and stories from classical antiquity. These works have a somewhat different, more heroic, style, which is also true of the brutal series entitled *The Life of Italian Bandits*. It was not this more temperamental, wild, destructive and barbaric side of Pinelli that captured the imagination of Marstrand, but rather the more peaceful, carefree and happy depiction of everyday life in Rome.[17] Pinelli has been selected as being the main inspiration for both *Oktoberfesten* (*The October Festival*) and *Roman Citizens Assembled for Entertainment at an Osteria*. Pinelli's print *Grape Pickers Returning to Rome after the Harvest*, first published in 1809, has naturally been linked to *The October Festival*. As inspiration for *Roman Citizens As-sembled for Entertainment at an Osteria*, we should turn to two details from Pinelli's collection *Life of the People of Rome*. The motif of the dancing couple can be found in *Saltarello nel mese di octobre, dentro la bottega de un café*, Rome 1821, whereas the space and architecture of the outdoor scene resembles more that of *Salta la Quaglia*, a motif of young Roman boys playing leap-frog. Here, for example, we can see the construction of the osteria with its large staircase, and other details, such as the use of the diagonal in the composition, by means of which Marstrand accentuates the depth of field in the painting.

In addition, we can refer to Bartolomeo Pinelli's series *Nuova Raccolta di Cinquanta Costumi Pittoreschi* from 1816. Here one can see *Saltarello Romano* as it is danced in *Baccanale di Roma in Testaccio*. Pinelli's depiction of the saltarello is

Saltarello Romano

Dancing on an equal footing. Bartolomeo Pinelli's dynamic picture of the joyous dancing couple was the main inspiration for Marstrand's treatment of the saltarello as "the finishing touch" of all that characterised Italian life and joy (*Saltarello Romano*, 1816, Thorvaldsens Museum, Copenhagen. Photo: Weis & Wichmann).

extremely dynamic and very forceful movements. The dancers' arms are stretched outwards and upwards, the body is bent forwards, the legs are lifted and everything that can be used to highlight the expressivity of the dance is incorporated.

Pinelli is a clear source of inspiration, but perhaps not the only source. German painters have produced several saltarello-dancing couples, and one that is surprisingly similar to Marstrand's painting is an etching by Adrian Ludwig Richter dating from around 1825. Richter came from Dresden and spent from 1823 to 1826 in Italy. [18] Although there are huge differences between Richter's *Saltarello* and Marstrand's *Roman Citizens* the basic motif is the same: Romans in picturesque national costumes, assembled in the open air in order to dance, sing and enjoy themselves. The dancing couple is pivotal in both works, although not such a dominant part of the composition in Richter's work as in Marstrand's. The major differences are to do with the perception of space and composition. Richter employs a relief-like composition, with a wide foreground bordered on a parallel to the plane of the picture by the characteristic architecture - a fantasy on a house from medieval Trastevere. This use of space and composition shows how Richter was influenced by Classicism.

In contrast, Marstrand is more modern and theatrical; he uses diagonals and boundaries that give a more closed, intimate space where the feeling of depth is underscored by the proportions of the dancing couple in the foreground and the tiny figures just entering the field of vision through the gateway of the building. Otherwise, the details and themes from folklore that fill Marstrand's pictures can also be found in Richter's: the saltarello-dancing couple, the musicians, the portly host, all sorts of people from young mothers with their babies to old women, the carriage with the new arrivals wearing their distinctive feather-decorated hats, the hunters and so on. It is simply a compendium of all the elements needed to make such a portrayal of a joyous gathering of folk complete.

The quantity of detail is not un-important in terms of meaning: the erotic dimension of the dance motif is set in relief against the family situations depicted - in part, the mothers sitting with their offspring, but also the presence of the young, unmarried girls. The dance defines the delineation between the acting-out of basic urges and human life with its social demands and obligations. Marstrand elevates dance to a sphere where it represents the expression of a harmonious

Classical enjoyment. Although A.L. Richter is more influenced by Classicism his paintings contain many of the folklore elements later found in Marstrand's pictures: life in the open with musicians, a portly host and a dog, mother and baby, new arrivals and above all the dancing couple (*Saltarello*, c. 1825, Munich, Staatliche Graphische Sammlung. Photo: Jørgen Watz).

balance between the life of the instincts and that of the family. It is not a question of dance as fatal seduction or damnation. Dance is a natural stage in the course of life. It is one of life's happy moments.

The saltarello

This period is, as mentioned earlier, rich in literary descriptions of the dancing Italian. Both fiction and actual memoirs and travel literature were partial to an *arm aber glücklich* portrayal of the Roman as the true descendent of the original population of antiquity. The essence of the carefree, outdoor life of these genuine Romans could be depicted by the saltarello-dancing couple. As such, Antoine Thomas, who published the richly illustrated book *Un an à Rome et dans ses environs* in Paris in 1823, mentions in his description of the saltarello that it is danced "en présence de nombreux spectateurs".[19]

Possibly the most important Danish book written about Italy during the Golden Age was published in 1835, the year before Marstrand set off on his journey. Hans Christian Andersen with his *Improvisatoren* (*The Improvisatore*) had suddenly put Italy on the agenda for the whole of cultured Copenhagen society. Danish authors including Schack Staffeldt, Oehlenschläger, Ingemann, Carsten Hauch, and Ludvig Bødtcher had written about the promised land, but with *The Improvisatore*, which laid the foundations for Andersen's fame, Italy made a breakthrough as never before. Through its lively descriptions, the novel leads us into Italian life in all its facets. The main character, Antonio, encounters the saltarello for the first time as a small boy still enjoying the innocence of a happy childhood. He has visited Trastevere with his mother. It is late when they return home, and the moon is shining so wonderfully:

> It was one of those evenings, of which one experiences but few in one's life, that without being any great event still makes, with all its colour play, an impression on the psyche. Whenever I think back to the River Tiber, I still see the picture as it appeared to me that evening; the

thick yellow water with the moon shining on it, the stone
pillars of the old ruined bridge that, with strong shadows,
loomed up from the stream where the big water-mill
sprayed the merry girls who sprang past with their tambourines, dancing the saltarello.[20]

Andersen masterfully succeeds in creating, in condensed form, an overall detailed
picture with undercurrents of something frightening and momentous, yet, at the
same time, idyllically happy. The essence of this is conveyed in the final description
of the dancing girls. Afterwards, the author gives a very exact explanation of what
the saltarello is:

A Roman folk dance performed to a very repetitive tune.
It is danced solo or in couples – though these never come
into physical contact with each other. It is usually two
men or two women who, with quick, springing steps
that get faster, move in a semicircle. The arms move just
as much as the legs, and continuously change position
with the grace that is so special to the Roman people.
The lady dancers usually raise their skirts a little as they
dance, or beat the rhythm on the tambourine themselves
– otherwise this repetitive drumming is performed by a
third person outside the dance.[21]

This account can be supplemented by a description by Th. Hentschke in his *Allgemeine Tanzkunst* from 1836. He recounts the fast tempo of the dance, its frequent
cross springs and – contrary to Andersen's description – the arms making bigger
movements than the legs.[22]

The classic works of reference tell us that the saltarello is a very widespread,
lively jumping dance, going back to the Middle Ages in Italy. The word *saltare*
means to make small jumping movements. Several variations are known, and in
the 17th century the dance disappeared from the courtly dance repertoire and
became a part of the folk repertoire in Romagna and Abruzzi.

In the 18th and 19th centuries, the majority of accounts describe a lively jumping dance for couples in either 3/4 or 6/8 time. There are apparently no fixed, obligatory patterns. The dance is performed in two basic steps: *doppio* - a double step - and *salteto* - the little jump - according to the description by Bianca M. Galanti in *Dances of Italy*. Joan Lawson also describes the saltarello in her book *European Folk Dance*. Here the two steps are called "balancé" and "step-hop" respectively. [23]

If we look at Marstrand's picture, we see that the painter has wanted to show the two basic steps of the dance. The woman is performing the doppio or balancé while holding her white apron gracefully; the rather heavier gentleman is jumping onto his right foot and his arms are held elegantly in the air, his fingers clicking. The woman with her back turned was already present in the first draft of the picture. The man, however, changes considerably from the first sketch to the final painting. In the sketch we see a man in white trousers, a black jacket and a tall, pale-coloured hat. He has his right arm in the air and his left to his side. The weight is on the left leg, while the right is slightly crossed over the left. In this version there is no attempt to show the characteristic hop-step, but rather more the balancé. In other words, in the first version both dancers are performing the same step. In the sketch in the Art Museum of Funen, this has been changed and we can see the differentiation in the steps that is found in the finished painting. This change, from both dancers performing the same step to each performing their own, different step, is remarkable. Pinelli usually lets his dancers perform the same step and - in accordance with Hans Christian Andersen's observations - he also shows two women dancing together.

The erotic game

If we look at other representations of the saltarello there are significant deviations. The available material is comprehensive. I have already pointed out that in Pinelli's works the positions displayed are generally rather more forceful. He emphasises the extremes of movement. While one can recognise the foot and leg positions of the men in his pictures, there are crucial differences among the dancing women.

In the first sketch for Marstrand's *Roman Citizens Assembled for Entertainment at an Osteria*
the man dances with the woman in a less challenging manner, as they are both performing the
same step. However, both he and the dog change as the dance and the painting progress (compare
illustrations on pp. 89 and 98), (1838, Private Collection. Photo: Jørgen Watz).

Most significant is Marstrand's rather subdued portrayal of the dancing woman. In many other portrayals the women are seen to whirl, rock and swing around like the maenads from the painted decoration on vases from antiquity. Marstrand is extremely discreet. Is this the cold Scandinavian who is afraid of upsetting the provincial, middle-class ideal of woman if the postures become too intense? The eroticism of the female dancer is only expressed indirectly, since she avoids the gaze of the spectator and exposes herself only to her male partner. He, on the other hand, is displayed quite openly and with an interesting contrast between his rather plump anatomy and the lightness of his jumps. He is as fine an example of the contrast between lightness and heaviness as can be conveyed in visual art. One should, however, be aware that the age and stoutness of the male dancer tends to tone down the erotic tension between the partners.

Marstrand had also worked with the saltarello in his drawings. In the Department of Prints and Drawings and in the Hirschsprung Collection we find many examples. Most of these drawings show outdoor or indoor scenes from the osteria with the dancing couple: she is holding out her apron and moving gracefully and discreetly; he alternates between holding his hand at his side or his arm in the air.

Only a few of the drawings show anything radically different. Here we see one of these more atypical drawings in which the artist captures the experience of a more forceful expression of movement than those encountered in the painting. This is particularly eye-catching in the representation of the female dancer. The drawing shows her turned to face the artist, turned to us, the viewers. We can, discern something of the flirtation, the graceful and erotic game, the fun and challenge that we know to be part of the dance. In the painting this is rather toned down, in part because the woman's movements are not at all forceful, but also because she has her back turned to us. In this modest portrayal of the woman, Marstrand sets himself apart from other portrayers of the saltarello - and perhaps this is one of the things he wanted to change in *The October Festival* where we can observe two dancing women facing one another. The strength of expression in the movements has, however, not become more brutal as a result.

This toning-down process is worth examining. Returning to Goethe, he writes about the dances in his account of the Roman carnival:

A more daring, face-on representation of woman dancing. In the drawing we can more readily discern the fun and flirtation, the graceful and erotic game, which are somewhat toned down in the painting (W. Marstrand, *Dansende par* (*Dancing Couple*), n. d., the Danish National Gallery, Department of Prints and Drawings, Copenhagen).

that in their pantomime they express something very
typical, for example, two lovers part and make up, they
leave each other and then return. In their pantomime
ballets the Romans are used to exaggerated gesticulation;
also in their party dances they prefer a form of expression
that we would regard as excessive and affected.[24]

That this pantomime element in the dance could still be seen in the 1830s can be
read in the description of the saltarello in Th. Hentschke's *Allgemeine Tanzkunst*.
Bianca M. Galanti also discusses this element in the book *Dances of Italy*. She
writes that the erotic dances were most widespread in Italy, dances which convey
flirtation, philandering, choices, sighs, playing-up. It is often the woman who performs
the mime, although in other circumstances it is the man who flaunts himself. Dances like the furlana, the saltarello and the tarantella belong to this erotic category:

The mime demands good acting in the love scenes both
for man and girl, the one pursuing, the other retreating,
the one ardently offering, the other, after much play with
her apron, at last accepting.[25]

While this mime and erotic game can be traced in some of Marstrand's
drawings, they are, as mentioned before, considerably toned down in the paintings.
Hans Christian Andersen, with his fear of sexuality, makes no mention of this
erotic game but suffices to note that the dancers do not actually touch one another.
 In her article, "The Difficulty of Saying Yes", which introduced the Marstrand
exhibition at Nivaagaard in 1992, Elisabeth Cederstrøm points out that enjoyment
never dominates at the expense of harmony:

Marstrand was profoundly fascinated by this interesting
dynamic between man and woman, since he painted it a
number of times (...) Every movement, every colour is
carefully chosen to fit in. This becomes somewhat removed from the Italians; but the intention was not ironic.[26]

No, it is not; but what is it then? To lift the veil a little, Cederstrøm brings in a scene from an osteria painted by Marstrand in connection with his second trip to Italy in 1847. Marstrand draws the motif from Goethe's *Römische Elegien*, from number XV in which he describes an interesting meeting of the sexes. The picture is regarded as one of the more unpleasant expressions of the increasingly sentimental enthusiasm for Italy. It forms part of the truth. The other part has probably something to do with the shyness - maybe even fear - that Marstrand harboured with respect to women. Fear of the truly tempting. An angst that typifies the provincial, middle-class, North European culture.

Marstrand and Bournonville

Roman Citizens Assembled for Entertainment at an Osteria is signed 1839. The painting was exhibited in Copenhagen in 1840. Thus, this is not the painting that could have inspired ballet master August Bournonville to create his first idyllic Italian ballet *Festen i Albano* (*The Festival in Albano*), premiered on the birthday of Marie Sophie Frederikke, the Queen of Frederik VI, on 28 October 1839.

This is puzzling if one reads Bournonville's libretto for the ballet, it really seems as though the ballet master wished to bring to life on the stage of the Royal Theatre as much as possible of what is found in the painting. According to the ballet master himself, it was Albert Küchler's painting *Scener fra Familielivet i Albano* (*Scene with a Family in Albano*), belonging to Thorvaldsen, that provided the source of inspiration. Küchler's painting was shown at Charlottenborg, where Bournonville may have seen it together with works like Marstrand's *The Feast of St. Anthony in Rome*, *En scene af det neapolitanske folkeliv* (*A Scene from Everyday Life in Naples*) also by Marstrand, and Jørgen Sonne's *Romerske landfolk, som drager til marked* (*Roman Farmers on their Way to Market*).[27]

Paintings of Italian subject matter were a significant source of inspiration for the ballet master, who had not yet visited Italy himself, as they not only offered the possibility to view the mime-like performances of folklore but also dances such as the saltarello and a tarantella in *The Festival in Albano*. The dance that inspired the picture, inspires once again a dance. Seen in this light, Bournonville and Marstrand stand side-by-side in the culture of the Golden Age. Marstrand uses the saltarello-dancing couple as a metaphor for the *joie de vivre* of the Italians, one of Bournonville's artistic high points is the tarantella in the third act of *Napoli,* in which he celebrates the joy of life in the South.

Marstrand and Bournonville shared, in a way, a basic aesthetic view. Harmony must never be jeopardized. Thus it was necessary, both morally and artistically, to tone down the erotic game. In 1840, Bournonville demonstrated how he wished to underplay the extremes of Spanish dance in the ballet *Toreadoren (The Toreador).* The lascivious and provocative that Bournonville experienced in the Spanish dance he had seen in connection with Christian VIII's coronation met its subdued counterpart in this ballet.[28] In *Roman Citizens Assembled for Entertainment at an Osteria* Marstrand also understates the extreme movements and the erotic elements of the mime.

These conditions illustrate that the period around 1840 was one of moral and aesthetic turmoil, of breaking with tradition. On an ideological level the upheaval occurred between the spent absolute monarchy and the democracy that finally saw the light of day in 1849. On the aesthetic plane, it can be observed that Classicist historical painting, the autocrat's form of expression *par excellence,* was now being replaced by genre painting, conversation pieces, the form of expression of the new bourgeois democracy.

Marstrand's use of dance as a pictorial motif also indicates these conflicts. On the one hand, the dance forms part of a classical composition where the artist, in attempting to show both the basic steps of the dance, is also trying to keep an overall view of the dance. On the other hand, it is part of a genre motif, its contemporary nature underscored, inter alia, by the seated tourists. Dance as a motif in Marstrand's art is, therefore, an expression of the development away from Classicism towards Realism.

Bournonville's use of dance, or more specifically the saltarello, displays the same development: away from the academic, Classicist expression and towards what he referred to as the natural, as is found in, for example, *Et Folkesagn (A Folk Tale).* Dance, either as a pictorial motif or with ballet, moves, in these decades, away from the heroic-mythological, the religious or the historical-literary, and moves towards the realistic. But, at the same time, the artist is nervous about revealing the erotic dimensions of dance. Dance as an artistic expression, whether on stage or as a pictorial motif, enters a period of liberation from the symbolic meanings of earlier times. It is regarded as being a significant part of the portrayal of everyday life and the interest in dance as a form of expression must be viewed in the light of past beliefs in national character and characteristics. Dance serves as a metaphor for peoples and their ways of life, but it was still necessary to tame the uninhibited aspects of the dance.

The other world that the Scandinavian found in Italy – nature, the authentic life of the people, the passions etc. – was ensnaring and full of promise; but in artistic works it was necessary to tone it down so that it could be presented in the right light, so that the hard-won harmony would not be jeopardized.

Notes

1. *Yearbook for Traditional Music,* Vol. 23, 1991.

2. Per Øhrgaard, *Goethe. Et Essay,* Copenhagen, Gyldendal, 1999, p. 105.

3. Friedrich Otterbach, *Die Geschichte der europäischen Tanzmusik,* Heinrichshofen, Wilhelmshaven, 1980, p. 215.

4. Bo Lindwall, *Barockens Epok* (sections *Borgerlig verklighetssyn* and *Genrebilden*), Stockholm, 1968.

5. This subject area was put into focus through the exhibition and accompanying catalogue *Realta e Fantasia nelle pittura Napolitana XVII-XIX secolo*, Naples, 1987.

6. See Øhrgaard op. cit., p. 113.

7. See also: *Gouaches napoletane del Settecento e dell' Ottocento*, Naples, 1985; *Il Mito e l'Immagine Capri, Ischia e Procida nella pittura del 600 ai primi del 900*, Edizioni Rai, Torino, 1988.

8. Charlotte Christensen, *Maleren Nicolai Abildgaard*, Gyldendal, 1999.

9. Carl V. Petersen, *Italien i dansk Malerkunst, Kunst i Danmark*, Copenhagen, 1932.

10. Hans Edvard Nørregård-Nielsen, *Jeg saae det Land. H.C. Andersens rejseskitser fra Italien,* Gyldendal, 1990.

11. Gitte Valentiner, *Wilhelm Marstrand*, Copenhagen, 1992, p. 32. Additional important Marstrand references are: *Wilhelm Marstrand. Breve og Uddrag af Breve fra denne Kunstner* by Councillor of State Raffenberg, Copenhagen, 1880. Karl Madsen, *Wilhelm Marstrand*, Copenhagen, 1905. *Nivaagaard viser Marstrand*, texts by Claus M. Smidt, Gitte Valentiner, Elisabeth Cederstrøm, Kirsten Nørregaard Petersen, Bent Holm and Erik Fischer, Nivaagaard Collection, 1992. Also utilised are: *De ægte romere, tegnet af Bartolomeo Pinelli og Wilhelm Marstrand*, text by Lisbet Balslev Jørgensen, Thorvaldsens Museum, 1968/69.

12. Karl Madsen, *Wilhelm Marstrand*, Copenhagen, 1905, p. 47.

13. Op. cit., p. 63.

14. Op. cit., p. 43.

15. *Billedhuggeren og Balletmesteren*, Thorvaldsens Museum, Copenhagen, 1992, pp. 50-55. Sys Hartmann, *I sydens land. Ludvig Bødtcher i Rom*, Cicero, 1993.

16. *Nordisk Salonkultur. Et studie i nordiske skønånder og salonmiljøer 1780-1835*, Odense, 1998, p. 201. See also Ursula Peters, *Fællesskabets ideal i Kunst og liv i Thorvaldsens Rom*, Thorvaldsens Museum, 1992, pp. 82-83.

17. *De ægte Romere*, Thorvaldsens Museum, 1968/69.

18. See further on the increasingly popular *genre* paintings with Italian themes: *Biedermeiers Glück und Ende, Die gestörte Idylle 1815-1848*, Munich, 1987, especially Barbara Eschenburg, *Darstellungen von Sitte und Sittlichkeit - das Genrebild im Biedermeier, Das Italiengenre*, pp. 177-179.

19. Walter Salmen, *Tanz im 19. Jahrhundert¸* in the series *Musikgeschichte in Bildern,* Bd. IV, Lieferung 5, Leipzig, 1989.

20. H. C. Andersen, *Improvisatoren (The Improvisor)*, ed. Mogens Brøndsted, Det danske Sprog- og Litteraturselskab, Borgen 1991, p. 23.

21. Ibid.

22. Th. Hentschke, *Allgemeine Tanzkunst*, Stralsund, 1836.

23. Bianca M. Galanti, *Dances of Italy*, London, 1950. Joan Lawson, *European Folk Dance,* London 1950.

24. Johann Wolfgang Goethe, *Italiensk Rejse*, anden del, Det romerske Karneval, Carit Andersens Forlag, 1962, pp. 156-157.

25. Galanti, *Dances of Italy*, op. cit., p. 10.

26. *Nivaagaard viser Marstrand*, op. cit., p. 11.

27. Hans Edvard Nørregård-Nielsen's text is interesting in connection with the painting in the New Carlsberg Glyptotek, *Italienerinde,* by Albert Küchler. Here the Danes' fascination with the lovely Italian girls is discussed: "We see the face as a mirror of all the world's tangled passions, from the tiny ferocious mouth to the unpredictable eyes." Hans Edvard Nørregård-Nielsen, *Dansk Guldalder Maleri*, Ny Carlsberg Glyptotek, 1995, p. 182.

28. Erik Aschengreen, "Når lidenskaberne tøjles. August Bournoville og det sydlandske" in *Vindue mod den romanske verden*, Gunver Skytte, Lene Waage Petersen, Nils Soelberg and Ebbe Spang-Hansen, eds., Museum Tusculanum Press, Copenhagen, 1994.

The Bournonville Passion: "You – here – dance"

Interview with Nikolaj Hübbe

by Monna Dithmer

Bournonville's ballets are generally regarded as an expression of joy, how do you see him, now that you're based with New York City Ballet?

There is basically the joy of dancing in this Apollonian art form. It comes from the sun, the joy, and it comes from Apollo, not from Dionysus. It's like a madness, just as you say in Danish you are "bindegal", literally meaning so mad - for dancing - that you have to be strapped down.

In Bournonville the overall atmosphere is so irresistibly the joy of dancing. It's an earthy, dare-devil mentality such as in *Napoli*'s third act and *A Folk Tale*. Bournonville dances when he is happy. There is almost triumphant joy in James' big solo in the first act of *Sylphide*, as he comes just after Gurn, his rival, "This is what I am and this is what I can do. I'll wipe him out. Here I come." But James doesn't do variations when the sylph is dead, Gennaro doesn't dance when Teresina has gone to the grotto. They do the variations when they are at the highest point of their love or when the wedding is celebrated. Dancing is the ultimate expression of joy. Bournonville makes sense psychologically - if you are depressed you don't go into physical vigour, you just sit, you become a hermit, the physicality dies.

Do you subscribe to the idea of the sunshine Bournonville?

His ballets contain the moral "stay on the path, don't walk on the wild side". But there are other more troubling sides. In *Sylphide*, for instance, when James wakes up, the sylph is gone and there stands Effy saying in mime, "You - your heart – me - no." James answers, "Calm down - I - you - love." There have been two interpretations of this. Is he lying to her or, as I've always believed, is he lying to himself? That's how I learnt it from Henning Kronstam, but afterwards people coaching me have said, "And now you lie to her." And I say, "No!" James is trying to convince her in order to convince himself. He is living a lie. That's much more tragic and detrimental than just telling a lie. This way of looking at it shows how much subtlety and psychological depth these ballets contain.

I've been away from the Royal Danish Ballet for such a long time (since 1992, ed.) and I haven't seen a lot, but the general consensus during the past ten years has been to make the ballets - I wouldn't say boring - but much too smooth.

When James runs after the three sylphs, it's extremely important that this young man runs in with a conviction and a devotion to this 150-year-old material. He has to believe that he is out in the forest, looking for the Sylphide. He has to believe in the moment he is in now, in the material, in the steps. He must really have a point of view and a passion. Otherwise it becomes a dusty old painting of a Scotsman running in from the wings. There has to be an urgency about this entrance. He just left his house and his home and his bride.

How do you see James and Gennaro in comparison with other romantic heroes?

When people go on about how great it must be to dance the masterpieces *Giselle* and *Swan Lake*, I have to admit that for years I had a hard time with Albrecht. I don't think it's such a fantastic role, and that goes for Prince Siegfried too. It's like, "Where do I come in and how many lines do I have?" Of course they are dreamers too, like James and Gennaro, but it's something you have to produce yourself. The female roles in the Petipa repertoire are much more meaty. The reason why the Bournonville male is so fascinating is probably that Bournonville himself starred in these ballets.

Doing James and Gennaro felt completely natural for me. There is so much to build on, they are elaborate and so well defined. In the first act of *Sylphide* Bournonville actually gives you a living room. You cannot get out, you are in a cell, surrounded by walls and with all three women around you: your mother, your bride-to-be, the sylph. It makes so much sense.

In Bournonville's universe everything is psychologically subtle and well-defined. The setting in *Sylphide* is a quite down-to-earth parlour, which closes in on the emotional escape artist James, surrounded by the sylph, the witch, his mother and his bride-to-be (Sorella Englund as Madge and Nikolaj Hübbe as James, 1988, Royal Danish Ballet, Photo: Erik Petersen).

This image of the closed-in space makes me think of Bournonville as the Biedermeier romantic, longing out but staying put?

Except for *Sylphide*, which isn't really his story anyway, Bournonville is more of a Biedermeier romantic. There is a lot of inner turmoil in his ballets, but very little is done about it. If it's resolved, it's resolved within the four walls of your house like in *The King's Corps of Volunteers on Amager*.

Do you see anything particularly Danish or Nordic in these ballets?

There is a certain modesty in the style, a minuteness, a subtlety and a sweet directness. It isn't like the Russian repertoire, there isn't any flourish or extravagant in the movement. It's the opposite of chic, it's pure and sparse. However, the ballets are sophisticated because of their unique peculiarity. If you just do the movement with the real technique, that's enough, and it's great. I love *The Conservatoire*, especially when the four boys finish by doing turns and then plié, fifth position, bras bas - finito! Just four boys in a little diamond shape, it's beautiful.

There is a wholesomeness about Bournonville, it's like Danish rye bread or dairy commercials from the 1950s. There is something very endearing about it. You feel kind of wholesome when dancing Bournonville, because the movement is so well constructed and fixed together like good timber. It's good craftmanship. But it's not carpentry from Versaille or the Winter Palace, it's more middle-class domestic.

The art of imitation

You emphasized the necessity of conviction and passion when dancing a Bournonville character, is it especially important when doing mime?

The mime is above all so musically timed - like little arias. Whenever you talk, you talk right on the music, "You are here - you want to dance?" When you make that gesture with the arms above the head, inviting the person to dance, you can hear the invitation to dance in the rhythm of the movement and the music. That is always the question, the eternal begging in Bournonville: "You – here – dance?"

"There is a certain modesty, a subtlety and a sweet directness." This is not only true of the style, but also of the relationship between man and woman as perceived by Bournonville (*The Conservatoire*, Heidi Ryom and Nikolaj Hübbe, 1991, Royal Danish Ballet. Photo: Martin Mydtskov Rønne).

Do you find that Bournonville's mime is more psychologically defined than mime in other classical ballets?

I don't think I have ever done mime in any other style, but one thing is for certain: you can say I love you in ten different ways - in Bournonville it's always so refined, precisely suited to where you are in the story of the ballet. Furthermore, it's categorically different when you go from dance to mime, that's very special. James in *Sylphide* is two people, one person dancing and another lost in his erring mime. That scizophrenia in the part is truly fascinating. When Effy is standing in front of him, it's as if he doesn't really know her, she could be anybody.

Generally, however, the music always defines the action. In *The Sleeping Beauty*, for instance, when the Lilac Fairy asks, "Why are you sad - why are you here - why are you alone?" and he answers, "I am sad - I don't know - I cry - I don't know - I don't have a love." At that point there is such a longing and such a sad tone in Tchaikovsky's music that there's not much else to do but follow the music.

Some people have a gift for it, some don't. I have a vivid imagination, I get into it very easily. I get very excited by mime. I think it's something that was instilled from the very beginning - when as a kid you stand in the wings and watch Sorella Englund, Arne Willumsen, Niels Kehlet and Lis Jeppesen - it will come out in you eventually.[1]

Because the body remembers? How much was impregnated through teaching and coaching?

A lot of my training was imitation. I have pictures in mind for all of Bournonville. In *Sylphide* I do my Peter Martins when I come to the hill, I do my Arne Willumsen when I'm looking for the sylph, I do a certain Niels Kehlet thing and then there is a lot of Henning Kronstam.[2] It's a copy, and then after a while it becomes you. And you don't even know that you're doing an imitation, but by that time it's yours, you've taken it on. You aren't a replica. I just remember the way Arne (Willumsen, ed.) used his feet and looked at his hand when the witch is standing there with the veil almost stroking it. It made so much sense the way he did it that I immediately thought, "Oh God, I'll keep this." He is running around looking for his girl, he is beside himself, very light on his feet as if ready to go somewhere else. It was such a great transition from realm to realm.

It was almost by osmosis that I picked up these images and kept them in my mind, plus things Hans Brenaa had told me. [3] You do that by osmosis and then later on, if you're lucky enough to have a brain, you think about it, and figure out the various traces and combinations. It was Erik (Aschengreen, ed.) who gave me a sense of what history means. At school he scolded us for laughing at Nijinsky's big thighs. He thought it was a sacrilege. I really respected him for that, he was into it, he meant business. It's exciting to get to know the links to history. Without the past we are nothing. You get a sense of where you fit into this great puzzle, it's like family.

The company is like family too, so it feels the most natural thing to copy. Just like I've inherited certain things from my parents and my nose from my grandmother, a huge beak.

So you'll make a perfect witch in twenty years time?

Maybe. Although tradition says the witch can be done by either sex, I think there is much more depth dramaturgically when she is done by a woman - then James is surrounded by four women. Anyway, sometimes it can also be very hard within the company family, it can be exactly like Norén. Familiarity can also be what screws the family up and makes the apple rotten. It's something you have to be very aware of.

You compare belonging to your old company to the Swedish dramatist Lars Norén, a modern specialist in family traumas. Does this imply that you feel it's a cross to bear?

Yes, it's so personal, you grow up with these people in the same house for your whole life, sometimes the relationship can go sour. It's like the royal families of Europe who became degenerate because they were too inbred.

Is this what you see happening now with the Royal Danish Ballet?

No, I think the problem there is overexposure. When the Royal Danish Ballet got so exposed, beginning in the 1950s, progressing in the '60s and '70s and accelerating into the '90s, all of a sudden Bournonville was a trade - you could talk about having a stock in Bournonville. He lost his virginity. All of a sudden it isn't by

123

Is there too much calculation behind the seductive steps? Bournonville lost his virginity when he became a trade, with *Napoli* and its infectious joy in dance as the gilt-edged trademark for the Royal Danish Ballet (Christina Olsson, Lloyd Riggins and Nikolaj Hübbe, 1992. Photo: David Amzallag).

osmosis anymore, it becomes so defined and exposed. When the Sylphide's wings are touched, they fall off. You have to realize that in any kind of art form there is always a vacuum of something indefinable. It's as if you know everything and you know nothing. In order to define something there is one box you are not allowed to look into, like in Bluebeard's castle, you cannot reveal all the secrets. If you do that, you've deconstructed it so much that you risk taking all life out of it. That's what happened to Bournonville.

Bournonville forever?

What is your solution to the question of how to keep Bournonville alive if you think he has become too defined and deconstructed?

You have to keep the ballets alive on their own premises. It isn't so much a question of defining, the important thing is to give each new generation - a James or a Sylphide - a real feeling for it. Then the ballet lives. I was taught these things by people who were into Bournonville all their lives. In the end you do it because you love it. You have to pass that on to new dancers. You must have that conviction.

I've just done *The Conservatoire* at the School of American Ballet - I love handing Bournonville's ballets on as if they were gold. My enthusiasm made them aware that this is great choreography. Of course, American dancers have a different approach from my more emotional attachment because they come from Balanchine and from an academic school, so I was worried that it wasn't sophisticated enough for them. But it involves a technique that is very hard, and it's also musical and makes sense. I felt home again, I miss Bournonville, he is part of my life.

When you stage The Conservatoire *or* The Bournonville Divertissement, *do you take certain liberties that you wouldn't dare to take in Copenhagen?*

I take no liberties. The steps are there, that's what you have to do, finito. When you are 28 and a big shot and your back is bothering you, you may change a step to make it more convenient. But if you start out changing the steps as a young boy, then by the time you are 25 you won't be able to recognize any ballet whatsoever. Anyway, why would you want to change the steps? That would be like taking a painting by Hammershøi and saying, "Well, the skirting board in the drawing room could do with a more lively colour."

This is nevertheless what has been happening to Bournonville all along. Steps and scenes have been changed over the years as the result of different attitudes to tradition.

True, if I was staging *Sylphide* I would cut the passage at the beginning when Gurn comes home from the forest and the others keep asking him questions in mime, "What did you see? - what happened?" "I - out there - saw a sylph," and then he sits down on the floor like an idiot. I always thought that was so strange, because I don't think anybody else can see her, they don't have that kind of awareness. Gurn could come in saying, "I saw James running on the hill like a crazy lunatic."

Then you do accept the possibility of making changes in the ballets?

Yes, it's a living art form, but I don't believe in change just for the sake of change. You have to have a valid reason. I saw a version of *Napoli*, and people were so enthusiastic about the changes they'd made, but all they did was to run in from the first wing for the pas de six. And I thought – what's that gonna do? You have this huge bridge with a great hole, what a great entrance, why do you want to run in from the first wing like a divertissement ballet?

The important thing, as I see it, isn't so much the steps, it's how you do the steps. It's up to the dancer and the director to colour it, to deliver it in such a way that the step is fulfilled. I think dance should have colour.

The latest production of The Kermesse in Bruges *tried to get away from a more trivial, humorous domesticity, reaching for a bigger ballet within the ballet.*

I haven't seen the new version, but of all the Bournonville ballets *The Kermesse in Bruges* is probably the most comical, like a farce.[4] I think they should do it like *The Olsen Gang (Olsen Banden*, popular Danish film farce, ed.). If you want to do anything to it you should go completely overboard, because it's extremely funny.

However, the main characters almost end up being burnt at the stake as part of an erroneous quest for happiness with spiritual overtones. Shouldn't there be some edge to the fun?

Of course, it should be brutally comical. If you try to make it into a moral case, saying art conquers everything because of the viola da gamba, it becomes too arty. The ballet is simply hilarious.

You cannot go in and really change the ballets, but you can change your attitude towards them. It's like singing *Lysets engel går med glans* (*The Angel of Light in all his Radiance*, Danish hymn, ed.). It's really about belief. You have to instil that in people. And this is where I sometimes feel they excuse themselves, "We have to make Bournonville better." No, we don't have to make him better, we have to better ourselves.

Nevertheless, a lot of people think Bournonville is too much of a burden from the past, suggesting that we just keep Sylphide, Napoli *and* The Conservatoire *and skip the rest.*

Why would you want to skip your roots? Why just turn the Royal Danish Ballet into any other company that does the same ballets as all over the world. If you go to the Paris Opera or Covent Garden or the Metropolitan - they do the same handful of ballets everywhere.

Ballet is for the few, a ballet audience will always be smaller than a theatre or opera audience. Dance is the least bankable, but it's a specialty, especially Bournonville. I'm sure that it doesn't appeal to a lot of people, but you cannot just produce what appeals to a lot of people. We have an obligation to keep Bournonville alive. We are the ones who can do it. You cannot let less knowledgable factors dictate what's going to happen.

You have to take great care of your heritage, evaluate and re-evaluate, and make sure that it makes sense. It's time for the Royal Danish Ballet to go back and dig into history in order to find out when and why they were at their best. It's very hard to have a tradition. But it should also be a great blessing, it should be a springboard. When you have a tradition you can afford to do other things.

If you wanted to convince a dancer from another tradition that they should do Bournonville, what would you say?

There are certain aesthetics that are eternal. Bournonville's choreography is of infinite value - his definition of how to be on stage, how to generate feeling, how to evoke an emotion, how to catch an audience and entertain them. Bournonville had such a gift for entertaining and for composing, his ballets are like paintings, perfectly composed.

In *The Conservatoire* there is a magnificent moment at the end: pas de bourrée and pas de basque and balloné and change of direction. It comes right before the finale, when it's getting a little repetitive and you just want everything to finish, and then - boom! - a boy does this step and you just go, "Wow! Did you get that!" It's as Balanchine said, "Surprise is a great ingredient." He also said, "Vulgarity can have its place."

Bournonville meets Mr. B.

Going from Bournonville to Balanchine, did you find your background a help or more of a hindrance?

I think it was a help. Balanchine is a different tradition, but there is a technical approach that is very like Bournonville. Balanchine entertained with steps too - he threw everything else away. A lot of Balanchine ballets don't have the big Russian jump for the men, but the petit allegro and the middle allegro seen in Bournonville. Musically it's also like Italian bel canto, very sharp and chiselled. Bournonville is fleet-footed and precise, and he has the French school with batterie and all that, so does Balanchine.

Although a ballet like *Jewels* is much more Latin, brassy and overtly sexual, there are elements that you can trace right back to something in a Bournonville ballet. In *Rubies* there is a passage that is just like the tarantella in the third act of *Napoli*, when they reach down for the foot. In Balanchine: the woman goes - the man goes - she dares him with the other leg - he dares her with the other leg - and they all go together. It's sort of the same, just another version.

In Bournonville you had this sense of a closed space, how do you feel space in Balanchine?

You have a sense of wide open spaces. It's huge, your eyes travel far. Like Bournonville he never stops but keeps moving, covering the space.

You characterized Bournonville as wholesome, is this also an element in Balanchine?

Sometimes. There is, for instance, something wholesome about the atmosphere and the execution in *Square Dance* and *Theme and Variations*. I have a colleague who calls it "the trained seal act," saying, "Oh, you're so good at that" – but I really enjoy it.

You never felt intimidated by dancing Apollo in Balanchine's home base?

No, it's a great feeling. I was fairly intimidated when I first learnt it from Henning Kronstam. [5] This man in his mid-fifties started moving about so supremely – I thought: why don't you do it yourself, why do I have to dance it? He was larger than life. I also felt that with Peter Martins, he was so beautiful. But you make it your own. If you thought like that every time you stepped on stage, you would never dance.

Dancing Balanchine here is very stimulating, precisely because there are so many people who have opinions about it. It's the same if you step into an Ashton or a MacMillan role at the Royal Ballet in London, or if you go to Denmark and Peter, Poul, and Hans are standing in the wings watching you.[6] That's tradition.

The other world – the life of the immediate

With Bournonville you go into another world of sylphs or dancing Italians, where do you go in an abstract Balanchine ballet?

That depends on the ballet. Mostly it's a more physical space. There is the element of partnering in Balanchine that I miss in Bournonville – but then it's much better for your back. It's a very physical partnering – the pas de deux in *Agon*, for example, which is like a contest or a fight where you measure yourself up against the woman. The tension is sort of aggressive. You don't get that in Bournonville, because you barely touch her.

Larger than life. It could be daunting to dance Apollo on Balanchine's own turf, but Nikolaj Hübbe is stimulated by the sensation that everyone standing in the wings has his or her own opinion of how it should be done, "That's tradition." (*Apollo*, 1999, New York City Ballet. Photo: Paul Kolnik).

Do you feel more a man of this century when dancing Balanchine with all his speed and abstractions?

I'm a man of this century when I do Bournonville. I'm a man of this century every time I step on stage - even in Balanchine's story ballet, *La Sonnambula*, which is set in France in the late 19th century. You don't go into another century, you go into another realm - you go into the life that goes on, the life of the immediate. What is right here on stage with you now is all exceptionally heightened. You don't think about what you prepared during rehearsal; you are just here, right now, in the moment.

Nevertheless, there are different approaches to this "life of the immediate", Sylphide offers a different universe from Agon.

It's all about the images you can play with as a dancer. In *Agon* it's called the knighting step - when the girl lifts her leg over your head and places it on your shoulder. Sometimes the dancer does it like the Queen Mum knighting you, another girl will do it as if she is sharpening a blade on your shoulder. What I have to think as a performer in *Sylphide*, when looking up at Effy and then looking at my ring, is, "Oh my God, this ring hurts so much that it's burning into my skin, I have to make my hand heavy." I have to make images for myself, but I can't speculate about the greater picture.

Is it because of your dramatic background as a Bournonville dancer that you also produce images when dancing more abstract ballets?

There has always been a theatrical dimension to my dance but, without sounding arrogant, I think basically it's a question of talent. You just do your little images and it's worlds apart: "Take her hand as if you love her - as if you would have nothing to do with her." "As if" is great.

Does this technique of make-believe sometimes take you into another world to the extent that you get high when dancing?

To get high on stage is the greatest experience, but it happens very rarely. It has only happened to me a few times. Everything stands still, so many images come into your mind, it's like opening up - something comes in and something goes

131

out. You are conscious, but you are actually unconscious. It's like something else has taken over your role. You are not living the ballet, the ballet is living you. Afterwards I don't recall exactly what happened, but the emotion stays there. It's a very private experience, it's almost like sexual fulfilment - it isn't anyone else's business. You go into another world, but it's a private world.

I treasure those unique moments, when the energy seems to jump onto another level. I thought it would be a shared moment - that when you feel high, so does the audience?

I'm not sure that although the dancer feels intoxicated the audience feels something special. Of course, I know the feeling of being ready to give yourself up completely to the stage. But does that mean that everybody else feels the same way? The other day I saw a colleague in Balanchine's *Ballet Imperial* - what she was doing was so beautiful, so musical and exquisite that I began to cry. Afterwards I thanked her for this sublime experience, and she just said, "Yes, I think it went really well today."

I always wanted to dance the boy in *Barocco*. I thought it was so beautiful and expressive, so lyrical and serene, it was like going to church. When I did it, it was nothing. All you do is lift and support and make sure that the girl's okay. You have very little to express, it's hard work, the opposite of a great, otherworldly experience - though hopefully it'll be so for the audience.

Isn't there another dimension to the hard work of dancing? I remember Nureyev saying that doing the daily barre was like saying a prayer.

Classical ballet is profoundly stylized, so rigourous and formal that it's like Buddhist mantras where repetition, the reiteration of a few words, gives a spiritual cleansing. You find strength and reasurrance in the steps which are built according to ancient hierarchic ideals, they contain in themselves the whole principle of order.

Let's do *Sylphide* one last time

Which ballets have been the most important in your career?

Sylphide, Romeo and Juliet, Apollo and *West Side Story.* I don't know if they are important for my career, but they are very close to my heart. I grew up with James, *Sylphide* was the first ballet I ever saw, and when I finally danced James it felt so natural, it was like family.

Romeo was like coming of age, "Yes, I will do this, yes, I will be a dancer." It started so many things - how to carry a girl, how to carry a ballet, how to carry yourself. I love that ballet and I prefer Neumeier's version to any other *Romeo and Juliet.*

Apollo was fantastic, naturally, because you're a god. I've done it so often that I feel I have conquered it. It's like a second skin. It's still intact, it never fails you, it never wears thin on you.

What's it like to be a god?

I feel I have complete power over the women, they just do as you tell them. No business tycoon on Wall Street could feel more powerful than me.

Originally, I didn't want to do Riff in *West Side Story.* I was so scared of singing and all that acting. I think Jerry (Jerome Robbins, ed.) had his eye set on me from the beginning. I learnt the role, and he said, "And now you start singing" - "I'm not gonna sing" - "SING!" It was wild. Some of his ballets are really not exciting, others like *West Side Story* just get better and better as you dance. I love doing it, and I love being able to span wide. One day you do *Theme and Variations* and the next night you do *West Side Story.*

It was fantastic doing *West Side Story.* Imagine - you're allowed to touch this material, meet this living legend. You feel you get a small portion of the fame connected to the greatest musical of our century. It's like a phantasm. You're touched by history, you were part of it.

"Let's do *Sylphide* one last time." Hübbe in his inner signature role as James, the man of passion with a belief in the revelation of the instant, the other world come true (Nikolaj Hübbe and Lis Jeppesen, 1989, Royal Danish Ballet. Photo: David Amzallag).

Does it sometimes make you wonder if this is for real?

It's always a bit like that. "Am I dreaming or am I awake," as Holberg said. [7] It's a dream to be on stage. Imagine – I'm allowed to do all these things, playing the hero roles. I felt that especially when I was younger, but you get used to it, even if somewhere you still feel like the happy amateur. You go on stage because you had the childhood dream that made you a dancer. It's your greatest desire: that people will like you. It's not much different from little girls in their tutus.

On a more general level, dancing is living another reality – it's a dream, imagination made real. It's strange that something so physical and strong can be based on something so delicate as hopes and dreams. That's the beautiful thing about dance, it isn't real and yet it is real. Dance and reality hold each other at bay.

Have you ever felt completely obsessed by a role?

Yes, James in *Sylphide* – I was completely obsessed. It was on my mind constantly. It was always operating. Even when I was doing other ballets I kept relating to James, comparing them to the feeling and the intensity I experienced there. It's become a sort of inner signature ballet. If I ever get the message, "Well, that's it, we're going to take away your knee and your calf and we're gonna cut off your toe, so it's now or never" – then I would say, "Lets do *Sylphide* one last time."

135

May 2000

Notes

1. The dancers mentioned were principals of the Royal Danish Ballet in the 1970s and 1980s.

2. The role of James in *Sylphide* was danced by Henning Kronstam (1934-1995) for the first time in 1956/57, by Peter Martins during the early 1970s and Arne Willumsen in the later part of the '70s. Niels Kehlet danced his James for the first time at the Royal Danish Theatre in 1973/74.

3. Hans Brenaa (1910-1988) was the most prominent director of the Bournonville repertoire from the mid-1950s until his death.

4. *The Kermesse in Bruges* was restaged in 2000, in a new version, by Dinna Bjørn, Anne Marie Vessel Schlüter and Jan Maagaard.

5. Henning Kronstam was Balanchine's choice as Apollo in his staging of the ballet for the Royal Danish Ballet in 1957. Nikolaj Hübbe's first appearance as Apollo was in the 1988/89 season.

6. Peter, Poul and Hans are common Danish boys' names.

7. Ludvig Holberg was a major Danish-Norwegian dramatist (1684-1754). His plays are still central to the Scandinavian repertoire.

The Human Dimension in Bournonville

Interview with Dinna Bjørn

by Monna Dithmer

What made you originally want to dedicate your career to Bournonville?

Dancing his steps made me feel so good, it felt so natural. It was a privilege to get the chance of travelling the world as a member of The Bournonville Group, and it's a privilege to stage his ballets.[1] Bournonville has meant everything to me, he has been the backbone of everything I've done.

What is it like to be inside a Bournonville character?

There is so much joy. He said himself that dance should be an expression of joy. Doing his choreography is a freedom and a joy that I haven't felt in other classical ballets, where it's certainly not always a joy. The sense of freedom comes from the feeling that you are communicating. It's not just a one-way thing when you're dancing Bournonville. Ever since I first danced Bournonville, I've always felt that the audience gets caught up by the joy you feel. Of course I'm now talking specifically about the actual dancing, not the mime. People become involved when watching Bournonville, it touches the heart.

The challenge with Bournonville is that you have to be aware of what to express. What is the story? It's not just a question of the placement of an arm, but a question of what you feel when doing the steps. What is this person trying to express? You should feel the roundness of the arm. The dancers start to feel like humans relating to one other, they aren't just dancers.

It almost sounds as if it was modern dance.

I've always felt that Bournonville was modern. Not that my teachers, Hans Brenaa and Kirsten Ralov, told me so, but when I started to teach I found out that everything comes from the centre.[2] At that time I was taking Martha Graham classes in New York and many of the things said in class were the same things I tried to explain when teaching Bournonville: the relationship to your centre and to a certain sense of feeling human - an idea that the movements come from your heart. They're not just ornaments. In that way it's very like modern dance.

Bournonville wanted to show the vulnerability of human beings. He didn't like all the bravura and superficiality that later became the trademark of the Russian style. Fantastic jumps eliminate the feeling that this is a vulnerable human being. In most traditional versions of *Swan Lake* and *The Sleeping Beauty* you don't become so involved with the characters as humans - they are much more beautiful cliché-figures. Bournonville wanted the dancers to be human rather than dancing machines. He made ballets about real people - that was really his starting point and a way to break down the wall between the stage and the audience. That's what I read from his style. He wants a dancer to communicate, not to show off and thereby lengthen the distance to the spectators. He wanted the dance to get much closer to us.

The ballets are designed for a certain size theatre and audience in a very little country, so everything is on a smaller family scale. If the auditorium is too big, you get too far away, losing the feeling of being part of it that was so essential to Bournonville. You need some kind of intimacy to tell his stories. People often think that in Bournonville you simply do everything smaller, but it's just as much a question of communication and contact. The rounded arm doesn't mean it should be small and protected, it should just look as effortless as walking.

If you shouldn't think of doing everything smaller, what feeling should you have?

The roundness of the dance makes it communicate. You are not just dancing out, showing yourself to an audience, you are also bringing in. There is something very inclusive in the style. The direction of your eyes, where you are looking, is very important. The way you use your eyes is just as important as the steps. I was

As a signature gesture of the Bournonville style, the rounded arm seems to embrace everyone, both those on the stage and in the auditorium. Rather than dazzle with superhuman virtuoso numbers the dancer suggests a more intimate and vulnerable human scale (Dinna Bjørn and Anne Marie Vessel in The Bournonville School, *Wednesday's Class*, 1973, Royal Danish Ballet. Photo: John R. Johnsen).

never told specifically about this, but I have learnt it from watching other dancers. Sometimes, though, Hans Brenaa would say, "You have to loo-ook towards your hand" - but it was not so specifically clear-cut as it is now, when the art of teaching has become much more specialized.

Where you look also includes the audience - you look down at your foot, making the audience look at your foot. You don't see that connection in other styles. That's a speciality of the style that gives the ballet another dimension, where you are including instead of just presenting.

Inner world and other world

Does this way of following the movement with the eyes make it more of an inner world?

Yes, it's an inner world, and at the same time you share it. In that way all of Bournonville is very much the other world. The ballets have to do with an inner world. That is why they can be interpreted in a thousand ways. It's almost like a dream with a lot of symbols. In the first acts of *Napoli* and *The Kermesse in Bruges* you are of course in an everyday situation, you are among people, but even then it has a lot to do with the inner world of those people. There is always an element of something else - in *The Kermesse* there is the alchemist, in *A Folk Tale* there is this underworld, in *Sylphide* you have this world and the other world.

Do you mean some kind of double presence? The sylph has something ambivalent about her, she can also be almost demonic and frightening, tempting this young man into the wild forest.

True, *Sylphide* is Bournonville's most interesting story although he stole the idea. You can interpret the relation between James, the Sylphide and the witch in so many ways. As I see it, the witch is the most interesting figure because she belongs in both worlds, she is the go-between. She is a quite concrete human being who comes to the house, and at the same time she is definitely part of the other world. She is in control and manipulates the sylph as well, whereas the sylph either hasn't got the power or doesn't have the desire to transform herself into a human being.

You see the witch and the Sylphide as doubles?

Exactly, they are two sides of the same thing – the witch is a fallen sylph, especially the way in which a dancer like Sorella Englund depicts her, with arms like broken wings.[3]

This isn't an interpretation I've learnt from Hans Brenaa or anyone else I've worked with, but it has become obvious to me when I have staged or seen *Sylphide* in other countries. Brenaa told so many different stories. In my time we were five different people dancing *Sylphide*, and I found out afterwards that he had told us all different stories about what she was like, according to our individual personalities. However, the steps were the same. He told me about the sylph's sadness, her desperate attempt to avoid losing James. It became a very human story. Another Sylphide could be much more playful or calculating and conscious of what she was doing. I think all interpretations are valid.

It's part of Bournonville's genius that he can create this picture. It's like a painting coming alive. When you watch this painting, there are a thousand little stories being told. Of course each story doesn't have the same value – one story is the framework, but you can show it from different angles.

In order to balance between these worlds you have to do things very simply, this is always the case with Bournonville. You can't change the steps or the story, but if the dancers have ideas about doubles, or hidden worlds, or whatever; it comes out in a kind of tension in the atmosphere. If you can make the dancers feel this, it communicates to the audience. If you explain too much, it becomes too concrete and loses its magic.

Mime – an unexplored language

What part does the mime play in creating these different worlds?

Bournonville's mime is as important as the steps. It's so special, again it goes back to the inner feeling. Mime has to be taught as something that you feel more than something you are instructed to do. In Russian ballet, mime is much more functional with gestures like a sign language – with Bournonville it becomes dance.

Bournonville's way of using mime was a revolution at the time, even if it was normal to do mime. In Galeotti's ballets more than two thirds was mime, but it was much more rigid, almost like tableaux. Bournonville transformed that into a kind of choreography.

Can the Bournonville mime language express more than the ordinary ballet mime? Is there a larger vocabulary?

It could be interesting to see just how many things are actually being said in all the existing ballets. In some of the forgotten ballets you can still see from the notation what was said in the mime scenes. I tried to reconstruct a mime scene from *Soldier and Peasant*, one of Bournonville's very first ballets, where, as in *Giselle*, a girl picks up a flower and pulls off the petals, asking, "Does my fiancé, who is far away, still love me - does he not – yes, no - yes, no?" It's like a solo, and there would seem to have been a lot of them. In the existing ballets it's mostly a case of conversations, probably because the solo mimes have been taken out.

What always fascinates me in the mime scenes is that you can feel the strength of these people from another age approaching us, making now and then come together.

Yes, suddenly it's like another world coming alive, a past world becomes a present moment. Mime is an unexplored part of the Bournonville tradition, it should come much more into focus because that's what makes Bournonville's ballets so different from the other classical ballets. It's a special trademark of his ballets.

It could be interesting to isolate the mime and look at this particular aspect of the ballets. There is as much mime as there is dancing in the ballets. Since the 1979 Bournonville Festival we have focused so much on the dancing, the steps, the style - now it's time to focus on mime and make it more valued.

The Conservatoire was recently reconstructed, with its mime scenes; however, now we are left with just the dance act once again.

Hopefully the mime scenes will come back, because they were really interesting. All the little meetings and dates based on mime in the second act - it was like three mime pas de deux in a row. We don't have this in any of the other existing Bournonville ballets.

143

Mime is an unexplored part of the Bournonville tradition. The Sylphide has many faces, depending on who is behind them. Dinna Bjørn revealed a sylph of sadness, making "desperate attempts to avoid losing James" (Dinna Bjørn and Flemming Ryberg, 1971, Royal Danish Ballet. Photo: John R. Johnsen).

Bournonville said that the steps expressed joy, whereas the mime represented the other feelings. Do you agree?

Yes, the actual pieces of choreography always come in moments of joy and celebration in his ballets. But it's too easy to say that whenever you dance in Bournonville you're happy. Of course there are other feelings, especially in *Sylphide*. James' solo in the second act certainly doesn't just tell a joyful story. He is losing himself in the dance. He becomes more and more like a sylph, losing his touch with reality. Another example is Birthe's solo in *A Folk Tale*, she is frightened and overwhelmed when the troll in her comes through in her dancing - it's certainly not a moment of joy.

Reinventing Bournonville?

You've worked on staging as well as reconstructing the ballets - what should be kept alive as the Bournonville tradition?

The legacy of the seven ballets that we already have and *La Ventana* should definitely be kept alive. The Danish Ballet has an obligation to keep that repertoire alive, although it was pure chance that these particular ballets were kept – they happened to be in the repertoire when Bournonville resigned and he made his successor keep them there. That's why they survived, not necessarily because they were the best. I think some of them actually weren't. *The King's Volunteers on Amager* is very sweet but not so strong, and *Far from Denmark* would also have been lost if it hadn't happened to be in the active repertoire.

The larger-scale ballets *Sylphide* and *Napoli* are now being put on around the world, like *Swan Lake* and *Giselle*, whereas *The King's Corps of Volunteers on Amager*, *A Folk Tale*, *The Kermesse in Bruges* and *Far from Denmark* have remained a Danish specialty.

Which of the forgotten ballets do you consider the biggest loss?

I would have loved to know them all. Bournonville's manuscripts are so beautiful, they are like little poems. Then there is the music. *The Valkyrie* has such lovely music that the ballet should be reconstructed. I couldn't do it because I'm not a

Lost in the grip of a fallen sylph. James, the dreamer, becomes more and more like a sylph, ensnared by Madge's manipulative grasp (*Sylphide*, Sorella Englund and Arne Willumsen, 1979, Royal Danish Ballet. Photo: John R. Johnsen).

choreographer – it needs a real choreographer of today, interested in doing it in collaboration with a Bournonville reconstructor.

How do you go about the reconstructions? What are your sources when trying to find out what the movements were like?

The reconstructions I have done have mostly been dances, based on notation. But in *The Kermesse in Bruges* I reconstructed mime scenes, and those conversations were written in the score. Some of the gestures had been lost, however, so I had to reinvent them. I basically used some of the mime language we know from the other ballets - there's a pattern you can work it out from.

It seems that the reconstructive zeal to dig out new old ballets has ebbed away?

I think people realized that maybe it wasn't the right way to renew the repertoire, because it's more likely to turn out as copies of the ballets we already know. Maybe they were very different, because Bournonville could allow himself to be very different. Now when we try to reconstruct a ballet we feel an obligation to be very faithful to the Bournonville tradition, and it ends up like a copy of *Napoli*. *Abdallah* is proof of that - it's a wonderful reconstruction, but it doesn't add anything to the Bournonville tradition.

It seems quite difficult to change anything in a Bournonville ballet, because everything is interconnected and suddenly you miss a point somewhere else?

When you're trying to rethink the ballets and make new productions of Bournonville, you may find an interesting new way of doing one of the scenes, but then you realize that the whole ballet was so logically constructed that if you take something out here, it's missing somewhere else. If you change it too much, it may upset the whole balance. Speaking in broad terms: the more things you want to change, the more you realize that you should keep them as they are.

But then again, over the years the ballets have been changed, and the question is why and how have they been changed, and should we try to recover the original? This has a lot to do with Hans Beck's administration of the tradition.[4] What we now love in *Napoli* with all its dances, well, they weren't there originally.

Do you mean that sometimes there is more Beck than Bournonville in the tradition?

No, but Hans Beck was very much in Bournonville's spirit and close enough to the tradition. At the same time he had that little distance to the ballets so that he could see what really could be done here and there. Maybe he has made the ballets better.

Then there was the period when everything was taken out, such as the mime scenes. That happened when Harald Lander, in collaboration with Valborg Borchsenius, was bringing the ballets back into the repertoire, and again a lot of changes were made. [5] We have now tried to reinsert those omissions in the new productions, but of course it will never be like it was.

What is tradition to you? Convention doesn't necessarily mean being true to the work?

I've been forced to rethink this problem about convention the more I have gone into restaging Bournonville's ballets. There is a danger here. You want to be so true to what has been done that you forget that this is just one outcome of a series of previous interpretations.

This is the challenge, but also the difficulty, of staging Bournonville in his own country: there are a lot of fixed opinions about how it should be done. It can be a problem if you are so ingrained with the tradition that you don't have sufficient distance and just take some things for granted. A certain distance is very important.

At this stage of the Bournonville tradition in Denmark there is a fear of losing tradition. I've felt a great responsibility not to let things go too far, whereas when I have staged the ballets abroad, I have found it interesting to see what the dancers would bring to them - often something different, but why not? I've been very strict with the style and the dancing, but not so much with the interpretation. Here I have to be the restorer - which can be a danger. You can kill the tradition if you try to preserve it too much. It has to be a living tradition.

One extreme way to keep Bournonville would of course be to say, "Now we have seven authorized versions of these ballets, let's put them all on film and that's it. We don't have to do another Bournonville ballet for ten years, because we can reconstruct him any time, just bring out the tapes."

147

That sounds more like canned beans?

If we just say that now we want to catch hold of Bournonville and keep him in exactly the right authorized way, we might risk losing him. Things have to be allowed some freedom.

Could you give a sort of recipe of how to keep the Bournonville ballets alive?

Keep the steps and the mime as precise as possible and then give a lot of freedom. The ballets can stay alive if you allow the dancers to interpret their parts differently from ways in which they have been done before. At best there should be different versions of *Sylphide* - in my time Hans Brenaa was doing one *Sylphide*, Lizzie Rode another, and Henning Kronstam was doing his. [6] They were all slightly different. There has to be a continuity, and things will change gradually. Every now and then it will be necessary to make a new production, but it will have a connection to the previous one. If we want to explore the various possibilities in the ballets, we could keep a closely reconstructed version of the ballet, as with *Sylphide* now, and then dare to make an extremely different version of it.

148

Like Mats Ek and his Swan Lake?

Yes, you can learn a lot from seeing both versions. You could also learn a lot about Bournonville - it can help us to understand things in a new way.

Dancers are the backbone of a living tradition

When is tradition alive, when do the ballets get too far away from Bournonville, where is the borderline?

I think it has something to do with the humanity. The changes must come from an inner feeling. You don't change to get an effect, but because you feel the person would do this, and it would be better. This is why it's very much up to the dancers who do the ballets - they should have the freedom to interpret. That's what keeps the ballets alive.

It's not only thanks to Hans Brenaa and Kirsten Ralov that we have these ballets, it's also thanks to all the dancers who have passed on their insight into the roles. These links are of tremendous importance.

Previously, there was probably greater freedom for each dancer to add something, do something slightly differently, and then it was passed on as tradition, even if it wasn't how Bournonville did it. There was a time when Gurn was played as a very comic figure, now he's played more like an equivalent to James.

To what extent should the dancers and directors be free to interpret?

You must know the ballets from the inside, not just from doing one part. You must know the classes, the music and know about Bournonville and his history. If you know all this, you can allow yourself to change things. Incidentally, it's fantastic to read Bournonville's books because sometimes it's as if they were written yesterday, with all the problems of politics, money and management.

Everybody who does Bournonville and thinks about what they do should pass on their experience, coaching new directors and dancers. Otherwise I fear there might not be a new generation of Bournonville ambassadors. At the moment there are dancers like Thomas Lund and Gudrun Bojesen who can do this - of course they'll look at Bournonville slightly differently, just as Anne Marie Vessel, Flemming Ryberg, Frank Andersen and I did in our time. [7]

Bournonville is interesting because it's a living tradition, otherwise it loses interest. But you have to keep him a part of daily life, let the dancers do Bournonville class and dance his ballets. The training must be day-to-day to be in your blood. It's not enough to say that you maybe learnt some Bournonville as a child.

But you were seventeen before you started to learn the Bournonville style.

Yes, and I would never have learnt it if it hadn't been for the daily classes. Furthermore, the ballets must be part of the daily repertoire. The tradition cannot live if you only do a ballet every third year. This is the home base for Bournonville, so it has to be the real thing.

Bournonville in the blood. The legitimacy for continuing to perform Bournonville depends on the ballets being a living tradition. Conservation and renewal must dance close together (*The Kermesse in Bruges*, Anne Marie Vessel and Dinna Bjørn as Marchen and Johanna, 1979, Royal Danish Ballet. Photo: John R. Johnsen).

How do you motivate young dancers - especially those coming from abroad - to do the Bournonville training? Apparently this has also been a problem for the Royal Danish Ballet.

Bournonville has to be taught in a different way to dancers who have another background. It can't just be a case of learning the steps - there has to be much more awareness about the feeling of the steps and the style. This has not been developed enough in the Bournonville training. But I can't imagine that Bournonville would be anything other than a challenge for any dancer.

A Bournonville training is definitely a good background for many other styles because of the required effortlessness. This apparent non-effort has to do with the way you link the steps, which is a very important part of the Bournonville choreography. There have to be big steps and small steps, they are not all the same big size. In other styles you can practise your assemblé battu a thousand times. When you do Bournonville, you can't do separate steps, you have to practice a sequence of different steps. That's how you master the style – it depends on the connection between the steps. If you can really master these nuances, you can master any style. It gives you a vocabulary that you can actually use in modern ballet and dance. It's not unlike modern dance, where it's the flow of movement that counts rather than each separate movement.

When you stage Bournonville abroad, you are dealing with dancers who not only haven't had Bournonville on a daily basis, but no Bournonville training whatsoever.

Sylphide is the easiest ballet to do because it's similar to *Giselle* and *Swan Lake*. It's far more difficult with *Napoli*, especially the first act with so much mime. However, growing familiarity with Bournonville's technique, moving in his style, will gradually give you the feeling of how to do the mime.

A question of longing

Apart from technique and style, what is the attraction of a Bournonville ballet compared to Swan Lake *or* Giselle?

When you compare *Sylphide* and *A Folk Tale* to *Swan Lake, Giselle* and *The Sleeping Beauty*, you find the same underlying universal stories concerning love, manipulation and morality, but they are told in different ways.

The *Swan Lakes* and *Sleeping Beauties* have been staged everywhere, so there are no longer any originals around, whereas the Bournonville repertoire has been kept in Danish hands for so long that we are still very close to the source here, even if we don't know exactly what it looked like in Bournonville's time. That makes it an interesting study object as well.

There have been critical voices, though, claiming that the original ballets didn't look as light and humorous as today?

There are certain indications of this - for instance, Birthe in *A Folk Tale* has become more of a comic character. It's actually quite a terrible solo, as she is trying to hide that she is scared about something inside her, the troll inside her. The other world exists in her mind.

The Kermesse in Bruges *has usually been staged as a purely comic number, although there is the story about alchemy, which basically deals with how to transform flesh into spirit?*

That story is definitely there, but I don't know if Bournonville considered it the most important story. He said that he wanted to make a comic ballet, people should have something to laugh at. There can, of course, be a danger if the comical side takes over. However, if *The Kermesse in Bruges* was turned into a completely serious, dramatic ballet it would be wrong, because Bournonville wanted the ballet to be humorous.

Although Chekhov wanted The Cherry Orchard *to be funny, there have been pretty serious productions ever since. Is Bournonville the ultimate authority on what his work is about?*

There has been a tendency to make the Bournonville ballets steadily more light and entertaining. In their new production of *The Kermesse in Bruges*, however, Dinna Bjørn, Anne Marie Vessel Schlüter and Jan Maagaard wanted to provide the comedy with a somewhat deeper dramatic intention (Gudrun Bojesen and Thomas Lund as Eleonore and Carelis, 2000, Royal Danish Ballet. Photo: Martin Mydtskov Rønne).

I think so. Of course in ballet it can be more difficult to find the author's intention, because we only have the synopsis, the steps and the mime that has been passed down from one dancer to another. Anyway, Bournonville wouldn't have been interested in just making something comic - in that respect he's like Hans Christian Andersen and his fairy tales for children. For those who can see it, there are other dimensions - others can just have a good laugh.

Could these other dimensions have something to do with the longing that colours much of Bournonville's universe?

Yes, that's true, it's a very strong element in all of Bournonville's ballets. The moment you don't long for anything - that's when you're dead. If there are two worlds there will always be a tension between them, which can be a longing - it can also be a fear. In Bournonville it's mostly a mixture of both.

Have the more existential dimensions in the ballets been toned down to the advantage of a more cosy and joyful Biedermeier Bournonville?

Bournonville was certainly not a cosy little Biedermeier choreographer, his ballets cover a much larger emotional range. There is joy, naturally, but also fear and longing. His ballets contain more than one world. I think this is the case with all the ballets we know - even *Far from Denmark* has stories about passion, guilt and longing. The ballets are like a kaleidoscope, you can turn them a little bit around and then you see something else. You can choose to focus on one world more than the other, but it's all there.

April 2000

Notes

1. The Bournonville Group, known outside Denmark as Soloists of the Royal Danish Ballet, was founded in 1976 by Dinna Bjørn and Frank Andersen. The group, comprising 8-10 young dancers and occasional guests, toured the world for a decade as ambassadors representing the Bournonville tradition.

2. Hans Brenaa (1910 -1988) was the most prominent director of the Bournonville repertoire from the mid-1950s until his death. After Brenaa, Kirsten Ralov (1922-1999), a Bournonville director and the Assistant Artistic Director of The Royal Danish Ballet (1978-88), took over the task as chief custodian of the tradition.

3. Sorella Englund danced the Sylphide for the first time in 1973/74, and in 1979 she also showed her gift as a character dancer in the role of Madge, which she danced regularly until 1994.

4. Hans Beck (1861-1952) was constituted Artistic Director of the Royal Danish Ballet in 1894, 17 years after Bournonville's retirement, and he remained in the post until 1915. He considered it his main obligation to enable Bournonville's work to survive. On the one hand he revised and shortened the ballets, cutting out mime scenes and adding new dances, on the other hand he collected combinations of steps in the so-called Bournonville Schools which became the basic training material for the company.

5. Harald Lander (1905-1971) was Artistic Director of the Royal Danish Ballet 1932-1951. Following in the footsteps of Hans Beck, he gave the surviving Bournonville ballets the form they have largely retained up until today, cutting the mime scenes and inserting new dances with a focus on the entertaining aspect of the ballets. Soon after Lander's appointment, he engaged Valborg Borchsenius (1872-1949), who had danced the leading Bournonville female roles at the turn of the century, to assist him in staging the ballets and to serve as an official notator of the Bournonville repertoire.

6. Hans Brenaa staged *Sylphide* in collaboration with a series of Artistic Directors: Frank Schaufuss in 1956/57, Flemming Flindt in 1967/68 and Henning Kronstam in 1987/88. Lizzie Rode, who was the Assistant Artistic Director of the Royal Danish Ballet 1971-78, was also involved in staging the Bournonville ballets.

7. Thomas Lund and Gudrun Bojesen were appointed principals in 2000 and 2001 respectively, whereas Anne Marie Vessel, Flemming Ryberg, Frank Andersen and Dinna Bjørn were prominent dancers during the period from the mid-1960s to the early 1980s.

The Man Who Fell in Love with a Bird

The animal in dance

Monna Dithmer

How does one avoid getting into deep water in *Swan Lake,* where animal and human unite in one great embrace? It says something about the art of dance that this ballet of ballets, this love drama of dizzying pathos, is about a man who falls in love with a bird. Shakespeare may make merry with the idea of a woman's infatuation with an ass, but one has to go to the ballet to find a bird that can turn a man's head so that it becomes great tragedy. The dance quickly carries man away to the borderlands of existence, where, liberated from the rational anchoring of the word, the spectator reacts with "the willing suspension of disbelief", as the wild romantic Coleridge called it. *Swan Lake*, with its magically spiritualized world, is the epitome of the rapturous spirit of romanticism. But the existential brink on which it teeters, in the form of the alliance between man and animal, is not the exclusive preserve of the romantic ballet. The question of the animal in dance is something with which the art form as such confronts us: where are the boundaries of human identity?

In calling dance the most "bête" (meaning both foolish and animal) of all the arts, the French choreographer Serge Lifar was referring to the fact that a dancing human being is like the animals, having abandoned himself to physical destiny rather than letting the head have its way. In Western thinking the crucial distinction between man and animal has been that man is a speaking animal. As the psychoanalytical philosopher Lacan has formulated it, we are not only "êtres" but "parlêtres", speaking beings. Dance is on the other hand, by tradition, the mute art; the dancing human being has renounced the word and the arguments of reason in surrender to the body. Thus there is a special affinity between dancer and animal.

This is evident from the wealth of different animals and other creatures that have swarmed over the stage in the course of time, all the way from mouse-kings and snakes to rats and cats - not just in the fairytale world of romantic ballet, but also elsewhere. The diversity of species in the fauna of dance is to some extent indicated by the titles of different ballets, although this of course tells us nothing of how animal-like these creatures have appeared on the stage: Saint-Léon's *Le Petit cheval bossu,* Nijinska's *Les Bîches,* Fokine's *L'Oiseau de feu,* Tetley's *Sphinx,* Cullberg's *Månrenen* (*The Moon Reindeer*), Cunningham's *Beachbirds,* Mark Morris's *Dogtown* and Lloyd Newson's *Strange Fish.* Other creatures, such as sylphs, naiads, fauns, witches and elf-girls, are also included in the zoo of the dance, being associated with nature through their animal-like features such as sexuality, instincts and sensual power. Just think of the tempting sylph, who takes her name from the Latin word "silva" (forest), and whose gossamer wings come from the insect kingdom.

Winged beings have quite naturally been in the majority in the bestiary of dance, culminating with *le ballet blanc* of romanticism and its swans, sylphs and blue birds, for in its essence ballet is about elevating mankind into another world. While it is true that a definition of man as "a two-legged animal without wings" was current in Antiquity, the ballet seems, as the origin of the stage dance of the West, to have been created to prove the opposite: man as winged soul. To mark his state of civilization and his spiritual longing, *homo erectus* - standing man - could hardly have thought of a more fantastic being to separate himself from the four-legged species than the totally artificial creature of ballet, walking on its toes and reaching for the sky. Beyond the earthly, carnal limitations, the human being of ballet is the image of the purely ideal, an airborne species that frequents the realms where winged angels and the dove of the Holy Ghost belong. As a denizen of the air and archetypal image of the soul, the bird is thus assigned the role as the dancer's second nature, because it can connect heaven and earth, spirit and body. This, as will become evident, is the crucial, connective role that the dancing human being fulfils.

The history of dance can be seen as a continuous attempt to come to grips with the animal, which has manifested itself with everything from ethereal feathers to a sensually sweating body, depending on the prevailing aesthetic ideal and image of the body. To characterize a manner of dancing as "animal" was traditionally a kind of stigma, as if the dance had a carnal, awkward or spiritless aspect, whether in the form of a ballet dancer with no *ballon*, Isadora Duncan's shamelessly naked feet, or Martha Graham's passionate contorsions as if pregnant with a cube. Yet the animal, by virtue of modern dance's re-evaluation of the physical, sensual qualities associated with the bestial, has now emerged on stage in all its complexity. Today the animal is more than bogeyman or winged vision; a deliberate animal image is now cultivated and explored. Over the last few decades we have seen this explicitly signalled by butoh dancers with raw fish in their mouths, dance theatre populated by hippopotamuses and barking dogs, postmodern chimeras with trunks and webbed feet, bikini'ed ballerinas with insect shells on their backs, or a real live sheep let loose in a minimalist pastoral.[1]

In Western culture the animal has always functioned as the mirror of man, or more precisely as a metaphor of the body, the animal body. But whatever skin the animals on the dance stage have appeared in, the animal cannot simply be dismissed as a harmless reflection in which, depending on the spirit of the age, we can recognize ourselves, as an expression of good, primal nature or evil, primitive nature. While *Swan Lake* and its creatures expressed a romantic fairytale world where people can be turned into animals and animals can be given human souls, the metamorphic art and transformative power of ballet and modern dance go much deeper.

When dance represents the animal as something other than spiritless matter, this is an indication that the animal symbolizes other forms of existence for man than our narrow individual template. Rather like the automaton - the body as the mechanical - the animal is one of the subtle bodies that is at play in dance. The animal represents the dark sides of humanity and shows us that the individual is a multi-faceted, mutable entity. This is where the mute speech of dance has its strength, in its alliance with the animal as the representative of the Other; dance speaks of those things our culture has banished into the darkness. The animal in dance epitomizes the ambivalence of Western culture towards the body, and the problem of maintaining a dualistic distinction between body and spirit. Dance as an art form expresses the idea that the body is permeated by the spirit, that man is a totality of mind, soul and body.

With my point of departure in classical ballet as an extreme expression of the civilizational fate of the Western body, and as an attempt to overcome the gulf between body and spirit, I will dip into *Swan Lake* to investigate how the animal in dance has developed as an existential metaphor from classical ballet to modern dance.

The body as trained animal

In terms of cultural history, the grappling of dance with the animal is part of the Western disciplining of the body as an element in a totalizing subjection of nature, where the animal has become subordinate as an image of mankind's raw instinctive nature and uncontrollable drives. Although the body in its animal nature has been the object of changing valorizations throughout the ages, it has fundamentally been regarded as a primitive, incalculable creature that must be mastered, disciplined and shaped. It has been the civilizing mission of man to control his animal aspect, with disciplining and sublimation as the burden of culture.

However, as the philosopher Michel Foucault has demonstrated in his historical analysis of institutions, this is far from being a matter of simple repression of the body; it has just as much been about the construction of a new body, the imprinting of the body with the prevailing knowledge technology of the age.[2] "Biopower" is based on the body as the locus for the exercise of power in society and functions by way of a disciplining pincer movement. The body's abnormal imbalances, erotic desires, sensual impulses, rage and madness become the object on the one hand of controlling investigation and verbalization, on the other of systematic ordering in terms of the dominant framework of understanding. This means that the disciplining of the body takes place through the engrafting of a normative gender, a normative soul and reason, by means of a specialized technology of body and soul. As a central concern of biopower, sexuality, for example, is not something that is purely and simply repressed, but rather something that is installed as a normalizing factor in relation to the erotic desires of the body.

160

Swans are not what they used to be. Diving into the flesh, Mats Ek's waddling creatures (m/f) reveal the other side of the winged animal as an existential metaphor; a radical contrast to the ethereal species of classical ballet, liberated from animal flesh (*Swan Lake*, 2000, Cullberg Ballet. Photo: Lesley Leslie-Spinks).

Biopower's normalizing hold on the body is manifested in an extreme way in dance and its disciplining of the animal body. For here it becomes clear that one not only shapes a body *secundum artem*, but also engrafts and coaxes forth a soul.

The animal in dance reflects the transformation that any body must undergo to be able to appear on the dance stage. While at one level the animal can represent the dancer's transformed body as it is manifested on the stage – light as a bird, supple as a panther – fundamentally it represents the raw, unprocessed body, the recalcitrant horse that must be tamed. Whatever the ideal for the dancing body - whether ethereal, fleshly, abstract or everyday-functional - a metamorphosis is necessary. The ordinary body with all its imbalances and flaws, habits and desires, is transformed to become the instrument of another cause – art, ritual, entertainment, or, as the ballet writer Rayner Heppenstall, with a typical animal metaphor, has said, the body and its "animal acts" are transformed into "mind".

162

> Man, in his natural state, plainly, is a thoroughly unsatisfactory piece of work: in form, in moving, far from express and admirable, as a rule and much less like an angel, in action, than a well-bred whippet is (...) And ballet, fundamentally is an attempt to defeat this fact (...) the emergence of non-cerebral Matter into such a condition of subtlety and sensibility that it can itself be called Mind.[3]

If, of all dancing bodies, the balletic body is singled out to represent spirit, this is because, as a child of the Enlightenment, it is the very image of the civilized, rational, disciplined individual. Each movement is controlled down to the smallest detail, formed according to an aesthetic codex and an academic vocabulary of steps – a sophisticated kind of body technology that makes the machine, like the animal, a favourite metaphor of the body. The balletic body is a "machine for manufacturing beauty," said the ballet writer André Levinson, as an extension of the Enlightenment philosopher Diderot's view of the body as a machine for manufacturing feelings.

As a precondition of the dancers entering the airy otherworld of the ballet, it is precisely necessary that they have control of their limbs. As the dance theorist Jean-Georges Noverre insisted in the best Enlightenment spirit, although his *Lettres sur la danse* (1760) was also influenced by the new pre-Romantic sensibility, "Unless the heads of the dancers control their feet, they will always get lost."[4] True, nature was the model for Noverre's rationally-coloured dance, but it was a nature typified by order and harmony, moderation and control. Even in romanticism with its cult of wild, unspoiled nature, the mind may storm, and sylphs may leap up to carry nests down from the trees; but behind this is the thoroughly controlled balletic body and a formalized choreography. When the black swan of *Swan Lake* whirls superhumanly in her 32 *fouettés,* she maintains a cool, collected overview thanks to the fixed-spot technique. The ballerina's spins do not lead to the transcendent loss of self one associates with the whirling dances of other cultures.

Nevertheless this is far from being a matter of total rational control exercised in a veritable round-dance of body, mind and soul. For the spirit that must flow through the dancer is not only the rationality of mind, but above all soul. The ballet dancer may maintain the technical control, but the dance carries her over into the other world where, ideally, she dances with her soul. The art is a matter of balancing on the knife-edge of the spirit; between mind and soul. The technical perfection and control count for nothing in themselves. If dance is only mechanics and the dancers pure dancing robots, the result is, in Noverre's warning vision, a "spectacle des singes", a mere dance of monkeys. Dance, as he repeatedly insists, must "speak to the soul".

> I want the steps to be executed with as much spirit as art,
> and to correspond to the story and to the movements of
> the soul in the dancer.[5]

In the history of the ballet Noverre stands as the crucial driving force behind what is to be understood as "soul" in ballet. Although he often makes it a question of aesthetic sensibility rather than divine spirit – in accordance with the later secularizing development – this does not alter the fact that ballet dances on Christian ground with Original Sin and Redemption as dead weight and vision of freedom respectively. This is inherent in both the body technology and in the universe of the ballets.

Viewed in this perspective, the dancing body thus has the potential to elevate itself definitively above the animal. This happens inasmuch as the spirit transfigures the flesh, whereby the dancer escapes the natural fate of humanity: death. Mortality is after all a condition of life we share with the animals. Ballet is an image of mankind rising above his physical mortality and fallen fate by dint of spirit. The balletic body is the incarnation of Western man's longing to appear as pure spirit – a body transformed into a spiritualized work of art, formed as a symbol of eternal youth, beauty, perfection and soul. It is civilization's tour de force: from its low state the animal body has been elevated to incarnate perfection, immortal spirit.

A dance on Christian ground

164

The miraculous metamorphosis of the body in the grip of ballet follows in the footsteps of the great transformation mystery of Western culture: Jesus Christ, both man and God. [6] Regardless of the mainly condemnatory attitude of the Western Church's writings and practice regarding the body, Christianity is at its core based on the sacralization of the body with its fundamental dogma of the resurrection of the flesh. It is not only the soul that achieves life everlasting, but also the body. The body cannot be written off as the prison of the soul; it is, as St. Paul says, the temple of the spirit, and quite crucially it involves the potential of being transfigured by spirit. This is evident from the idea of the resurrected body, the spiritualized flesh purged of sin. Christ showed this as the great exemplar: mankind too has this dual nature - body and spirit can become one.

The sacralization of the body comes through sacrifice. Physical suffering or the mortification of the flesh is the way to sublimity, as prescribed by Christ on the Cross; no other religion has the suffering body as its central symbol. From this fundamental idea of sacrifice the Church has produced a comprehensive technology of body and soul, where medieval scholasticism with its ambition to unite the Christian faith with Aristotelian rationalism has formed a particularly crucial

Civilization's tour de force. The Prince triumphantly lifts his Swan Princess into the air, demonstrating the elevation of the animal body to pure spirit. The sinful, mortal body has become a symbol of perfection, eternal youth and spirit (*Swan Lake*, Andrew Bowman and Silja Schandorff, 1996, Royal Danish Ballet. Photo: Martin Mydtskov Rønne).

pivot. Ingenious prescriptions were drawn up for how one could mortify and purge the weak, fallen body, which was stigmatized as bestial. By virtue of a correct and erect posture the Christian could bear witness to his upward aspirations; the head was to control the limbs, the upper body was to rank higher than the lower body with its lustful loins, the right side was elevated above the left side, the left foot was more diabolically unpredictable than the right foot, etc. All in all, a bodily symbolism was developed which, with increasingly marked body-spirit symbolism, has influenced the civilized individual in our culture.

In this light the balletic body can be seen as an extreme version of the castigated, upward-aspiring body, transformed into spirit.[7] Beyond the splitting into spirit and body, the idea of the resurrected body is here kept alive as an aesthetic ideal. The body is raised up, but on the condition that the darkness of the flesh, all the sexual, physically sensual and instinctively animal, is purged away.

There is no question of a total purgation; rather, ballet excels through its capacity to channel the animal-like, the carnal, into a socially acceptable, aesthetically stimulating form, in a particularly refined sublimation. As the romantic poet Heinrich von Kleist puts it in his brilliantly imaginative story about the nature of dance, *Über das Marionettentheater* from 1810, it is a subtle balancing-act when the body has to dance with its soul.[8] A ballet dancer can easily come to dance with "his soul in his elbow", because he is controlled by his limited, sin-burdened consciousness. By contrast the dancing puppet is able to follow "the path of the soul" because it knows nothing of "the dullness of matter", the gravity of the awareness of sin that has been engrafted on man since the Fall, knowing his sex and his mortal difference from God. Similar to the marionette, even a fencing bear is cited by Kleist as an example of a perfect accord between body and spirit. The bear is invincible, since by almost scanning the soul in its opponent's eye, it can predict his next movement.

The marionette and the bear represent two different aspects of the dancing human being – form and geometry on the one hand, physicality and instinct on the other. By following the abstraction of form or physical sensing, the dancing human being can transcend the individual consciousness and the idea of the sinful, imperfect body. Man can recover the supreme balance between soul and body, maintains Kleist, if he again eats of the fruit of the Fall. In the context of dance this can be interpreted to mean that dance involves the possibility of acknowledging the body, sex and death anew as something other than an indication of our fallen state. Therefore, one must not purge away the animal, but dance with it as a carnal kind of knowledge. Just as the fencing bear demonstrates.

The romantic ballet, is, like the whole romantic *Sturm und Drang* about the divided being of humanity, a place where one can dance with the animal. As *Swan Lake* shows, though, this does not happen without a struggle. It is striking that the hunting of the animal also appears as a motif in ballets such as *Giselle*, *The Sleeping Beauty*, *A Folk Tale* and *Sylphide*. The animal is both pursued and coveted.

Fallen woman on her toes

The white ballerina in *Swan Lake* is the paradigm of the resurrected body: totally purged, disciplined and perfected, she is liberated from her animal flesh. According to the Biblical primal scene, the Fall, when man became one with and aware of his flesh, and thus became mortal, the woman as the carnal temptress must bear the wound of the Fall. In response to Eve's seductive behaviour with the fruit of the Tree of Knowledge, which opens Adam's and Eve's eyes to gender and sexuality, the serpent bites her on the heel. Bearing the mark of the beast, the body is now bound by death and the earth - a fallen woman with a wounded foot. It is not for nothing that the primal scene is literally described as a fall.

But the ballerina can elevate herself above the fallen fate of man, vile matter and its death-related horizontality. She is a spiritualized being, liberated from sex and death, just as the author and dance critic Théophile Gautier paid homage to the "Christian", "virginal" dancer Marie Taglioni in *La Sylphide*.

> Mlle. Taglioni is a Christian dancer (...) she flies like a spirit in the midst of transparent clouds of white muslin (...) she resembles a happy angel who scarcely bends the petals of celestial flowers with the tips of her pink toes.[9]

There is not much of the animal left there, while Gautier very tellingly taunts those dancers who can only soar with the aid of the hoists and swings of theatrical machinery, comparing them to "stuffed crocodiles" or "toads out of their element". Not all dancers, it is true, are equipped with a Taglioni's pink toes; on the other hand they have adopted her exquisite item of body technology, the pointwork shoe, which with its symbolic content crucially helps to manifest the ballerina as icon. Thanks to the ballet shoe, the sinful female body is raised above deathbound earthly matter, and the white silk sheath of the shoe can be seen as the bandages that heal the wound of the Fall. The fallen body can now take to the air with ethereal resilience or stand in balance with minimum contact to the ground. The ballerina's partner lifts her high into the immortal sphere as a demonstration that she is completely liberated from the heavy burden of the Fall. In addition he can now show her in obscene positions, legs apart in the tutu, for which a Hamlet would be banished from the stage if he dared to do anything like it with Ophelia[10] This is a clear demonstration of the purgative transformation of the dancing body. For the immaculate body in dance, sex is almost non-existent; to the pure, all things are pure.

However, the animal has a habit of rearing its head again, heralding the return of the repressed, the animal, instinctive, unconscious self, as Freud so revolutionizingly proclaimed just a few years after *Swan Lake* had its breakthrough in Petipa's and Ivanov's version of 1895. While the Swan Princess may appear as the epitome of soul, perfection and grace, she is still an animal. She is bound by day to her swan-skin, to nature, the depths of the water, and a warlock in the shape of an owl. Amidst all the grace of beauty the movements of the Swan Princess also signify the animal – just think of her signature position, half-lying, folded in upon herself like a sleeping bird. Where else does one see a ballerina in such intimate contact with earthly matter, unless she is close to death? And doesn't she strut with bird-like grace on her long legs as her arms flap and undulate while the small instinctive jerks of her head indicate the timidity of the wild animal?[11] Here she has nevertheless reached the limit of her animality; she is utterly chaste, with the typical elusive romantic female nature.

However, the black swan appears as a hidden shadow side, animal in the sense that it is erotically aggressive, shameless and faithless. Other famous romantic heroines also have their ominously animal-like sides, which even seem to bear death within them: the witch lurks behind the sylph, and behind Giselle the wilis

Temptress on her toes. Thanks to the exquisite item of body technology, the pointwork shoe, the ballerina can achieve her vertiginous balancing act in order to overcome the cultural gulf between body and spirit, animal and man, Fall and resurrection (*Swan Lake*, Heidi Ryum and Martin James, 1996, Royal Danish Ballet. Photo: Martin Mydtskov Rønne).

manifest themselves as fanatical killer females. Odette's fellow swans show no similar desire to attack, but in their white, anonymous homogeneity the flock of swans show what the transformation to animals involves: loss of individuality. This too is a kind of death.

The animal nature of the flock of swans appears when, quite contrary to the frontal codex of the ballet, they take up back-turning postures as if insisting on showing the reverse side of humanity. They can cultivate the cat leap, the so-called *pas de chat,* or advance in ranks with down-to-earth hops on flat feet, as if they really were a flock of birds at a lakeside. The nature of the swans is also manifested in a special gaze on the world, mainly along the vertical axis, so that the swans look up and down. This can give the impression of a disconcertingly alien scrutiny that sees everything in a bird's-eye view. The other world of the animals is forcing itself upon us.

The ideal world of ballet with its dream of love, harmony, beauty, youth, purity and immortal perfection takes that which is rejected along like a shadow. This is evident from all the stories of madness, jealousy, evil, death and sexuality. The artful balancing-act of the dancers is thus an existential imperative, since man is here cast out to move between the poles of existence, from the most spiritual to the bestial. As a space for human identity the ballet is a world in vertiginous balance.

The Swan Princess as an image of yearning

If the ballerina is, for once, to reveal her animal side by assuming the shape of an animal, the swan must be said to be an ideal choice. It is the perfect symbol to unite the dual, or rather multiple, nature that is characteristic of the dancing human being. First and foremost, the swan can connect the two borderline zones in human existence: animal and spirit, the most physical and the most ethereal. It is distinctive in its white grace, whether it glides over the water or up into the airy regions where mortals cannot follow. In addition, in the Christian conceptual world, it is a symbol of the Assumption of the Virgin Mary - her apotheosis. Despite this immortal status the swan at the same time bears death in the shadow of its wings, known as it is for its swan song just before it dies. This is evident from Fokine's *The Dying Swan* (1907), which can be seen as a last vanishing act for *Swan Lake*, a solo elegy for the Swan Princess as that which must not be lost, yet *is* lost and disappears.

The Swan Princess is a unique, precious being because she is animal, spirit and human being in one, an image of longing able to unite the elements that have been culturally set at war with one another. She is a vanishing legendary creature who points to a unity of the natural, the cultural and the supernatural that has been lost. As an animal-woman with a soul she falls outside the sphere of culture, impossible to capture for civilization's swan-hunters – as anything but dead prey – and only visible as something much more than an animal for the young prince who is prepared to go beyond the protective walls of the court culture and lose himself in the female, moon-dark forest, drawn by the romantic vision of the unified human being.

Siegfried is the archetypal youth who must leave "mother" and set off into the world to meet "woman", integrate nature, confront the father-figure and become a man. He is not free, but fenced in by his mother and the marriage-hungry maidens, and without a father-figure to provide backbone. But the Swan Princess is similarly unfree, trapped in her bird form by the animal father-figure Rothbart. Her human status depends on Siegfried, just as his spiritual and carnal manhood depends on her. Love sets them free and gives them the potential to unite the culturally separated elements of human life, body and spirit, animal and human.

The pas de deux is the meeting-place where the union of man and woman, human, animal and soul is displayed and celebrated. The Swan Princess's deep dives into *arabesque penchée,* her upward-striving *cambrées* and airy lifts show the tension between earth and heaven, animal and spirit, with the Prince providing the human scale and support. Only with his bird in his arms he can really dance. Nevertheless, the union of the different dimensions of existence is only possible for a short while.

As a typical romantic tragedy, *Swan Lake* also bears witness to the impossibility of the man becoming one with his bird in this world, whether the two lovers end up abandoning themselves to the waves or not. The ballet is fundamentally in the grip of an ambivalence towards the animal. Odette loses her animal self, but thereby also her swan-like supernatural status, the moment she can be united with a faithfully loving man. Although the swan feathers lock Odette in a state of animal enslavement, it is at the same time this dual nature that can liberate the Prince and give her direct access to another, supernatural world where the spiritual forces rule – even if it is in the form of Rothbart's sorcery.

During the nocturnal swan-hunt Siegfried refuses to shoot the great white bird with his crossbow, as his distant romantic cousin, Coleridge's Ancient Mariner (1798) did - having to wander through eternity as a punishment for killing the albatross. In contrast to this tale of a man who killed the bird with a soul, we here have the man who fell in love with it. The question is, however, whether the Prince really wants the animal as such, or whether he is only interested in the white, purged model. At all events the black, carnal swan appears with all the capacity of the repressed to return, strong and destructive. She forces her way into the heart of the court and the Prince, and wreaks havoc as a reminder that the Prince must embrace the whole animal.

172

Even here, at the heart of the ideal white ballet, which at its core is about the purgation of the carnal, the route goes through the animal, precisely as an indication that it is not just a matter of repression, but also of sublimation. *Swan Lake* thus becomes the story of the animal as an existential imperative. As much as a love drama, it is a drama of identity where the love between Prince and Swan is an image of man dancing with his soul – that is, with the animal as a kind of "sleeping partner," a sleep that results in the flooding of the identity. Prince and Swan perish in the Swan Lake. They must drown in the primal womb so they can later rise again to eternal life in the kingdom of the spirit.

The realm of metamorphoses

Thus, in immersing oneself in *Swan Lake,* one risks being swallowed up in the no-man's land of identity where a prince, if he is not turned into a frog, is at least set upon by a horde of swans until he learns to balance between the different dimensions of existence, between the physical and the metaphysical. However, this does not only apply to romantic ballet, where people are usually surrounded by supernatural, fairytale phenomena. It is true in general that the human being

The animal as an existential imperative. This is what *Swan Lake* is all about, whether it be the beast Rothbart or the pure creature Odette. A drama of identity, asserting the individual as a multivalent, mutable entity, in which body and soul are essentially an integrated whole (*Swan Lake*, Silja Schandorff and Peter Bo Bendixen, 1996, Royal Danish Ballet. Photo: Martin Mydtskov Rønne).

in dance moves out to the fringes of identity, under constant metamorphosis. Compared with other art forms, dance is a privileged locus for transformation of identity, as it is here manifested in corporeal form. That the self is not a fixed, demarcated entity is quite evident.

At the abstract level the dancing body dissolves and becomes forms, lines, rhythms, energies and shifting figures with the shifts in the flowing sequences of motion. At a more concrete narrative level, dual beings emerge – mechanical puppets, living statues, fairytale creatures and monsters, thematicizing the transformations of the identity. Transition and transformation are precisely the themes of the great ballets – *Giselle, The Nutcracker, Napoli, La Sylphide, La Bayadère* and *The Sleeping Beauty* can all be classified as tales of transformation, balancing on the borderline between youth and adult life, flesh and spirit, life and death, earth and heaven, and, not least, human and animal.

"Where does the dance come from, where does it go?" reflected Martha Graham. It is spirit that becomes body, becomes animal, becomes energy, becomes pure form and rhythm in a chain of transformations. "How can we know the dancer from the dance?" asked the poet Yeats. In the dance identity becomes fluid, a multivalent, mutable entity, the bodies constantly change form and glide together in configurations beyond the normal notions of individuality. This is visualized in the so-called "peacock", the final figure in Balanchine's *Apollo*, where Apollo and the Muses, man and woman, bodies and limbs appear as one figure consisting of several beings.

One can – more theoretically yet no less imaginatively – attempt to pin down the mutable creatures of dance by referring to the postmodern philosopher Baudrillard's description of "the body of metamorphosis" – a fluid, non-psychological body which he sees as a dying phenomenon in a culture characterized by fossilized identities, but which can still be found for example on the dance stage as "a chain of appearances, fluid forms beyond time and gender."[12] When Baudrillard emphasizes that the metamorphic body is liberated from psychology, this is to say that the dancing body can become one with the movement and express something other than the usual self-expressive subjectivity. This is equally true even if the body, at the storytelling level, takes the form of a Giselle or Petrouchka. The metamorphic body's absence of sexuality does not mean that the body in dance is a de-eroticized entity. It is simply not subordinated to a phallocentric structure of meanings and drives, but can flow more freely, "given over to all seduction". It is interesting in connection with the animal in dance that the body of metamorphosis is asserted to have an "animal felinity", related to pure, non-subjective motion.

The philosopher Deleuze and the psychoanalyst Guattari directly describe a fluid, non-psychological identity as a "becoming-animal", since the animals are primarily characterized by their "movements and vibrations" and their ability constantly to create new "lines of flight", moving outside the familiar landscape of fixed ideas of identity and gender.[13] With reference to among other things the Kafka story *Die Verwandlung (Metamorphosis)*, about the man who wakes up one morning and has become a beetle, the body is described, in its state of becoming-animal, as a complex of liberated energies, "a world of pure intensities", "a non-formed matter" in constant transformation. What happens is "an absolute deterritorialization of man".

The crucial point about the becoming-animal phenomenon as a tool for pinning down the animal in dance is that the animal is described as more than a metaphor. It is "a capturing, a possession, an added value, never a reproduction or an imitation". Man is not in some simplistic mimetic sense an animal; at another level we *are* animals. This is a far more dangerous and challenging affinity than if one places the Swan Princess in a harmless fairytale bower as if she were simply a romantic reflection-figure at a safe distance, in terms of identity, from us in the spectators' seats. The swan points directly to the fact that the human being in dance is a hybrid, a fusion of different existential forms.

At the level of the aesthetics of dance, the essential feature of the animal in dance has in fact never been a banal mimetic metaphor, where the body is to imitate an animal as true to nature as possible. Although there have been widely differing interpretations of how bird-like the Swan Princess should appear, the question has never essentially been the external resemblance to the zoological swan, but how to create a being on stage who can embody another dimension of reality.

175

The animal in modern dance

Whereas ballet attempts to transcend the physical earthbound state and pass over into pure ideality, modern dance turns towards the earth, the body and the animal, to express a self that is situated in a modern reality. At the beginning of the twentieth century the pioneers of modern dance demonstrated the earth-bound connection with their barefoot dancing; later veterans such as Martha Graham and Doris Humphrey - with her "fall and recovery" - cultivated the earth-connection by putting the body in extreme off-balance states, and in recent decades the fall rather than the leap has actually become a virtuoso number. The body in all its materiality, sensuality, weight, disharmony and instinctiveness has come to the foreground; in recent dance even with accentuation of the imperfect, embarrassing, distorted and anything but ideal. The animal has increasingly been let in from the darkness outside.

This is obvious in a contemporary *Swan Lake* like the Mats Ek version with the Cullberg Ballet from 1987; it is not necessary to be an ornithologist to note that swans belong to the duck family. Flat-footed, waddling with bare feet and slightly bent legs, they come sweeping along, cocking a leg like a dog, wriggling luxuriantly with their tutus, females and males in one great confusion of flesh. These swans have an extremely physical look with their bald, fleshy scalps like an obscene dot above the i. They may be carnal, but with the child's playful kind of eros. Comedy, otherwise alien to the white ballet – swan princesses are normally no joking matter – is part of the Cullberg swan's distinctly animal characteristics. The back-turning and down-to-earth postures of the classic *Swan Lake* are grotesquely magnified, the whole corps zestfully turning its back – and rump – on the classical, upward-aspiring frontality. The legendary small bird-like head jerks of the Swan Princess are now propagated to the whole flock as head-shaking and jittering as if the swans had an attack of Parkinson's; an indication that uncontrollable, instinctive physicality has them in its power.

Ek's Swan Princess looks more like an ugly duckling than a swan; she is playful and robust, furnished with an aura of inviolability and a vitalistic soul. But there is also a tragic beauty to her and the other swans' majestically earth-sweeping gliding and a magnificent desperation about their wild thundering leaps – their take-off could knock a prince for six. There is no doubt that the animal is in control. The Prince is sidelined into the role of an infatuated voyeur or a small boy falling flat on his face before the Great Beast of Revelation. It is his internal, oedipal drama that is in focus with Ek. Thus the Prince's fateful dilemma is not a matter of choosing between the white and the black swan, but of rejecting the mother.

The white swan and the black swan (which is simply bolder and more seductive) are cut from the same sensual cloth, for the point of Ek's *Swan Lake* is that the world is not dualistically divided into white and black, nature against culture, the ideal world vis-à-vis the real world, evil and good, high and low. It is a fluid world where the people are shape-shifters, gender-benders, change places and roles; the court and the swans by the lake merge into one, accentuating the fact that this is all taking place on the Prince's mental stage. The ballet is a long chain of trans-formations, the courtiers become swans overnight, the mother turns into Rothbart, and out of dark, rigid mother-figures with oversized wombs that will not release their offspring, the swans finally appear as in a liberating rebirth.

Although liberated from the mother, the Prince is left with his white and his black swan. Not an ending with tragic self-abandon, but with a more down-to-earth, divided individual who, standing with his white swan-bride, gazes longingly after the tempting black swan; a sign that the animal has to a greater extent been integrated, although this does not result in a happy menage à trois. It is a primarily merry, unthreatening excursion into the animal kingdom, where Ek does not venture too far into the irrational darkness of the body. That the work seemed very provocative at its premiere in 1987, however, tells us something about how much the view of humanity and the body has been changing in recent years.

One could ask how much soul remains in Ek's swans. But there is more at stake than simply an amusing reversal of the classical ballet in a world apparently without depth or heaven. The strength of Ek's *Swan Lake* is that it insists upon the animal – here meaning the power of the senses, the physicality of the body and the play-ful eros of the child – as the key to a spiritual dimension. For what happens when the Prince meets the Swan in the great love pas de deux? They stand side by side and shiver, as if in the grip of something all-powerful. The bodies are utterly shaken, with their shoulders up around their ears, completely enraptured. In fact the whole flock of swans is seized by an internal storm, which, in the form of

Triumph of the black beast? Bald and barefooted, the black Swan has got the upper hand of the prostrate Prince as well as the codex of ballet. As opposed to the traditional body/spirit dualism, Mats Ek's black swan and white swan seem to be cut from the same sensual cloth (*Swan Lake*, Julie Guibert and Carl Inger, 2000, Cullberg Ballet. Photo: Lesley Leslie-Spinks).

Tchaikovsky's passionate music, sweeps through them, sending body and soul into spasms: the spirit in the flesh as unequivocal physical manifestation. The swans undergo an agitation of the soul, but in vitalistic manner it takes the form of a convulsion of their corporeal life.

A hybrid species

As an icon for ballet as an art form, the Swan Princess is today still untouchable, a symbol of purity and grace whose global aura is evident from something as down-to-earth as the way the swan icon can be used to sell anything from toiletries to exclusive watches. Mats Ek's version nevertheless signalled that it was time to deal with the animal side of the icon. Later Matthew Bourne in 1996 actually made the Princess a man who passionately lures the Prince out into deep water. The whole ballet was given a sexualized appearance thanks to the swans' sensual, maleness-exuding bodily world as a space of dangerous, tempting freedom. Just as Ek made the animal in dance take its point of departure in a taboo area in the codex of ballet – the sensually corporeal – Bourne placed it in homosexuality.

179

The animal kingdom, with all the forbidden, marginalized aspects of humanity, is gradually being circumscribed and dammed-in, although this is happening much more tardily in ballet than in modern dance. The question is whether spiritual animals like the swan have become an endangered species, since a number of carnal, less gracious creatures have occupied the stage? Is the soul being ousted as the animal emerges in all its bestiality? But developments have in fact been moving towards a negation of the dualistic opposition of spirit and animal.

If we look at Nijinsky's faun, which served as a pioneer for this animal liberation front, it has an overwhelmingly sensual physicality that strains against the rigorously two-dimensional, almost abstract ornamental form in which it is inscribed. The animal seems to be bursting out of the choreographic form with all its carnality and thus becomes an emblem of modern dance in the effort to give the excluded dimensions of human life their say. The faun takes only a single leap on the spot, but although it and its fellows in modern dance are not bearers of ballet's dream of flight, they are still bearers of another reality, with a body that has overstepped the physical and mental boundaries to which an ordinary body is subject, and has moved into another state where it is possible to be a metamorphic body and give expression to animal, soul, automaton or perhaps even cyberman. No matter how close postmodern dance has rubbed up against the impure everyday body, dance constitutes a space – by virtue of the body and the stage – where the identity can unfold in another dimension of reality so that the human being can become a totality of body and spirit.

That the conspicuous entry of the animal into recent dance may actually be the equivalent of dancing with the soul, is shown in an exemplary way by the Japanese butoh dance which, since its introduction in the 1960s, has had a striking influence on the dance scene. Animal, spirit and the metamorphosis of the body take on a key position here. The starting-point is the corpse which, exposed in the darkness of carnality and culture, attempts to raise itself up. This is a distorted body whose limbs seem to go their own way, governed by organic impulses, but at the same time it is a body suffused with spirit – and a body technology that also works directly with mental techniques. To dance butoh is to empty the individual self to make room for other beings that exist within and outside the body. The dance is explicitly about the continuous metamorphoses, from embryo to dotard, man to woman, stone to sea and not least to animal. It is a matter of penetrating through to the layer of nature, inhabited by mankind. Butoh is presumably the first form of stage dance that actually sets up the animal as ideal – by virtue of its senses, instincts, intuition and presence. By opening up to surrounding nature, delving down to the body's ancient organic memory and sensing the fish, bull or bird, the butoh dancer tries to express a more authentic state of existence.

The actual origin of butoh as the dance of darkness was indicatively enough Tatsumi Hijikata's *Forbidden Colours* (1959), where a chicken was choked between the legs of a young man as a consequence of his erotically charged encounter with an older man. The animal had to die, but not in the spirit of *Swan Lake* and the romantic ballet, where the animal may have functioned as a suggestive image of longing, but eventually had to be purged out, just as the body had been. In butoh it is rather a matter of moving through the animal and the darkness of the flesh as a profound natural force in man, which is permeated by spirit. The pain connected

The soul is the animal. What started off as "the rebellion of the flesh" turned out to be the resurrection of the flesh. From the hidden night-sides of carnality and culture, the butoh body emerges in its continuous metamorphoses, the animal manifested as the epitome of soul (Carlotta Ikeda in *Also sprach Zarathustra*, 1982. Photo: John R. Johnsen).

to the sacrifice of the animal has to be suffered and lived through in reaction to civilization-dulled modern man. The object, however, is to resurrect the animal through dancing; the path to the soul goes through and deep within the body.

Swan Lake had already shown, with its irreconcilable oppositions and its tragic failure of consummation, that the soul cannot be separated from the animal, although at one level this is the declared ambition of the story and of the prince. While romantic ballet cultivated the tragically unconsummated in a perfect aesthetic form, modern contemporary dance rather cultivates the imperfect, both the un-consummated – no happy-ending union of body and spirit – and the torn, frayed form. This is done with bodies which - in contrast to the classical ideals of smooth, incorporeal perfection - sweat, groan, writhe and agonize as if in spasms in the confrontation with the nasty, the embarrassing, the ugly and the clumsy. Rather than ballet's heroically invulnerable, divine superbody, dance now puts the body at stake by stressing its vulnerability, perishability and exposure. But at the same time it is a body that, thanks to its aroused animal senses and vital instincts, points to another kind of authenticity and spiritual power. It is a body that gains its strength by acknowledging its fundamental dividedness.

Compared with the classic notion of the whole, homogenous individual, confronted today by the instability and ego-weakness of the modern subject, dance, as mentioned above, has always been a place where the dividedness and multidimensionality of the individual have found expression; but precisely not primarily as a sign of frailty and dysfunctionality. The dancing chameleon body can be a powerful animal. Dance can show the forces that are unleashed when one ventures into marginal zones.

Romanticism, with its idea of the unbounded self, had a more spacious, fluid view of humanity where the individual could form an alliance with animated nature and its creatures by more or less anthropocentrically absorbing them as part of himself. *Swan Lake* was in fact the definitive last call for the romantic ballet: Reisinger's original version from 1877 came twenty years after Darwin's much more earthbound view of the relationship between human and animal. On its publication in 1859 *The Origin of Species* marked the emergence of a more sober, scientifically-minded spirit. Darwin presented Western, rational man – as he still was, despite the emotional storm of romanticism – with the ultimate horror scenario: that we are in reality the offspring of apes. With evolutionism's view of humanity as biologically determined and controlled by heredity, the animal seemed, rather than romantically formed in the image of man, to have invaded mankind.

Today the animal seems once more to be biting its supposed spiritual master in the heel. Research in genetic engineering has demonstrated how close our relationship with animals really is; the genetic material that separates us from the anthropoid apes is no more than 1.6 per cent – less in fact than the difference between the African and the Indian elephant. With biotechnology and the possibility of xenotransplants and cloning across species, our kinship with animals has also begun to invade mankind at the external level of reality. The question now seems to be whether we are ready to develop our status further as a biological hybrid.

This is where one begins to look at the feathered creatures in *Swan Lake* with renewed interest; not as a clinical, biological spare-parts bank for the enfeebled individual, but because at another existential level they help to clarify the question of human nature. The swan can repair our inadequate insight into man's fundamental dimensions.

From swan to choked chicken, from ballet to butoh. Through the ages dance has shown the longing for and the cost of confronting the animal sides of existence. Yet nowhere is this as tragically seductive as in *Swan Lake*, an archetypal image of man reaching out for that which must not be lost, the other reality where man can be animal and soul at one and the same time. This is an image of longing with renewed attraction in today's prosaic reality dominated by one great metaphysical hole, where any dream of humankind as a multidimensional totality of body and spirit appears to be a lost kingdom. That is why we shall continue, like the man who fell in love with a bird, to immerse ourselves in *Swan Lake*.

183

Notes

1. With reference to *Sovrana* (1989) by the Danish choreographer Anita Saij, *Arien* (1979) and *Nelken* (1982) by Pina Bausch, *Codex* (1987) by the Frenchman Philippe Decouflé and *Das Glas im Kopf wird vom Glas* (1990) by the Belgian Jan Fabre, and *Sonata* (1993) by Michelle Anne de Mey, Belgium.

2. Michel Foucault, *Seksualitetens Historie I. Viljen til viden,* Copenhagen, Rhodos, 1978, p. 154 , (*Histoire de la sexualité I, La Volonté de savoir*, Paris, Gallimard, 1976). With regard to Foucault's presentation of the soul as a cultural construct, this article operates with a broader concept of the soul as something which is not just installed but shaped in dialogue with an already present spiritual element.

3. Rainer Heppenstall, "The Sexual Idiom", 1936, in *What Is Dance?*, Roger Copeland and Marshall Cohen, eds., New York, Oxford University Press, 1983, pp. 287-88.

4. Jean Georges Noverre, *Lettres sur la danse et les arts imitateurs* (1760), Paris, Lieutier, 1952, p. 94: "tant que la tête des danseurs ne conduira pas leurs pieds (...) ils s'égareront toujours."

5. Ibid., p. 193: "Je veux encore que les pas soient placés avec autant d'esprit que d'art et qu'ils répondent à l'action et aux mouvements d l'âme du danseur."

6. The transformation of the body is the central ritual of theatre as a whole, with obvious religious references to the Eucharist in which bread and wine are transformed into the body and blood of Christ, the so-called transubstantiation.

7. See Pierre Legendre, *La passion d'être un autre*, Paris, Éditions du Seuil, 1978, and Monna Dithmer, *Mennesket i Dansen*, unpublished Ph.D. dissertation (magisterkonferens), University of Copenhagen, 1989.

8. Henrich von Kleist, *Sämtliche Werke und Briefe*, vol. III, Carl Hanser Verlag, 1982, p. 340.

9. Théophile Gautier, "Revival of *La Sylphide*" in *What Is Dance?*, op. cit., p. 437.

10. The word "tutu" is derived etymologically from "cucu", French colloquialism (children's language) for bottom.

11. Through the performance history of *Swan Lake* there have been different interpretations of how birdlike the swan princess should actually be. With regard to this question as well as the ballet in general I am referring primarily to the *Swan Lake* by the Finnish National Ballet (directed by Josette Amiel, 1993, from the Vladimir Burmeister version 1960) and by London Festival Ballet (directed by Natalia Makarova, 1989, from Frederic Ashton's version) as well as Peter Martin's version for the Royal Danish Ballet from 1996.

12. "The body of metamorphosis, the one of a pure chain of appearances, of a timeless and sexless fluidity of forms, the ceremonial body brought to life by mythology, or the Peking Opera and oriental theatre, as well as by Dance (...) Not a psychological body, not a sexual body, a body freed from all subjectivity, a body recovering the animal felinity of the pure object, of pure movement, of a pure gestural transparition." Jean Baudrillard, *The Ecstacy of Communication*, New York, Semiotext, 1988, pp. 45-46.

13. "Becoming animal means to transgress a treshold, to reach (...) a world of pure intensities where all forms and also all meanings, signifiants and signifiés, are dissolved in favour of a non-formed materia." Gilles Deleuze and Felix Guattari, *Kafka – for en mindre litteratur*, Aarhus, Sjakalen, 1982, p. 27 *(Kafka – pour une littérature mineure*, Paris, Minuit, 1975).

Paradise Lost?

Dancing in Stockholm around the turn of the 19th-20th century

Lena Hammergren

By the turn of the 19th – 20th century, the image of classical ballet as a delightful vision appears to have faded. Sylphs, enchanted swan princesses, and wilis no longer accompany the audience into magic worlds beyond the everyday problems of reality. Instead these supernatural beings seem to have taken entirely concrete, physical shapes with chubby legs, rounded hips, and ample bosoms, and they move across the stage floor in dance forms that apparently "lack" artistic value. The euphoric dance paradise of the 19th century seemed to have vanished.

The turn of the century is usually regarded as a period of decline, judged from ballet's point of view.[1] The question is, however, whether this was actually the case, especially with regard to the dance culture as a whole? How did people experience it at the time? How did the arbiters of taste around the turn of the century express their evaluation of the aesthetics of dance at the time? In this article I examine how Swedish critics and journalists assessed not only classical ballet, but also other dance genres that were frequently appearing on various stages. Furthermore, I reflect on how historical writings have treated cause and effect in analyses of the development of dance. As the dance culture had become highly international by this time, foreign tendencies will also be recognised and woven into the Swedish context.

A multi-faceted dancing culture

Although today we may agree with dance historians' judgement of the turn of the century as a period lacking an artistically-distinguished classical ballet, we often forget that it was a time when a multitude of dance genres mingled on various kinds of dance stages. On the basis of these conditions, the turn of the century should not be categorised as a period of decline, but rather, it should be seen, from a broader dance perspective, as an extraordinarily rich time. The Swedish dance audience of the time could choose to go to the Stockholm Opera to watch ballet features in the operas or shorter one-act ballets often based on saga motifs or with pantomimic action. They could watch various guest ballerinas or exotic female dancers at the variety shows; or they could go to a range of musical comedy stages to watch the latest fashionable dances incorporated into the action. They could also watch the new plastic dance springing up – a dance form that was originally often called barefoot dancing. In various ways, this broad spectrum of different dance forms was reflected in the way in which dance was discussed and reviewed in the press. In 1906 a journalist at the women's magazine *Idun* argues that:

> in nine out of ten cases, the mass display of women's legs
> and arms wriggling and flailing about in the opera and
> circus ballet is a bizarre kind of gymnastic, choreographic
> experimentation, but a dance which allows the lines and
> shapes of the human body to reflect subtle states of mind
> (…) the modern art of dance is far from this goal.[2]

This acerbic criticism of ballet as a circus art form dominated by women must be seen in a quite specific context. It was written in connection with Isadora Duncan's visit to Stockholm. As the audience is given the chance to watch a new dance genre, the writers of the Stockholm press are presented with an excellent opportunity to discuss the dance ideal of the time. For many critics, Duncan stands as a guarantee that new sublime movement ideals will once more appear on the public stage. However, not all spectators agree on this point. The leading critic Carl G. Laurin, who continually reports from the theatre stages of Stockholm, is very critical.[3] He finds Duncan tedious and ungraceful, she has "slouching shoulders, ugly arms, ugly legs and very ugly feet"; furthermore, she is too good-natured to be capable of expressing the ferocity and suffering that Laurin wants to see in the dance. Indeed, he loves passionate dancing. He finds this neither in Duncan nor in the classical ballet but on the variety stages. "It is the folk dances that are fun, the

A multi-faceted dancing culture. "Rythmical gymnastics" and "ballplaying" are listed alongside *Offerdans* (*Victim's Dance*) and *Valsetude* (*Waltz Etude*) in the programme for a student performance at Miss Anna Behle's Plastikinstitut (Institute of Plastique), (*Idun*, 1908, The Dance Museum, Stockholm).

Spanish dances, the cake-walk, the cancan, the mazurka, the czardas and, as for ourselves, the Swedish peasant dances."[4] Folk, character, or national dances, as they are alternatively called, are some of the most popular dance forms on the theatre stage around the turn of the century. Laurin is not alone in his approbation, although only a few of his colleagues publicly state their preference for character dances above Duncan's dance art inspired by antiquity.

This mixture of dance genres in reviews and commentaries is very typical of the Swedish press around the turn of the century and also reflects international conditions. The German dance historian Karl Storck claims that it is on the variety stage that the art of dance is rediscovered. Thus, he counts ballerinas, barefoot dancers, Spanish dancers, and cancan dancers as exponents of the art of dance, whose different dance expressions he seems to find equally appealing.[5] Here, then, we find a mixture of genres which is hardly matched during the rest of the 20th century, be it in discussions on dance aesthetics, dance history or in the repertory plans of the various theatres. Around the turn of the century, there is a lively discussion concerning the advantages and disadvantages of the different genres and even the increasingly popular social dance is drawn into the debate. The German Albert Dresdner, whose article about Duncan and the dance of the time was translated and published in the Swedish press, moves untroubled between the genres when he defends Duncan against those who defame her and criticises the ballet and social dance of the time. Dresdner thinks that the ballet has "developed into a cancan style whose affected twists of the joints (…) merely express a far-reaching coarseness."[6] Even ballroom dancing has degenerated. The social dances consist of nothing but a senseless spinning around, while, according to Dresdner, they should "express feelings of joy and festivity", and thus dance in all its forms has lost its influence on life.[7] The same critical tone is also found in a Swedish critic who thinks that the true dance has disappeared. In earlier times, the rhythm of life was found "in one single plastic movement", but all that is left for the contemporary audience interested in dance is the ballet, and that is merely a matter of physical drill with a sexual foundation.[8] According to the same critic, ballet is neither nature nor art.

Thus, around 1905-08 the general opinion appears to have been that both Swedish and international ballet were in a state of decay. The much sought-after

A state of decay? The critics at the time lamented the vanished ideal of beauty and the loss of the 19th-century dance euphoria (Victoria Strandin and Robert Köller, c. 1905-1908, Royal Swedish Ballet. Drottningsholm's Theatre Museum, Stockholm).

euphoric experience was found on the variety stage rather than at the opera house. Strangely, there does not seem to have been much difference between the dance ideals expressed on these stages. In both cases, the dances were short, almost fragmentary and they often consisted of the same movement vocabulary and sequences of steps. Nevertheless, it was on the ballet stage that a vanished ideal of beauty was lamented. The historians of our time have chosen to explain this condition by pointing to the classical dancers' lack of technique at the time and the miserable repertoire policies demonstrated by many European opera houses.

Certainly, there were specific reasons for repertoire plans and technical skills, beside the judgement of the artistic status of ballet at the time. By the turn of the century, the Royal Swedish Ballet had almost no male dancers, which made it impossible to present full-length ballets with a great number of both men and women. In 1901 the German-born ballet master Otto Zöbisch was the only male leading dancer. In 1902 there were four boys at the ballet academy, of whom only one succeeded in being appointed leading dancer in 1907. In 1911 still only two out of about thirty students at the academy were reported to be male.[9] Although male dancers were always better paid than the women, the wages were generally low, and this was commonly thought to prevent young men from choosing dance as a profession.[10] According to the views of the time, the lack of male students and dancers also had other serious consequences. It was thought to cause an insufficient increase in the profession of ballet master, a profession that was obviously perceived as suitable primarily for male dancers.[11] Consequently, the technical skills of dance could be endangered, as the ballet masters usually led the daily practice. This, then, is a social context which can be used as a complementary and partial explanation for the low status of the ballet.

The Russian ballet

It did not take long, before the waning interest in ballet was challenged and the problem of the lack of male dancers was solved. In May 1908 the ballet of the Russian Marinsky Theatre arrived for a visiting performance at the Stockholm Opera. This was the Stockholm audience's first opportunity in a long time to experience parts of the great romantic ballets and even full-length ballet performances which, as earlier mentioned, did not figure in the repertoire of the opera house (*Coppélia* was the only exception around the turn of the century. It was staged in 1896 by the ballet master Max Glasemann and was performed in its entirety only three times during that season).

The Russian visit was preceded by an intensive information campaign in the Swedish press. A French expert was quoted saying that only the Russian ballet demonstrated all the praiseworthy aesthetic criteria that the classical ballet had once possessed, even in Europe.[12] Thus, in St. Petersburg all the requirements of true art were fulfilled as the Russians had succeeded in administering the classical values that had once been formulated by Jean-Georges Noverre himself. Furthermore, it was pointed out, ballet was not merely a matter of technical perfection – a dancer must also be a dramatic artist, as the true dance includes a dramatic narrative.[13] In an interview with one of the stars of the ballet, Anna Pavlova, she stressed precisely this, "there must be temperament, feeling (...) soul in the dance, not just empty movements."[14]

Thus, dramatic ballets were the new attraction which would hopefully entice the Stockholm audience to return to the ballet stage. Among the pieces in the repertoire offered during the visiting performance were Act II from *Swan Lake* (it had not yet been given its present title and was called the *Swan Pond* in the press), *Giselle*, *Halte de Cavalerie* and *Paquita*, but also a number of divertissements which emphasised the dancing more than the narrative. In the information given beforehand in the newspapers, it was pointed out that there were detailed accounts of the content of the ballets which the audience could read in advance in order to prepare themselves for the performances. Possibly, this could be seen as evidence that there was some uncertainty as to whether you could follow a course of action that was only represented through dance. One critic also noted that the audience in Sweden was little accustomed to this form of dance and that for this reason alone, it might be difficult to understand the narratives.[15]

How did the critics receive the mimic and plastic wonders presented in the advertising campaign? Although the opinions differed with regard to certain pieces, the critics were generally rather negative towards the dramatic dance sections of the programme. They found that the action was poorly composed. In *Swan Lake* the plot was absurd and banal, in *Paquita* the action was thought to be a naïve excuse for dancing in colourful costumes.[16] Pavlova, however, was convincing both as Giselle in the "Mad Scene" and as Swanilda in *Coppélia*.[17] The discussion that most clearly seemed to divide the critics had to do with which female dancer was considered the best, a discussion that also demonstrated the various differences in how critics perceived dance aesthetics and the role of dance as an art form. The two dancers mostly discussed were Anna Pavlova and Eugenia Eduardova, and the form of dance that they respectively represented divided the public in two camps. Did one prefer Pavlova and her dramatic dancing, or the demi-caractère dancer Eduardova's lively appearance in various character dances?

Two of the Swedish dance critics are particularly interesting to deal with in this context, as both of them wrote from the perspective of a distinct dance aesthetic in which their respective dance ideals clearly come across. One of the critics was Gunnel Gerd-Holzhausen, who was a student at the Swedish Royal Dramatic Theatre. The other critic, Anna Behle, was a dance pedagogue who had opened her own school in Stockholm for rhythmic, plastic dance for children and adults the year before the Russian visiting performance and after having finished a short education with Jaques-Dalcroze and Elisabeth Duncan, in turn.

Gerd-Holzhausen, who studied dramatic and plastic *Gestaltung* (embodied interpretation) herself at the theatre school was disappointed with how the Russian troupe administered this art form. She thought that it was mostly dancing for the sake of dancing, which she apparently did not like at all. However, confronted with Pavlova in the role of Swanilda, even Gerd-Holzhausen had to admit that the dancer's art of interpretation was convincing.[18] But that was not enough to convince this particular critic that the art of ballet was undergoing a renaissance. In Gerd-Holzhausen's opinion, a true capacity for embodied interpretation, both artistically and choreographically, was to be found in other places than St. Petersburg. In her review, she made an eloquent comparison between the Russians and the art of ballet she had experienced in Copenhagen. As her point of departure, she used a love scene between Anna Pavlova and Adolph Bolm. In this scene, at the very moment when Bolm kissed Pavlova, the audience "suddenly saw the tip of her toe behind his head. The next moment she leans over his arm all the way down to the floor, only to run away diagonally backwards on the tips of her toes like an automatic doll."[19] Here, Gerd-Holzhausen claimed, the movements had no dramatic motivation, whereas in Bournonville's ballets you would never have to see such tastelessness. She remembered a scene from *Sylphide* in which the exact same movements were used as those employed by the Russians, but with a dramaturgic motivation behind the choice of movements. When the Sylphide sees the sleeping James, she runs towards him light-footedly on point so as not to wake him up, and when he "drops a flower from his hand, she bends backwards to the floor for it, as if she dare not take one step out of fear that she might wake him up."[20] Both the pointe work and the deep bend backwards were thus incorporated as organic parts into the dramatic choreography of Bournonville's ballet, while the Russian ballet company used features such as the "difficult promenade on point" at every entry and exit, irrespective of which story was being presented.[21]

Anna Behle did not find Pavlova's art of dancing completely convincing but for reasons other than those emphasised by Gerd-Holzhausen. In the review of the opening performance, Behle compared Pavlova and Eduardova. Indeed, Behle found Pavlova a radiant classical ballerina, but not "even the most graceful dancer can make us quite forget the usual unnatural tastelessness of the art of ballet."[22] Eduardova, on the other hand, who – in Behle's opinion – danced the most beautiful dance of the evening which was a Hungarian czardas, "founds her artistry more on the expression of an immediate feeling through the natural rhythm of the body."[23] Behle did not appreciate the pantomimic art of dance, but rather the dance that created an outlet for more abstract feelings which the audience perceived through the musicality and rhythmic sensibility of the dancers. According to Behle, the Slavic national dances stimulated the feeling of life. It is evident that she discussed the dance by means of the terminology she had learned, studying with Jaques-Dalcroze. For Behle, it was the rhythmic, plastic dance – even in the shape of character dances – that was the dance form of the future, the classical ballet belonged to the past.

Although certain critics thought that the visiting performance had been a success, it was mostly the dancers' technique and their discipline when training that critics found fascinating.[24] The rebirth of the art of ballet promised by the advertising campaign did not take place. Nor did critics agree that the admired art of ballet from the 19th century still existed in Copenhagen. In contrast to Gerd–Holzhausen, an anonymous critic thought that indeed there was both a good

196

How to interpret the modern dance hieroglyphs? Egyptian *Iris* performed by students of Anna Behle, who believed that the new plastic dance was the dance form of the future (*Idun*, 28/12-1913, The Dance Museum, Stockholm).

dancing school and a "tradition in terms of ballet" in the Danish capital, "but how lacking in beauty is it not".[25] The important question is: what sort of beauty were people actually looking for? Was it really the charming, supernatural sylphs with pretty feet and melancholy smiles that the audience of the turn of the century wanted to encounter at the theatre? Or did people long for a different kind of dance – a new art of dance that would stage the exciting future called the 20th century?

A modern Swedish ballet

In traditional Swedish dance history, Michel Fokine's visit at the Stockholm Opera, which took place for the first time in 1913, is seen as an event that was to influence the development in a positive direction. However, later historical descriptions have demonstrated the small significance of the visit.[26] Indeed, the Swedish audience was given the opportunity to see a number of examples from the repertoire of Diaghilev's Ballets Russes danced by the Swedish ballet company and by Fokine himself and his wife, but when the visitors had left, the company returned to the more modest ballet culture of earlier days, as none of the ballet masters or choreographers were capable of continuing Fokine's work in the same spirit of genius. This was the situation according to the alternative strand within the writing of history, and even if its conclusions mostly seem correct, there is room for certain modifications.

It is true that no ballets created at the Stockholm Opera at this time have survived as landmarks in dance history. If, however, a more detailed examination is undertaken as to how the audience of the time evaluated the development, it becomes evident that other types of changes took place, a fact which undermines the prevalent description of the turn of the century as a period lacking important renewal in ballet. Above, I described how Anna Behle, in lyrical terms, pointed to the rhythmic, plastic dance as the art form of the future. This dance form was practised by Isadora Duncan, by the students of Jaques-Dalcroze, by Behle herself and her students and even by Eduardova, the great ballet star of the Marinsky Theatre. However, as it turns out, Swedish critics perceive this plastic form of expression as an important and positive source of influence even in the context of ballet at the Swedish opera. This happened during the period from Duncan's visiting performance in 1906 to Fokine's arrival in 1913. Thus, it is reasonable to speak of a significant period of change that began even before Fokine staged his ballets in Stockholm.

In the beginning of the decade 1910-20, the Swedish press brought descriptions of the influence of the plastic, or, according to our contemporary terminology, modern, dance on ballet. The ballet academy put on plastic dances in classical style at the annual displays. The dances had been choreographed by Gunhild Rosén, the head of the academy, and they were very much appreciated as the new style gave the dance "a different kind of grace and plastic" from what was usually seen in ballet. [27] The new dance forms had also been incorporated as ballet features in operas, choreographed by the ballet master of the time, Otto Zöbisch, who had been studying abroad between 1905-1908 when he did not work at the Stockholm Opera.[28] The reformation of the ballet, as it was expressly called, was perceived as a direct adaptation of Duncan's, and to a certain extent also Jaques-Dalcroze's, ideas. The result was that the ballet had been elevated to a higher artistic level, point work had become rarer, and stereotypical ballet costumes had been replaced by costumes that were more suitable for the content of the ballets.[29] It was even believed that "the chaste nudity of the barefoot dancer has gained a foothold in ballet."[30]

From a dance historical perspective, this information – which was printed in the press in 1912 – is especially interesting as the reforms are roughly identical with some of those we ascribe to Michel Fokine, published as late as 1914 in the newspaper *The Times*. The fact that the Swedish reforms were being discussed in the press also shows that both the reviewers and the audience had understood that important changes had taken place within the art of dance. It was, however, a different sort of renaissance in ballet aesthetics that people spoke about then compared to what the historian of today usually means by the concept of ballet renaissance, which implies a renewal of the dance through a return to so-called classical ballet ideals. The term "classical" is particularly interesting to examine in relation to the decades around 1900.

When Pavlova came to Stockholm in 1908, she was interviewed about her view of the dance of the time. On one occasion, she described the way in which her own dance genre differed from the Slavic national dances that were also danced by the ballerinas of the opera house. Pavlova emphasised that her genre was "the classical dance, more or less like madame Duncan, you know?"[31] What Pavlova probably aimed for was to show, through a comparison between herself and Duncan, that despite their differences, the two of them sought a common dance expression which did not find its inspiration in the romantic ballets of the 19th century but in a classical dance embracing the ideal of antiquity which stressed "beauty, feeling, life in the dance".[32]

This use of the term "classical dancing" is also repeated in other sources related to the turn of the century. In the historian J. E. Crawford Flitch's book on dance around the turn of the century, Isadora Duncan and Maud Allan are listed under the heading "classical dancing". Flitch underlines that, in order to avoid mis-understandings, he uses the term "academic dancing" to refer to classical ballet.[33] Maud Allan, whom we now primarily associate with the erotically coloured and dramatic dance of Salome, also described her dancing as "classical".[34] She probably saw the term both as a mark of quality and a genre designation with a new content. In Flitch's analysis of the situation, he pointed out that while Duncan "propounded the gospel of the classical dance, Maud Allan promulgated it with the greatest popular success."[35]

If the 1910s are included into the phrase "the turn of the century", it is evident that one could speak of a renaissance of the Swedish art of ballet. Rather than a revival of the classical ballet ideal of the 19th century, the renaissance signified that a vitalisation of dance was aimed for through the use of various means influenced by the new dance styles of the time. Beauty, feeling and life in dance were under-stood from new perspectives.

A paradise regained

The starting point for this article was to question whether the romantic ballet's vision of a pleasurable paradise beyond the everyday had disappeared from the audience's imagination by the turn of the century. This also raised the question of what kind of danced beauty the audience really wished to see on stage: a reborn romantic ballet or something quite different? When Anna Behle and Gunnel Gerd-Holzhausen discussed the Russian ballet's visiting performance, they exemplified the opposition between two dance ideals that has existed in the dance world for ages and has not yet disappeared. Against the dramatic and narrative dance stands a more abstract dance that emphasizes dance for dance's own sake, the kind of aesthetics we usually call *l'art pour l'art*. Gerd-Holzhausen found what she was looking for in certain parts of Bournonville's ballets, Behle found her ideals in the character dances of the Russian ballet. None of them, however, thought that traditional classical ballet could completely satisfy the dance-goers of the age.

By way of introduction, I mentioned how dance historians later in the 20th century have offered a specific causal explanation for this phenomenon. It is, however, fully possible to explain the negative responses of the ballet audience as having other causes than a deficient choreography and the lack of a refined dance technique. Perhaps the audience around the turn of the century no longer wanted the metaphysical world beyond the everyday – the magical dimension that the spectators found so stimulating during the romantic epoch of the 19th century? Did the audience, rather, search for the danced beauty ideal of the new age? If so, what was this ideal like?

Concurrently with the new century, a number of different changes had taken place. Everyday life was full of industrialisation, urbanisation, and technical innovations, factors which all in a very concrete way physically moved people into new worlds and changed their view of their own bodies. If Swedes around the turn of the century visited the world exhibition in 1900 in Paris, they could walk on moving walkways, try the escalators and roller coasters before seeing Loïe Fuller perform her "innovation", the serpentine dance (which had actually already been performed by a Fuller imitator, the dancer Miss Minnie Vivian, in Stockholm in 1893). It seems reasonable to think that the new technical and mechanical development of the age was integrated into people's experience of their own and other people's movements. The desire for speed, weight, flowing energy, physicality, and accentuated rhythm could thus be seen to have replaced the fascination with the more floating, soft and ethereal qualities of the romantic ballet.

In Flitch's dance history from 1912, I have found one of the most fascinating descriptions of a dancer, characterised by the new century's desire for innovation and interest in studying bodily expression in detail. The object of description is not Fuller or any one else among the so-called dance pioneers. Instead Flitch dedicates his enthusiastic analysis to a dancer from variety culture, a French can-can dancer by the artist name of Nini Patte-en-l'air:

> Five, ten, twenty times her foot flew above her head; then it remained suspended at the level of her face (…) as though it possessed a life independent of the leg; it was a prisoner and struggled to escape; the dancer watched its contortions, an amused spectator of its restlessness; at last it was released (…) and resumed its command of the dance.[36]

What is noteworthy in this quotation, besides the richness of detail in the description of movement which is rarely seen in early 20th century dance texts, is the distinction between the movement and the dancer. One part of the body, the foot, has a life of its own and controls the dance to such a degree that it seems independent of the dancer's own will. The typical high cancan kick is observed by a dancer who appears more preoccupied with studying the physical laws than with selling herself and the dance as a risqué gesture to a primarily male audience. Five, ten, twenty times the foot repeats its movement in the air – to read this description is like watching Muybridge's photographic series on the human body in movement. Muybridge did this work in the middle of the 1880s and it includes – not surprisingly if you look at the contemporary dance – both a woman "kicking above her head" and "dancing fancy".[37] In the quotation from Flitch's book, both the spectator and the dancer seem to be fascinated by the dancing body as an object of study which, moreover, can be the source of new, innovative ways of moving – rather than seeing the body as an erotic object on display or a hallucinatory vision.

The view of dance as a technical innovation actually constitutes the basis for how Flitch conceptualised his entire book on dance of the turn of the century. In the same way as the contemporary Swedish critics mixed so-called "high" and "low" dance forms in their discussions, so Flitch mixed these dance terms into his

On the look-out for the danced beauty ideal of the new age? A lone male in modern dance clothing surrounded by female dancers who also on the modern dance stage outnumbered the men. (*Dansfantasi* (*Dance Fantasy*), Anna Behle's Institute of Plastique, *Idun*, 28/12-1913. The Dance Museum, Stockholm).

historical writing. The decisive factor, as to whether a dance form should be included in the book or not, was whether it involved any kind of technical renewal of the dance or other scenic elements. Both skirt dancing, which belonged to the variety culture, and the serpentine dance, which was characterised as art dance, were rather a matter of innovation and science than of artistry. But precisely for this reason, Flitch thought, both of these genres vitalised the dance and had a self-evident place in its history. Skirt dancing introduced a new medium, the long dress, and in the serpentine dances Fuller proved her intelligence in her choice of a new technique, lighting, etc., despite the fact that the dance had "no steps, no gestures, no poses, none of the usual criteria by which dancing can be judged."[38]

The paradisiac world beyond the everyday which the dance audience of the 19th century encountered at the theatres was thus replaced by a more down-to-earth euphoria that accompanied the journey into the physical, into the plastic, or vital, rhythmic dance. In other words, the reason for the low status of the ballet could also be that the dance audience around the turn of the century desired the body of the future and experienced a state of mind in which ecstasy mingled with an interest for novelty and richness in technical innovation. The integration of the machine rhythms of the new age into the bodily experience of the common man may have been so strong that the scenic dance expressions simply had to change. Flitch described the people of his age more or less in this way, "Human motion nowadays tends to be not flowing but angular, jerky, abrupt, disjointed, full of gestures not flowing imperceptibly one into another, but broken off midway."[39] If all of this powerful change is taken into consideration in the evaluation of how the dance culture around the turn of the century developed, perhaps we should not speak of it in terms of how people lamented a lost paradise but how they applauded a newly discovered paradise – a danced world that did not lie beyond everyday life.

203

Notes

1. See e.g. Mary Skeaping & Anna Greta Ståhle, *Balett på Stockholmsoperan*, Stockholm, 1979, and Susan Au, *Ballet & Modern Dance*, London, 1988.

2. Anon., "En danskonstens prästinna", *Idun,* vol. 19, no. 18, 1906, p. 220.

3. Carl G. Laurin, "Från Stockholms teatrar", *Ord och Bild*, vol. XV, 1906, p. 386.

4. Carl G. Laurin, "Från Stockholms teatrar", *Ord och Bild*, vol. XVII, 1908, p. 336.

5. Karl Storck, *Der Tanz*, Bielefeld & Leipzig, 1903, p. 89.

6. Albert Dresdner, "Dansen som bildande konst", *Ord och Bild*, vol. XIII, 1904, p. 532.

7. Ibid., pp. 532-536.

8. *Svenska Dagbladet*, May 12th, 1908.

9. Kungliga Teaterns matriklar, Kungliga Teaterns Arkiv, Drottningholms Teatermuseum.

10. H. Glimstedt, "Operabaletten", *Scenisk konst*, no. 18-19, 1912, p. 178.

11. See e.g. signature Celestin, "Baletten", *Scenisk konst*, no. 2, 1902, p. 6. These opinions are expressed in an interview with Theodor Marckhl, who worked as ballet master at the Royal Swedish Ballet between 1870-86.

12. *Svenska Dagbladet*, May 6th, 1908.

13. Ibid.

14. *Svenska Dagbladet*, May 11th, 1908.

15. *Dagens Nyheter*, May 12th, 1908.

16. Ibid., and *Dagens Nyheter*, May 13th, 1908.

17. Gunnel Gerd-Holzhausen, "Om plastik och mim", *Skådebanan*, no. 9, 1908, p. 16.

18. Ibid.

19. Ibid.

20. Ibid.

21. Ibid.

22. *Dagens Nyheter*, May 12th, 1908.

23. Ibid.

24. See e.g. *Svenska Dagbladet*, May 18th, 1908.

25. *Dagens Nyheter*, May 11th, 1908.

26. Erik Näslund was the first to make this different evaluation of Fokine's visit, see Erik Näslund, *Carina Ari, Ett lysande liv*, Stockholm, 1984.

27. Signature: Chip, "I operabalettens elevskola", *Scenisk konst*, no. 11–12, 1911, p. 96.

28. Glimstedt, 1912, op. cit., p. 182.

29. Ibid., p. 181.

30. Ibid.

31. *Svenska Dagbladet*, May 11th, 1908.

32. Ibid.

33. J. E. Crawford Flitch, *Modern Dancing and Dancers*, 1912, 2nd ed., London, 1913, p. 103.

34. Maud Allan cited in Felix Cherniavsky, *The Salome Dancer: The Life and Times of Maud Allan*, Toronto, 1991, p. 150.

35. Flitch, 1912, op. cit., p. 110.

36. Ibid., p. 94.

37. Eadweard Muybridge, *The Male and Female Figure in Motion: 60 Classic Photographic Sequences*, New York, 1984, pp. 109, 112.

38. Flitch, 1912, op. cit., p. 86.

39. Ibid., p. 104.

Subverting the Dream-of-Elusive-Women Scenario

Vaslav Nijinsky's *L'Après-midi d'un faune*, Jerome Robbins's *Afternoon of a Faun* and *Antique Epigraphs*

Deborah Jowitt

The heroes of nineteenth century ballet scenarios pursued their supernatural objects of desire into zones of erotic promise and psychological danger. These forbidden landscapes - the forest of Bournonville's *Sylphide*, the Blue Grotto of his *Napoli*, the river where the heroine of Filippo Taglioni's *La Fille du Danube* made her home - represented a "natural" world immune to the civilized discontents that beset the hero, or, as in Petipa's *La Bayadère*, a dreamworld in which an impossible love became possible for a while. The terrain was defined less by the painted scenery than by the ubiquitous bevy of identically dressed women - the heroine's companions. Their choreographed rivers and glades became mazes, obstacles, or ordeals of temptation through which the usually doomed hero sought his elusive ideal. And in such ballets' supernatural acts, unfettered by realism, classical dancing grew in daring as a metaphor for beauty.

Vaslav Nijinsky's *L'Après-midi d'un faune*, premiered by Serge Diaghilev's Ballets Russes in 1912, subverted this Romantic narrative and catapulted it into the precincts of emerging modernism. Nijinsky also bypassed the hothouse orientalist scenarios of Diaghilev's reigning choreographer Mikhail Fokine (in whose ballets he had made his reputation as a dancer). The male protagonists of *Cléopâtre*, *Thamar*, *Shéhérazade* did not chase a wispy ideal; they gave their lives for a night of passion with a sexually ravenous femme fatale.

Nijinsky's brief encounter between a faun and some nymphs come to bathe is cool - cooler than the fragrant Mallarmé poem that lent it a title and an ambiance, and the already well-known orchestral composition by Claude Debussy to which its minimal action unrolled. The reticent performing, together with a weighted muscularity unusual in ballet, a denial of virtuosity (a single jump by the ballet world's most notable jumper), and the limitations imposed by its formal premise of two-dimensionality rubbed against the music's sensuous evocation of antiquity and the audience's familiarity with Mallarmé's delicately erotic poem to create a startling theatrical tension.

The subject of *L'Après-midi d'un faune* is not the pursuit of an ideal or a suicidal dedication to passion. It is the sexual awakening of a naïf, compressed into a living frieze - the flatness of the choreography almost more of a bar to capture and fulfillment than the leading nymph's tendency to flee. In reference to Mallarmé's poem, Debussy titled his work *Prélude à l'après-midi d'un faune*; his impressionistic waves of sound evoke the faun and his woodland landscape before the scene revealed in the poem (Romola Nijinsky is not alone in asserting that her husband never read Mallarmé's 1876 work; whether this is true or not, Diaghilev, his lover and mentor, knew it).[1] Mallarmé's lonely faun remembers, or dreams, an evanescent sexual feast with two nubile nymphs. The poem hints at the onanism that unsettled the ballet's first-night audience, when the faun carried the chief nymph's dropped scarf to his rock, arranged it in the semblance of a recumbent female, and lowered himself onto it. The poet's nymphs slipped away from the faun before he could fully consummate his lust with them. Perhaps there were no nymphs:

> But think, these nymphs, their loveliness. . . suppose
> They bodied forth your senses' fabulous thirst?
> Illusions! which the blue eyes of the first,
> As cold and chaste as is the weeping spring,
> Beget: the other sighing, passioning,
> Is she the wind, warm in your fleece at noon?[2]

There is another ballet to consider in relation to Nijnsky's *Faune*: Fokine's *Narcisse*, which premiered in Monte Carlo in April of 1911, with Tamara Karsavina as Echo and Nijinsky as the eponymous Greek youth, punished for his indifference to a nymph who could only repeat his utterances back to him, and doomed to fall in love with his own reflection. According to Njinsky's sister Bronislava (the chief

Bacchante in *Narcisse*), Vaslav had been trying out ideas for his ballet, with her as principal nymph, in Russia in the winter of 1910, well before Fokine began work on *Narcisse*.[3] Regardless of chronology, it seems likely that Nijinsky's vision of the faun influenced his portrayal of Narcissus and vice versa. Few photographs exist of *Narcisse*, but Valentine Gross drew Nijinsky kneeling in a pose that, although pliant and drooping, hints at the angled arms and torqued torso of the faun. Nijinska, in her memoirs, noting that "It could have been dangerous to portray in a dance the sensual and erotic Narcisse driven to ecstasy by his own reflection in the water," believed that the plastic beauty of her brother's gestures softened any disturbing implications of self-love;[4] artist André-E. Marty presented another view. His drawing shows Nijinsky stretched out, chin to the water, like a panther about to drink; the pose (if accurately rendered) is sweeter than the faun's final gestures, but fully as sensual. Apparently, too, the hero's skimpy tunic startled some members of the audience as much as the form-fitting spotted unitard with its erect little tail that Leon Bakst designed for *Faune*. Charles Ricketts reported that in *Narcisse*, Nijinsky "leaps like a faun with such rare clothing on that Duchesses had to be led out of the audience, blinded with emotion, and their diamond tiaras all awry."[5]

Subverting the chase

In *L'Après-midi d'un faune*, Nijinsky honoured tenets that were to define modernism in dance as well as in architecture and design: economy of means, clarity of shape, an embracing of angularity, and, on a deeper level, the notion that a work's subject matter (or function or material) informs its style. Our knowledge of the doings of fauns and nymphs comes from handed-down legends, but our vision of them is colored by the friezes and innumerable painted vases that stock the museums of the Western world. With a boldness perhaps born of inexperience (he was about twenty when he began work on the ballet), Nijinsky put those two-dimensional images on-stage.

He is reported to have told a London reporter that his ballet was "simply a fragment drawn from a classic bas-relief."[6] Whatever his exact inspiration, and whatever the extent of Diaghilev's influence and that of designer Léon Bakst, the severe twist of the dancers' torsoes against their heads and legs amounted to a

210

Not only is Nijinsky's faun a threat to the chaste nymphs, the ballet's two-dimensionality and angular shapes are also a violation of classical form (*L'Après-midi d'un faune*, 1912, Ballets Russes, Jerome Robbins Dance Division. The New York Public Library for the Performing Arts, Astor, Lenox and Tilden Foundations. Photo: Baron Adolphe de Meyer).

violation of balletic convention. In the shallow downstage corridor defined by Bakst's painted backdrop, the faun arranges and rearranges himself on his rock, plays his flute, eats his grapes in profile. The six nymphs venture into the space three by three, hands linked; even when not touching they seem tied to one another, as if the viewer were turning a vase whose figures therefore "travel" yet remain perpetually equidistant from one another in their circular progress. Wishing to approach these bewitching creatures and their leader, the faun, constrained by the flat design, must stay within his horizontal path. They pass him in their own track, but he can't step forward without violating the form (the dancer "cheats" a little on turning corners so that he gradually arrives on the nymphs' path). His pursuit is utterly unrealistic in terms of time – he walks deliberately, taking small, articulated steps – but his lack of haste only accentuates the drama of his advance. As the nymphs hurry anxiously in and out as if pulled by strings, he makes his only contact with their leader, who has dropped some of her veils to bathe. No pas de deux ensues. His arms can't curve around her, they can only pen her temporarily like parallel fence rails. There is a stylized chase. For a moment, the two link arms, she kneeling and recoiling. Then she flees, leaving him the scarf.[7]

Faune was something of a succès de scandale in Paris, performed twice on opening night and at many subsequent performances, but whether shocked or not by the ending, members of the public did not expect a living art object from the Ballets Russes, they expected dancing – either exotic like *Shéhérazade* or pretty like *Le Spectre de la rose* – and romance. Nijinsky's acting, called "miraculeux" by Cocteau, did not offer the thrills of the stunning leaps he had accustomed them to.[8] Given the premise of a faun pursuing nymphs, they may also have expected a more traditional scenario: the hero united with the woman of his dreams or perishing in the attempt to attain her. He was not supposed to watch her leave and retreat into a private and satisfying erotic dream of her. What Kirstein called the ballet's "lean and artificial grammar" resonated against the unmistakable expression of sexual release.[9]

Nor was Nijinsky's use of the score conventional. Waves and rivulets of sound often lapped against still figures; although the nymphs' patterns seemed to flow on and off the stage, their abrupt gestures, panicky or annoyed, formed accents spikier than those of the music.[10] Wrote Hugo von Hofmannsthal, "... Debussy's music seems to fade away gradually till it becomes merely the accompanying element – a something in the atmosphere, but not the atmosphere itself."[11]

A program note invited the audience not simply to observe this landscape but to implicate themselves in its fantasy: "Le rideau baisse pour que le poème commence dans toutes les memoires."[12] This faun's awakening to desire may have incited memories of Mallarmé's faun among well-read spectators; it also became a golden mirror in which spectators might see and recall their own burgeoning sexuality.

Through the mirror

Jerome Robbins conceived his *Afternoon of a Faun* to the same Debussy score over forty years later. The period during which he readied this small masterpiece for its premiere by the New York City Ballet on May 14, 1953 overlapped a troubling event in his personal life: on May 5, he was summoned to testify before the House Committee on Un-American Activities about his early membership in the Communist party; terrified – and perhaps badly advised – he supplied his inquisitors with names of some members of his cell.[13] Whether coincidentally or not, his *Faun*, all delicate sensuality, takes place in the ivory-tower world of the ballet – comfortingly far from politics, yet subtly "American" in tone.

If the otherwordly scenes in nineteenth century ballets promoted classical dancing as dangerously beautiful, Robbins's duet presented it as a sanctuary – a safe, enclosed, ordered world in which desire is sublimated into art, and physical intimacy is part of a dancer's day-to-day routine. The ballet also acknowledges, but in contemporary terms, the danse d'école that Nijinsky jettisoned.

Robbins's faun slumbers not on a rock but in an idealized ballet studio. His nymph, his vision of beauty, is another young dancer, come to practice some steps. What Arlene Croce has called "the ballet's discovery of a correspondence between realism and artifice"[14] is beautifully abetted by Jean Rosenthal's set and lighting. The room where the young man in tights sleeps curled up on the floor is bare, white, and transparent; a breeze catches at a filmy white curtain on the side "wall" with the barre. The scrim that veils the scene casts us as voyeurs, but as it rises, and the man wakes and stretches to the music's opening notes, the audience understands itself to be the studio mirror in which he begins to regard himself (so mysteriously potent is this illusion of the mirror as invisible divider between spectators and performers that it is surprising to discover that Robbins originally considered placing it at the side of the stage).[15] The mythical Narcissus became enamored of his reflected image. A dancer's gaze into the mirror rarely betokens self-love. *Afternoon of a Faun*'s two dancers look for what they might be, at how they transform themselves through the ritual of ballet. We see through the mirror into their desires.

A choreographer who did extensive homework before beginning any ballet, Robbins studied Nijinsky's *Faune* and Mallarmé's poem (as Croce has implied, he probably also noticed the oblique connections between *Narcisse* and the earlier ballet).[16] While his choreography is three-dimensional, the dancers, continually appraising their actions in the mirror, stress the two-dimensional legibility that is vital to ballet's image on a proscenium stage. Robbins's *Faun* too occupies a drowsy sunlit space that is suddenly infused with a reticent, but unmistakable, sexual tension. Except for the absence of attendant nymphs, it echoes the structure of Nijinsky's ballet. Nijinsky's chief nymph drops her veils to bathe; Robbins's "nymph" presses her shoes into a resin box, fixes a ribbon, adjusts her shoulder strap in a gesture that recalls the classic statues of women adjusting the clasp of their tunics. The suggestion of water also invades the 1953 work. At one moment, the ballerina is seated on her partner's shoulder; as he gazes up at her and she down at him, very lightly paddling her feet in the air, they might be seeing each other as reflections of the ambition they share.[17] Later, standing behind her, he frames her head almost awkwardly within his angled arms, and, in the next instant, lowers and tilts that frame to catch her stretched body as she dives through it. A few years after the premiere, Robbins added a movement just before the end; it is the arch upward from the floor with which Nijinsky's faun expressed his sexual release, but executed simply as a last satisfying stretch.[18]

Lincoln Kirstein has written cannily of Robbins's gift for "the artificed use of the apparently accidental".[19] Nowhere in his ballets is that gift more brilliantly and unpretentiously displayed. Instead of the predetermined inevitability of Nijinsky's scene - that careful chase around the vase - every movement in *Afternoon of a Faun* looks as if the protagonists were dreaming it up on the spot, trying this movement, suddenly drawn into that one, and always returning their eyes to the mirror to calculate the effect. They perform the classical steps, none of them virtuosic, with an unaffected ease more related to marking in rehearsal (a look Robbins loved) than to "performing".[20] The original cast, Tanaquil LeClercq and Francisco Moncion, could be said to embody most fully Robbins's idea.[21] An excitement quivers beneath their apparent calm. Moncion conveys a restrained yet intense sensual interest in LeClercq from the moment he starts awake at the sound of her footsteps to the moment when she starts to back out of the room and he, kneeling, raises his head slightly, as if scenting the trail of her perfume. She seems at times innocent, hastening away from him, but a minute before, she has slowly turned one bent leg in and out, watching him in the mirror watching her, very aware of her own seductiveness. It is possible to interpret Mallarmé's chaste little nymph lying interlaced with her more knowing companion as two aspects of the eternal feminine; whether or not Robbins and LeClercq consciously followed this reading, they reembodied it as the play of conflicting feelings within one young woman.

214

Unlike Nijinsky, Robbins felt no need to invent a vocabulary. The dynamics of discovery - the ballerina's spin suddenly stopped by her partner's arm, her introspective attention on how a lift feels, the speculative glances at the mirror - build narrative onto classical steps and strategies. Robbins's originality, his contemporaneity, lay in mating the elegance of ballet with the casual athleticism of young Americans one might see on the street. All the gestures but one allude to the dancers' life as dancers. The exception is the climax, when they are kneeling on the floor, and the man leans softly forward to kiss the woman's cheek. She watches in the mirror, turns to look at him, and, gazing back at their reflections, touches the spot with her hand. Robbins, who came to ballet from modern dance and Broadway, handled the moment with the fastidious theatricality that marks all his finest works. Ah, we think, so intent are these dancers on their reflected otherness that even an intimate gesture must be studied for its effect. And we feel the irony: while the two are feeling out their pas de deux, he often must grasp her body and press it to him; yet at the moment "real" life unmistakably enters the studio, the suddenly electric point of physical contact is very small - the size of two lightly pursed lips.

Reaching for the ideal. Set in a rehearsal studio, Jerome Robbins's faun might clasp his coveted nymph, but they both pursue the ideal - the ideal dancer - through the mirror (*Afternoon of a Faun*, 1953, Francisco Moncion and Tanaquil LeClercq, New York City Ballet, Jerome Robbins Dance Division. The New York Public Library for the Performing Arts, Astor, Lenox and Tilden Foundations. Photo: Fred Fehl).

In this scenario the hero – if he can be considered one – may even be dreaming this lovely girl, his ideal partner. Robbins leaves that open to interpretation. She is not exactly unattainable. She simply leaves, having finished what she wanted to do, and he, unregretting, perhaps unchanged, goes back to sleep. They may dance together another day; it is the audience, and Robbins, who feel on their behalf the perfection of this afternoon's interlude.

Island epilogue

Debussy's evocative piece lasts about ten minutes. On a typical New York City Ballet program, Robbins's *Faun* was therefore usually paired with another ballet from the repertory rather than being framed by intermissions. Following it with a galloping bit of virtuosity, such as George Balanchine's dazzling *Tarantella*, did not allow its spell to sink in. In 1984, Robbins choreographed another short ballet and made it clear that the two works were to be programmed as one.[22] For *Antique Epigraphs*, he returned to Debussy: the composer's flute melody *Syrinx* (used as both overture and finale) and *Six Epigraphes Antiques* (the orchestral version). The latter were musical impressions of selections from *The Songs of Bilitis*, erotic prose poems evoking an island community of women resembling Sappho's on Lesbos; because the writer "Bilitis" later became a prostitute, some of the poems also deal with love between men and women. The real writer was a fin-de-siècle Frenchman, Pierre Louÿs; perhaps for that reason, the poems have a slightly voyeuristic, occasionally decadent cast. A blind old man speaks to Bilitis of nymphs:

> Their necks were inclined beneath their long hair.
> Their nails were as thin as the wings of grasshoppers.
> Their nipples were hollowed like the cups of hyacinths.
> They trailed their fingers upon the water and drew up,
> from an invisible vase, the long-stemmed water-lilies.
> Around their parted thighs, the ripples slowly widened.[23]

After the chase - the gaze. Instead of being prey to seduction, the frieze of nymphs in Jerome Robbins's *Antique Epigraphs* embodies the familiar statue-come-to-life scenario (1999, New York City Ballet. Photo: Paul Kolnik).

Having choreographed an *Afternoon of a Faun* without the attendant nymphs who created agitated border designs and rhythmic punctuation for Nijinsky, Robbins now considered "nymphs". His suite of dances for eight New York City Ballet women is not as astringent as his *Faun*, nor is it as suffused with eroticism as Louÿs' poems. Like Debussy's music, the ballet is mysterious, nostalgic, voluptuous only in the most refined and formal ways. What Robbins has taken from Louÿs is a certain ambiance: a sunlit isle where desirable women exchange confidences and meditate on love. Here the dream of beauty does not belong to some fictitious hero, but to a poet and a choreographer. These nymphs are not to be pursued and won or lost; they are simply there to be gazed at as they go about their dances. The only link between sections is the pervading gently lyrical tone – as if someone had said, "Sing us another song, Bilitis." The women give a semblance of agency until the end, when choreographic artifice gradually congeals them into a frieze. They strike various archaic poses borrowed from life-sized sculptures of women with enamel eyes, which Robbins had seen in the National Museum in Naples (among Robbins's copies of the score are pictures of these statues), and then gently link themselves into a chain. It is the old statue-come-to-life scenario, seen retrospectively and promoting a nostalgic vision: how lovely they were just seconds ago, how alive! The artful conclusion, a few earlier postures, and the vaguely Grecian tunics are Robbins's only concession to Louÿs' embrace of fabled antiquity.

Robbins made *Antique Epigraphs* during his later years when he was suppressing his bent for dramatic dance, wishing, like Balanchine, to deal with ballet's innate capacity to reveal elusive human feeling. His approach to his subject is echoed in an essay about the music filed among his papers, which links "... classical clarity and the supple finesse of the modal melodies, Greek or oriental" in an illusion of timelessness.[24] As in many of his works, he builds a semblance of community. Dancers watch one another dance. In the beginning, the women stand at one side of the stage, staring toward the other and gradually moving in that direction; they might be pondering some distant shore or wished-for ship, or simply taking in air. The solo created for Stephanie Saland to the music titled *The Nameless Tomb* is tinged with darkness, the dancer echoes Debussy's arpeggios with incantatory gestures to the ground and toward the end seems infected with the dread captured in falling chromaticisms.

There is not a trace in the ballet of the eroticism that informed the poems. The choreography creates an illusion of simple, fluent utterance typical of Robbins's lyricism. The dancers make an attitude turn on pointe, looking as if they were sailing on invisible wind. Three women holding hands, entwining, have the chasteness of young girls frolicking on a beach; two lift another in a leap; all of them together fit their rhythms to the waltz Debussy chose to embed in Bilitis's pastoral song to invoke Pan.

Robbins's vision of these women – or, rather, of these women dancers – is certainly idealized. They are young, lithe, gracious, gentle. They inhabit the *danse d'école* as if it were a convent with all the windows open to the sun and breeze. There's a startling moment close to the end in which they move into a line, holding hands exactly the way Nijinsky's nymphs do: their arms are curved, and, crossing, form an oval, their fingertips not quite touching. But these women's heads and feet are not twisted into profile. They face us, enigmatic yet forthright. Their gazes breach the separation between performers and audience, but acknowledge that divide. It is almost like a warning. Perhaps they mirror our desires, but they are dancers, dancing. No prince would dare to thread his way among them.

Notes

1. Romola Nijinsky with Lincoln Kirstein, *Nijinsky*, New York, Simon & Schuster, 1934, p. 239. Arnold Haskell expresses the same view and credits Diaghilev and Bakst with the choice of the poem. See Haskell's *Diaghileff: His Artistic and Private Life* (1935), New York, Da Capo Press, 1978, p. 246.

2. Stéphane Mallarmé, translated by Aldous Huxley. Reprinted in Adolphe De Meyer, *L'Après-midi d'un faune, Vaslav Nijinsky, 1913: Thirty Three Photographs*, New York, Dance Horizons, 1983, pp. 45-48.

3. Bronislava Nijinska, *Early Memoirs*, edited and translated by Irina Nijinska and Jean Rawlinson, New York, Holt, Rinehart, & Winston, 1981, p. 353.

4. Ibid., p. 367.

5. Richard Buckle, *Nijinsky*, New York, Simon & Schuster, 1971, p. 262.

6. *Pall Mall Gazette*, February 15, 1913. Cited in Nesta MacDonald, *Diaghilev Observed by Critics in England and the United States 1911-1929*, Brooklyn, New York, Dance Horizons/London, Dance Books Ltd., 1975, p. 79.

7. Descriptions of the ballet are based in part on three versions of *L'Après-midi d'un faune* available on film or videotape: one staged by Leon Woizikowski for the Ballet Rambert in 1931, *Paris Dances Diaghilev*, performed by members of the Paris Opera Ballet in 1992, and a third staged in 1989 for the Juilliard School by Jill Beck from Stepanov notation.

8. Erik Aschengreen, *Jean Cocteau and the Dance*, Copenhagen, Gyldendal, 1986, p. 28.

9. Lincoln Kirstein, *Nijinsky Dancing*, New York, Alfred A. Knopf, 1975, p. 125.

10. Lynn Garafola posits a possible influence on Nijinsky, via Diaghilev, of Vsevolod Meyerhold's concept of "static" or "motionless" theater. See Lynn Garafola, *Diaghilev's Ballets Russes*, New York, Oxford University Press, 1989, pp. 53-56.

11. *The Standard*, February 2, 1913. Cited in MacDonald, op. cit., p. 80.

12. Romola Nijinsky, op. cit., p. 173.

13. U.S. Congress, House Committee on Un-American Activities, *Investigations into Communist Activities in the New York City Area,* Washington, U.S. Government Printing Office, 1953.

14. Arlene Croce, "Three Elders," *The New Yorker*, March 26, 1984. Collected in *Sight Lines*, New York, Alfred A. Knopf, 1987, p. 183.

15. Nancy Reynolds, *Repertory in Review: Forty Years of the New York City Ballet,* New York, Dial Press, 1977, p. 147.

16. Arlene Croce, op. cit., p. 183.

17. I am indebted to Yaping Chen for alerting me to the reflection imagery in this lift, in her unpublished paper, "Jerome Robbins's *Afternoon of a Faun*: From Male Mythological Narcissism to the Sublimation of Female Beauty", New York University -Tisch School of the Arts, 1991.

18. The change can be noted in a 1961 kinescope for Granada TV's *Personal Appearances.* The performance is by Kay Mazzo and John Jones of Robbins's Ballets U.S.A.

19. Lincoln Kirstein, *The New York City Ballet*, New York, Alfred A. Knopf, 1973, p. 97.

20. Interview with Jerome Robbins conducted by Deborah Jowitt in August, 1974, in preparation for her article "Back, Again, To Ballet," New York Times Magazine, December 8, 1974.

21. *Afternoon of a Faun* with LeClercq and Moncion was filmed c. 1953 at a performance in Trieste, Italy.

22. Robbins, papers. Noted among suggestions sent by Robbins to Peter Martins concerning the repertory for the New York City Ballet's spring season, 1989.

23. Pierre Louÿs, *The Songs of Bilitis*, translated by M. S. B. Privately printed 1919.

24. From a xeroxed essay found among Jerome Robbins's notes. Attributed to Harry Halbreich, its format suggests that it may have come from a record jacket.

Other Worlds – Sounding the Spirit

The aural-visual dilemmas of dance

Stephanie Jordan

> Does the thing heard replace the thing seen. Does it help
> or does it interfere with it...Does the seeing replace the
> hearing or does it not. Or do they both go on together.[1]

Could these obsessive questions of Gertrude Stein represent the dilemma of watching one of Erik Aschengreen's highly theatrical lectures, the speaker telling an amusing point of history with a flamboyant flourish of the hands and enthusiastic bob of the torso or dancing the lithographic image of a long-lost sylph? It could, certainly, but it also reminds me of a conceptual issue posed in particularly colourful fashion during my first encounter with Aschengreen. It was July 1974, the occasion of the first graduate dance history seminar at the University of Chicago, "The Romantic Ballet in Europe" led by Selma Jeanne Cohen, Mary Grace Swift and the indefatigable Aschengreen. It was also my first major dance history experience, my first contact with Bournonville and the Danish ballet tradition, whilst providing many new insights into what little I then knew about the French romantic ballet. The seminar raised a number of fascinating issues about how audiences listened as well as watched their ballet in those days and how different voices and kinds of voice came to their attention. As much as anything, different worlds were evoked, worlds distanced too beyond the immediacy of the plot enacted on stage, and those aural voices could at times achieve an importance that we today might find surprising.

Customarily, we associate the romantic ballet with the enhancement and integration of aural and visual narratives through the use of motto themes associated with characters and situations, and with the drive towards musical unity and organicism that leads later in the century to the figure of Wagner. Music could now transport us into another world. Bournonville called it "the most excellent organ of imagination" and celebrated the link between sound and physicality through "the body that sings," surely the body of the ideal dancer who possesses sound to make us hear it more acutely.[2] Yet this is the master narrative of history, what we have been taught to take as the so-called improvements of the romantic ballet era. We have forgotten what today seems a far more fascinating feature, that of the "airs parlants". A device stemming from the 18th century and still used during the 19th century romantic period, these are voices from outside the story, literally "speaking tunes" borrowed melodies which, because of their known associations, would help explain the action on stage and which were gradually abandoned for the ideal of originality.

Airs parlants held associations from the operas to which they originally belonged (presumably familiar to the audience) and thus they would succinctly enhance the story of the dance or even occasionally inform the audience of a fact in a story that could not be told through dance without great difficulty, a parallel having been drawn with the same event in the opera. In Ferdinand Hérold's *La Fille mal gardée* (1828), for example, Lise's entrance on tiptoe so that she does not wake her mother is aptly illustrated by the opening chorus from Rossini's *Il Barbiere di Siviglia* (1816), "Piano, pianissimo". Or, in *La Tempête* (1834), when Oberon asks Lea to tell him what troubles her, she mimes her response to the orchestra playing "Voi che sapete" from *Le Nozze di Figaro* (1786).[3]

Take this a stage further and, according to the terms of today, we have a veritable intertextual experience as outside stories resonate with the narrative of the ballet in question, as other worlds. There is also the notion of an opening up of space and dialogue between what is seen and what is heard. I say "according to the terms of today", because it would be ahistorical to assume that 19th century audiences experienced the playful, open intertextuality and knowing, analytical frame of mind that seem to be the temper of our own times. Much more to the point is that such audiences needed the explanatory values of music in order to comprehend what was happening on stage (and likewise recitative style music that sounded like the speech so regretfully lacking from the stage). There is evidence too that they listened with a different kind of attention in those days. When, for instance, in our century, Charles Mackerras borrowed tunes from Sullivan operas for John Cranko's *Pineapple Poll* (1951), we cannot assume that audiences have been alert to the references in the same way that they would have been in the 19th century.[4] However, after the dominance of 19th century models of unity and autonomous, hermetically sealed artworks, we are at least reminded by such devices as airs parlants that unity is a created myth and that the spaces between music and dance are negotiable spaces, ambiguous, and offering exciting potential for different kinds of encroachment and rupture.

My thanks to Aschengreen and that seminar for not only transporting me into the world of ethereal visions and sylphian fantasy but for opening up that other world of play between the aural and visual - the sounding of the spirit. Since the 1970s, my own field of interest has moved into the 20th century, but I am still preoccupied by those 'spaces between', the notion of multi-voiced experi-ence and by Stein's aural/visual dilemma. This leads me to summarise some relevant theoretical models.[5]

The subversive power of music

Certainly, until recently, Western culture has tended to consider the eye superior to the ear as a perceptual mechanism. The modern-dance pioneer Doris Hum-phrey said as much, "not only is the eye faster, but, in a contest with the ear, will invariably take precedence."[6] The theory extends back to the Greeks, who related the eye to the ordering structures of consciousness, whilst the ear was perceived as unmediated and having direct access to the soul from which emotions spring. This model was accepted for centuries and sustained as scientific thinking of the 19th century valued objectivity (which the eye promised) over subjectivity (connected with hearing). Thus, for instance, until only recently, "visualism" has dominated anthropological research.[7] Likewise, until only recently, film theory has prioritised the visual over the aural too so that, as Christian Metz has pointed out, the very term "voice-off" is telling, meaning absence or lack rather than presence.[8]

Music's relationship to the screen has been for years discussed as a one-way relationship, in terms of its parallelism and counterpoint to the primary visual image. Does the music support the visual image or does it not? However, this view has been challenged on a number of occasions, and increasingly so recently, through ideological and psychoanalytic criticism. Theodor W. Adorno and Hanns Eisler, and later Jacques Attali, have proposed the power of music to deceive and manipulate, indeed precisely because it seems less mediated and more direct in its impact, and thus they recognise the subversive potential of music.[9] Using psychoanalytic theory, Claudia Gorbman has pointed out how music, because of its ability to connect the individual with the pre-oedipal imaginary (a state of integration or wholeness), helps the spectator to slip into the world of the film.[10]

Today, a number of film theorists reject the parallelism-counterpoint model. Instead, they propose models of mutual implication or interdependence. Dance can draw usefully from film theory here. Humphrey herself already understood the issues: she admits the power of music:

> to completely distort the mood of a dance. Suppose the dancer has a sequence arranged which is quite serious, a small segment of one of life's major encounters. Accompany this by trivial music which patters along without any depth of feeling. The result is that the dancer does not become stronger by contrast; rather he seems empty, silly and pretentious. Such is the power of the sound to set the mood. This same sequence, accompanied by jaunty, slightly jazzy music, can make the dancer look cynical; he is pretending to be serious, but actually it is all bluff, and he believes in nothing. The variations on this kind of thing are endless.[11]

The implication here is that music infects the dance so deeply that it looks different as a result: movement is not seen for its own independent values. This is one whole experience, music and dance inextricably combined. Humphrey also notes the power of music when the effect is more of separation or disjunction between music and dance, in other words, of two opposing voices:

If soft sound supports strong movement and vice versa, a curious effect is produced. The music seems to be antagonist; the figure of the dancer fights to be strong without encouragement; and in his more vulnerable moods the music seems to seek to destroy and dominate him.[12]

Why did the faun jump?

Now I want to examine the metaphorical concept of space, separation or disjunction between music and dance. How does it affect our response? Here is Brecht writing about the Wagnerian *Gesamtkunstwerk* tradition:

> The process of fusion extends to the spectator who gets thrown into the melting pot too and becomes a passive ... part of the total work of art. Witchcraft of this sort must of course be fought against. Whatever is intended to produce hypnosis, is likely to induce sordid intoxication, or creates fog, has got to be given up. *Words, music, and setting must become more independent of one another.*[13]

Brecht suggests that independence between art media allows our perceptions to remain acute.

We might now replace Wagnerian opera, words, music and setting with dance, movement, music and setting. Of course, as we know, for Brecht, this issue of separation or 'space between' was a polemical issue, not at all about questions of musicality, but might there be less overt politics stemming from techniques of independence or separation?

In relation to this issue, we might be reminded of Nijinsky's *L'Après-midi d'un faune* (1912) to Debussy's famous score, and surely one of the most radical works of the century, not least in its approach to music. Debussy did not approve.

Imagine if you can see the discrepancy between a sinuous, soothing, flexible musical line on the one hand, and on the other a performance whose characters move like those on Greek or Etruscan vases, ungracefully, rigidly, as though their every gestures were constricted by the laws of plane geometry. So profound a dissonance can know no resolution![14]

Any number of other people also noted the element of disjunction whether approvingly or otherwise. Here was the symbolist ethos of Debussy's music set against the new modernism of a much younger Nijinsky, a perceived aesthetic break that was not common practice at the time, indeed the term "cubist" had been applied to the choreography.[15] There is also clear structural disjunction. These are the kinds of 'spaces between' most prominent in this work. Now today, we might argue that we do not experience any major effect of disjunction from *Faune*, but there is no doubt that this was the case for audiences in 1912. The choreography is full of sudden starts, shocks, abrupt nervous movements that come from nowhere in the musical structure. At the climax of the work, the faun and chief nymph stand face to face, absolutely motionless for an exaggerated amount of time, then she bows down and rises to arch back very slowly, the restraint pulling against the emotional power and high volume, the 'witchcraft' of the music. And why did the Faun jump? He leaps once, passion let fly for one moment: the moment stands out like a blasphemy, just after that climax, and again comes out of nowhere in the music.[16]

One could say that the disassociation of sensibilities between music and dance in *Faune* contributes to a new modernist objectivity, leaves space for the analytical attention, even voyeurism, of the audience. *Faune* is a dual experience. Viewers at the time were quite clearly captured by the charismatic performance of Nijinsky and the nymphs, but the juxtaposition of choreography with music operates in bracing dialogue with this. Is there another kind of musicality here? My suggestion is that *Faune* looks forward to the future of a Merce Cunningham aesthetic where music and dance are totally independent and we experience each with a new clarity and objectivity.

Politics of perception – From Mickey Mouse to Merce Cunningham

I pay tribute to the important article by Roger Copeland "Merce Cunningham and the Politics of Perception" in which he claims that Cunningham's art "insists on maintaining an ironic detachment from the...'natural' world" and gives us perceptual training in a world cluttered with information and imagery. Copeland claims that the importance of Cunningham's work "lies not only in what we're given to see and hear, but in *the way we see and hear what we're given.*"[17] Cunningham encourages us to make our own choices, to see and hear differently (there is that wonderfully unmuddied physicality, for instance, movement dynamics unmediated by the clutter of sound beat) and to be aware of our perceptual processes. For a while too, until we got used to his model of independence, his work was a comment on the tradition that he broke. The breaking of conventions reminds us of those conventions.

Then, in the 1990s, Merce trumped himself. A 1998 London Barbican event concluded with a big joyous ensemble dancing emphatically to the happy beat of Latin American music.[18] When we experience music and dance together in Merce's now conventional world of disjunction a very odd thing happens. We are reminded of their separateness, by default! It is the breaking of the convention that is all-important, within the particular aesthetic tradition created by Cunningham. Indeed, a similar effect can arise out of a very different aesthetic tradition, when music and dance structures are commonly expected to match very closely. In the work of the British Indian choreographer Shobana Jeyasingh, the dancers stamp out apparently 'classical' foot rhythms in silence, without the expected, traditional rhythmic prompt of the music, and, once again, the space between choreography and musical score is highlighted.

Other choreographers are more secretive about changing their tactics. Mark Morris is most renowned for his wonderfully ironic, knowing commentary on the Mickey Mouse tradition. Any number of his pieces 'visualize' the rhythmic and melodic patterns of his music. But he also created *Drink to me Only with Thine Eyes* (1988, Virgil Thomson) for American Ballet Theatre, and how many people

Dancing around Cunningham's politics of disjunction. His *Beachbirds* (1991) breaks with the usual "detachment from the 'natural' world", as indicated by the costumes and Cage's music, reminiscent of pebbles rattling in the surf (1991, The Cunningham Company. Photo: Michael O'Neill).

have noticed that this is a study in counterpoint, dance and music sharing a pulse but working in different metres? Almost the whole of this little ballet appears to be structured in this way. Such structural separation of music and dance is perhaps less easy to perceive - this kind of dialogue after all seems so friendly, so close - but it too creates the experience of different voice lines.

The work of Balanchine surely tells us this too. In the trio Coda to the Triple Pas de Quatre in his *Agon* (1957, Stravinsky), the ironic gigue rhythm articulated by the solo violin has already been 'heard' in the dance in the skipping and 'soft shoe' steps. In the same trio, there is a striking passage where a series of entrechats springing down the line of dancers anticipates four shrill repeated B-flats on the flutes. Further accented kicks and relevés then become echoes or reverberations of those high notes. Then the metre of three canon passages is three beats to a bar (created by the three dancers), against two beats in the 6/8 musical bar. The contrapuntal effect between music and dance is very clear because the dance beats are marked by strong accents: entrechats, leg kicks, sharp relevés in attitude, and/or pirouettes. The effect is especially restless in the closing section of the Coda. The canon here begins with the man and then shifts the eye to the right and then to the left as it moves to the women on either side of him. We notice too the 'space between' music and dance on hearing the footfall during musical silences and sustained notes. And then there is an instance of genuine Mickey Mouse, as all three dancers huddle together and gesture with alternating shoulders, down, down and down into a low stoop, to a series of three descending musical accents.

Again, these are not the only tactics of Balanchine. A piece renowned for its much more consistent visualization of music is *Symphonie Concertante* (1945), with two solo women representing Mozart's violin and viola. It was conceived like an audience training piece "to show the relationship between a classical symphony and classical dance" for a programme of the National Orchestral Association called "Adventure in Ballet".[19] When the music repeated, so did the dance. The relationship between music and dance has particular meaning: it can emphasize closure, harmony, balance, security - it does in *Symphonie Concertante*. In *Agon*, it does quite the opposite: it means tension and argument. "Agon" literally means contest.

Bodies that sing

Space between, making us hear and see more acutely, aware of our perceptual processes, deconstructing tradition, even a choreographer's own tradition, these are the tactics of a number of choreographers today. My last example is Siobhan Davies, currently one of our most esteemed choreographers in Britain. The piece is the 1996 *Affections* and I describe how it opens.[20]

The lighting is secretive. We can just make out a figure on a high platform upstage, partly in silhouette, sometimes hovering, sometimes leaning over the guard-rail to watch below. Down in the dancing space, a woman emerges from the gloom, tossing, turning and snaking impetuously through her territory close to the floor. Soon, she springs up, lashes out as if throwing off some burden, then reins herself in. She places a hand on the front of a hip as if clutching a deep wound, another time, her feet jump apart and she thrusts her hands down her centre like a dagger into the pelvis - the low centre - or she touches her breast thoughtfully - high centre - or her rippling hand traces the line of a lively abdomen. And the voice! The physicality, the grief in that voice! "Cara sposa, amante cara, dove sei?" ("Dear wife, dear love, where have you gone?") What is this miraculous voice? Whose is it? Who is the person on the platform? Dressed like the dancing woman, in 18th century style skirted jacket and trews, is it another dancer? Is it man or woman? Is it the singer? The tripartite relationship between the two figures and the "voice-object" is tantalising, the more so as the dancer's gestures add pressure to sustained melodic highlights, the more so as she seems drawn upstage by that hovering, increasingly involved, even predatory figure above.[21]

The dancer is Gill Clarke, the figure, who turns out to be a singer, mezzo soprano Buddug Verona James. It is Handel's music that we hear, an aria from the opera *Rinaldo*, hence the title *Affections* after the "affections" of baroque art theory. Gerald Barry's arrangement, for piano and string trio, and the microphone amplification, removes us from the "natural world" of the baroque like Peter Greenaway's film *The Draughtsman's Contract*; we are both back in the past and definitely not back in the past. Heritage is skewed. Thus, the music is both close and distanced, of two worlds, past and present, and the duality accentuates perceptions of time and space.

There seems to be something particular too about the solo voice, whether singer or instrument, that it can insinuate itself into our darkest and most private regions. And James' "Cara Sposa" renders precisely that kind of experience. I am reminded of Roland Barthes' classic 1972 essay "The Grain of the Voice", in which he proposes an aesthetics of musical pleasure, "jouissance" (with all the erotic connotations of that word), or deep physical feeling, after years of a performance practice culture that demanded dry execution.[22] "Let's get back to 'the body in the voice'" is Barthes' apparent manifesto, and he writes about this possibility as if it is transmitted directly from the body of the performer to become an embodied musical feature. Dance can illustrate this intensity visually, as the dancers hear what we hear.

Perhaps Davies' exploration of deep internal regions, organs and cavities within the body as well as its surfaces would be Barthes' ideal in dance terms. Thus, "Cara Sposa" presents a fascinating, complex example of mutual possession, a rapprochement of forces, Clarke taking the sound into her own body (like Bournonville's "body that sings"), and I take both physicalities - from sound and dancing bodies - into mine. Such an idea of being possessed is far from the aesthetics of Brecht and Merce.

Yet this is not the whole story of the relationship between sound and body and between one body and another. Here too are tactics of separation and rupture. Later, during the musical repeat (the music is in ABA form), Davies presents a pared-down version of her first section A, selected moments elaborated, but with many long pauses, including a passage where Clarke simply lies for a long time on her side. Davies conceptualised erasure as the way out of such a deeply felt affection of love and stress, but we might also find that we listen more or at least differently during the pauses. And the body is distanced from sound; perhaps we might read this bodily disappearance as the ultimate indication of loss or dislocation. When the singer takes her breaks, there is a similar effect: in one passage, the piano takes the lead, like a voice suddenly from the outside. At the end of the aria, the tie is definitively cut, Clarke moves towards the audience, and James turns her back. But then, literal spatial distance has always been an issue between them.

With its many ambiguities, including the distance and rapprochement between singer and dancer and the fusion and distinction of voices, *Affections* plays with the conventional relationships between music and dance. Thus, like so many of my examples in this article, it draws attention to those conventions and devices.

With Davies, we have come a long way since the musical debates surrounding the 19th century romantic ballet, but she tells us that these debates are still with us, even if in different guise. She also confronts the aural/visual dilemma that Gertrude Stein faced earlier on in our own century. She understands rupture, but she plays too with the irony that sound deepens the physical sense, 're-bodying' the dancer, as it were, whilst the dancer also embodies the spirit of sound that we associate with the singer. Meanwhile, the spectator-listener negotiates her/his own route through the aesthetic, connotational and structural worlds that merge and separate from each other. There are still "bodies that sing" and voices that sing despite those bodies.

Notes

1. Gertrude Stein, "Plays" (1934) in *Stein*, ed. Patricia Meyerowitz, *Writings and Lectures 1911-1945*, London, Peter Owen, 1967, p. 63.

2. August Bournonville, "New Year's Gift for Dance Enthusiasts" and "Choreography: A Faith", quoted by Ole Nørlyng in "Music is the most excellent organ of imagination" in *Salut for Bournonville*, The Royal Museum of Fine Arts, Copenhagen, 1979-80, pp. 109-110.

3. Marian Smith, "Borrowings and Original Music: A Dilemma for the Ballet-Pantomime Composer", *Dance Research*, 6/2 (Autumn, 1988) Los Angeles, pp. 11-12. See also Smith's *Ballet-Pantomime and its Kinship with Opera in the Age of Giselle*, Princeton, Princeton University Press, 2000; stemming from the 1974 Chicago seminar is Jordan's "The Role of the Ballet Composer at the Paris Opéra: 1820-50", *Dance Chronicle*, 4/4, 1981, New York, pp. 374-88.

4. For a discussion of the Sullivan tunes used as sources in *Pineapple Poll* see Larraine Nicholas, *The Lion and the Unicorn: Festival of Britain Themes and Choreography in the Postwar Decade*, unpublished Ph.D. dissertation, University of Surrey, 1999.

5. For further discussion of a methodology for analysing relationships between music and dance see Jordan, *Moving Music: Dialogues with Music in Twentieth-Century Ballet,* London, Dance Books, 2000.

6. Doris Humphrey, *The Art of Making Dances,* New York and Toronto, Rinehart, 1959, p. 161.

7. James Clifford, "Introduction: Partial Truths", in Clifford and George E. Marcus, eds., *Writing Culture: The Poetics and Politics of Ethnography,* Berkeley and Los Angeles, University of California Press, 1986, pp. 11-12.

8. Christian Metz, "Le Perçu et le nommé", in Metz, *Essais sémiotiques,* Paris, Editions Klinckseck, 1977, pp. 153-59.

9. Hanns Eisler and Theodor W. Adorno (the latter uncredited), *Composing for the Films,* London, Dennis Dobson, 1947, pp. 59-61 (in the original English edition, Adorno's co-authorship is unacknowledged); Jacques Attali, *Noise: The Political Economy of Music*, trans. Brian Massumi, Minneapolis, University of Minnesota Press, 1985, p. 6.

10. Claudia Gorbman, *Unheard Melodies: Narrative Film Music,* Bloomington, Indiana University Press, 1987, p. 64. See also Kathryn Kalinak, *Settling the score: Music and the Classical Hollywood Film,* Madison, Wisconsin, University of Wisconsin Press, 1992, pp. 20-39.

11. Humphrey, op. cit., p. 80.

12. Humphrey, op. cit., p. 80.

13. Bertolt Brecht, *Brecht on Theatre: The Development of an Aesthetic,* ed. and trans. John Willett, London, Methuen, 1964, p. 38.

14. Interview in *La Tribuna,* February 23rd, 1914, quoted by Jean-Michel Nectoux, *Afternoon of a Faun: Mallarmé, Debussy, Nijinsky,* ed. Nectoux, New York, The Vendome Press, 1987, p. 35.

15. Charles Tenroc, "Nijinski va faire dans *L'après-midi d'un faune* des essais de chorégraphie cubiste", *Comoedia,* April 18th, Paris, 1912, p. 4.

16. For an extended analysis of Nijinsky's *L'Après-midi d'un faune,* see Jordan, "Debussy, the Dance and the Faune" in James R. Briscoe, ed., *Debussy in Performance,* New Haven, Conn., Yale University Press, 1999, pp. 119-34.

17. Roger Copeland, "Merce Cunningham and the Politics of Perception", (1979) in *What Is Dance?,* eds. Copeland and Marshall Cohen, Oxford, Oxford University Press, 1983, pp. 310, 322.

18. The date of the event was October 6th, 1998.

19. *Choreography by Balanchine: A Catalogue of Works,* New York, Viking, 1984, p. 179.

20. For a fuller discussion of *Affections,* see Jordan, "Body and Voice" (with notes by Helen Thomas), *Dance Now,* 6/1, Spring, 1997, pp. 28-31.

21. The term "voice-object" has been taken from Carolyn Abbate, *Unsung Voices: Opera and Musical Narrative in the Nineteenth Century,* Princeton, Princeton University Press, 1991, p. 10.

22. Roland Barthes, "The Grain of the Voice" (1972) in Barthes, *Image-Music-Text,* trans. Stephen Heath, London, Fontana/Collins, 1977, pp. 179-89.

The Marriage of Music and Dance

Understanding the world of choreomusical relations through a gendered metaphor

Inger Damsholt

The act of yearning and reaching for a world which lies beyond reality and everyday life, is a characteristic feature of ballet as an artform. In the ballets of the romantic era, the longing for that which cannot be grasped is exemplified in stories about man's love for a fairy-like creature. Characteristic of all ballet is that this bodily practice represents an attempt to defy gravity and rise into a world of ideals. Using the art of ballet as a general metaphor for the artistic experience, we might say that when we perceive a work of art, we are allowed to sneak a peek at a world that lies beyond anything that might be understood rationally. Thus according to one of the classical theories of perception, we may speak of an aesthetic experience as one which goes beyond intellectual apprehension.[1] However, much like the romantic heroes in *Sylphide* and *Swan Lake*, we - the audience, listeners, spectators, critics and scholars alike - have a desire to grasp and understand that element of art which might never be completely captured by our intellect.

As a general theory of understanding it has been proposed that human thought-processes are largely metaphorical. In other words, when our minds are exposed to something with which we are not familiar, we seek to understand it by means of a metaphorical transference of structures that we know from other phenomena.[2] The relationship of music and dance is one of the intriguing elements in a dancework that we seek to grasp, a dynamic encounter between two non-verbal phenomena which cannot immediately be explained in rational terms. This article examines how the relationship between music and dance has long been understood by means of a gendered metaphor, more specifically as a male/female relationship. Furthermore, the article investigates some of the consequences flowing from this gendered understanding of the choreomusical world.

Desire and attraction

The metaphorical understanding of the music/dance relationship as a relationship between male and female emerges from writings on dance and music throughout history. The talk of a "marriage between music and dance" can be traced at least as far back as the 17th century and is a metaphor which suggests a physical bond between the two art forms.[3] Where there is dance there is music. The relationship between music and dance is, however, also informed by notions of seduction and pleasure. Within the 20th century the fixed roles of dance as female and music as male are essential to the marriage metaphor. However, prior to the 20th century, the understanding of the music/dance relationship is predominantly informed by notions of desire and attraction which are less firmly rooted in the notion of male and female. Creating an image of a sensual relationship between two individuals Noverre writes:

238

> music...transports, exalts and inflames me...These are the natural effects of music on dancing, and of dancing on music, when two artists are attracted to each other and when the two arts blend, unite and mutually exchange their charms to captivate and please.[4]

Music awakens the dancer's desire to follow its rhythms. Similarly Magri explains how music compels the limbs to extend and to move according to its beat. Bournonville even defines dance as a desire to follow the rhythms of the music. If we turn to the actual narratives of ballets, the notion of desire and attraction in the relationship between music and dance is often highlighted by the story itself. As an example, in the Bournonville ballet *The Kermesse in Bruges* (1851) we encounter this notion when Carelis makes all present dance to the sound of his enchanted viola.

While music and dance exalt and inflame each other, the combined activities of the two form a coherence which is pleasurable to perceive. Thus Noverre explains how the relationship between the two captivates the spectator in the same manner as if watching a sensual pas de deux:

Desire and seduction inform the relationship between music and dance. In *The Kermesse in Bruges*, Carelis compels the two reluctant maidens, Marchen and Johanna, to dance by playing his viola da gamba (Henriette Muus (left), Lis Jeppesen and Lloyd Riggins, 1992, Royal Danish Ballet. Photo: David Amzallag).

their combined effect offers animated pictures to our eyes
and ears; these senses convey to the heart the interesting
pictures which have moved them; the heart in turn communicates these images to the soul, and the pleasure which
results from the harmony and intelligence of these two
arts captivates the spectator and makes him experience
the most seductive pleasure.[5]

Noverre's statement suggests an eroticism in the coupling of music and dance on
stage as well as in the relationship between the coupling and the spectator, who is
watching and listening - a position comparable to that of the voyeur.

In her analysis of ballet's staging of story and desire in *Choreography and Narrative*
(1996), Susan Leigh Foster argues that dance assumed an increasingly feminine
role throughout the 19th century. At this point it might be supposed that, when
compared to the natural sciences, all of the arts are conceived of in feminine
terms - Terpsichore as well as Polyhymnia and her other sisters. However, Foster
argues that:

the other arts' capacity to edify and educate their audiences
and to leave behind definitive documentation of their
composition carried a masculine weight and authority
that the pleasure-filled and ephemeral dance could not
match.[6]

As an extension of Foster's argument I suggest that within the context of dance,
music assumes an increasingly masculine role throughout the 19th century. The
notion of music as male primarily emerges in its role as the other part of the
dichotomy - the role of "other half" of a sensual or seductive relationship. Thus it
is particularly within the context of dance that music has come to assume its mas-
culinity. The masculine role of music is, however, supported by other factors.

Foster suggests that music carried a masculine weight in its capacity to edify
and educate its audiences and to leave behind a definitive score. To this it might be
added that the masculine status of music had long been confirmed by the fact that

Dance is female, music is male - listen to his master's voice. Jerome Robbins's *The Concert* (at the piano Julian Thurber, 1999, Royal Danish Ballet. Photo: Martin Mydtskov Rønne).

music theory was founded on the science of accoustics - a hard natural science. Moreover the status of music had long been institutionalised in its inclusion as one of the seven liberal arts. Another element that ought to be stressed is that the Hegelian scheme of arts which dominates the 19th century, enshrines music as the central romantic art, thus in music the spirit dominates its material embodiment.[7] As such it seems that the Hegelian scheme reflects the notion of music as male/spirit whereas dance is female/body.

Finally I should like to underline that the metaphorical understanding of dance as female and music as male is encouraged by historical circumstances. Thus during the late 19th century - at the Paris Opéra in particular - the division of gender is no more metaphorical than the fact that the ballet stage is filled with alluring ballerinas, while the orchestra pit is full of men playing their musical instruments. And as such the understanding of music as male within the context of dance is further enhanced.

Liberation and equality

In the 20th century there is still talk of the marriage between music and dance. However, while the understanding of the music/dance relationship is informed by notions of seduction, attraction and desire prior to the 20th century, the gendered understanding of the dance/music relationship is a question of liberation, power and equal rights in the new century. Thus the roles of music as male and dance as female become much more fixed. A dominant feature of 20th century choreomusical writings is the notion of a linear historical progression towards the liberation of dance from music. Curiously this history of the relationship between dance and music is constructed as a progression similar to the "liberation of women" and change of gender roles in the 20th century. Thus a consequence of the metaphorical understanding of music/dance is that the resistance or ambivalence towards musical accompaniment becomes a question of gender politics. In the following paragraphs I shall expand on this argument.

Generally speaking, there is a widespread consensus throughout most of the 20th century that dance should not follow music too closely. In 1936, the British ballet conductor and composer Constant Lambert writes:

> I am sure there must be innumerable musicians beside myself, who experience the same feeling of exasperation when the choreographer turns the stage into a vast lecturer's blackboard and, by associating certain dancers with certain themes, proceeds to underline obvious formal devices in the music which any one of average intelligence can appreciate with half an ear. Literal transla-tions from one language into another are always unsatis-factory and usually ridiculous.[8]

In the specialised writings on dance, a one-to-one relationship between music and movement is considered simple, banal and childish. The dance composer Norman Lloyd explains:

> carried to an extreme it becomes a kind of musical cartooning. In fact among film composers such a technique is called Mickey Mousing (although the technique predates Mr. Disney by many thousand years).[9]

Being too preoccupied with the music is not an ideal within the 20th century world of dance. As a general tendency of modernism in the 20th century artists have distanced themselves from the representational art of previous centuries. They have turned their gaze inwards in order to examine art's own premises, its material, its compositional procedures etc. Art has examined itself as an autonomous phenomenon and has tried to eliminate every kind of reference to anything but itself. As a special feature of 20th century dance, the silent dance work becomes a norm of its own within modern dance circles, thus to some artists the only truly autonomous dance is one which is unaccompanied. In 1953 Susanne Langer writes:

> the existence of an intimate relation - identity or near-identity - has indeed been repudiated, vehemently denied, by some dancers and dance enthusiasts who maintain -

quite properly - that theirs is an independent art; and
those few defenders of the faith have even gone so far as
to claim that the world-old union of music and dance is
a pure accident or a matter of fashion.[10]

One choreomusical poetics which becomes widely accepted in the second half of
the 20th century is the notion of the "non-relationship", insisting that dance and
music can operate as autonomous entities. This choreomusical paradigm is identified
in the works and thoughts of Merce Cunningham:

> The non-reference of the movement is extended into a
> relationship with music. It is essentially a non-relation-
> ship. The dance is not performed to the music. For the
> dances that we present, the music is composed and per-
> formed as a separate identity in itself. It happens to take
> place at the same time as the dance. The two co-exist, as
> sight and sound do in our daily lives. And with that the
> dance is not dependent upon the music. This does not
> mean I would prefer to dance in silence because it would
> strike me as daily life without sound. I accept sound as
> one of the sensory areas along with sight, the visual sense.[11]

In the statement above dance is allied or combined with music, however it is
thought no less independent or autonomous because it co-exists with music.
Thus the concept of chance procedure and indeterminacy is thought to be the
guarantee of choreomusical independence and autonomy. These creative procedures
are also thought to provide equal rights for the dancers/muscians or choreographer/
composer; to the extent that anybody can control the productive outcome of
their collaboration everybody has the same rights.

What is of particular interest here, as this article concerns the metaphorical
understanding of music/dance, is that the choreomusical progression towards
liberation and equal rights for dance and music resembles the progression towards
the "liberation of women" and change of gender roles in the 20th century. Just as

the institution of marriage between man and woman is questioned by the feminist movement, so is the marriage between music and dance. In this way the talk of marriage between music and dance in the 20th century is a matter of equality rather than sensual attraction:

> (Dance) is not an independent art; it is truly female, needing a sympathetic mate, but not a master, in music...The ideal relationship is like a happy marriage in which two individuals go hand in hand, but are not identical twins. (D. Humphrey)[12]

> The association of music and the dance is a partnership, a marriage between two arts...An ideal partnership is one in which mutual respect and support are so firmly established that it never even occurs to the partners to discuss them. But ideals are not of this world. (E. Evans)[13]

> Egalitarian collaboration is an arbitrary and ultimately pointless process. Every work has its primary apparition, to which all other virtual dimensions are secondary. There are no happy marriages in art - only successful rape. (S. K. Langer)[14]

245

As can be seen from the quotations above, the power struggles of choreomusical poetics resemble those found in feminist politics. Parallel with the women's liberation and fight for egalitarianism in the 20th century, the music/dance relationship is conceived in terms of power. And primarily this is a relationship in which the dance is in danger of being ruled or governed by the music.

It should be underlined that the ambivalence towards musical accompaniment is predominantly found within the world of modern dance, and as such modern dance is conceived as a sort of feminist art form. There are several elements to this conceptual formation. First of all, the modern dance pioneers were women - the forerunners of modern dance being Isadora Duncan and Ruth St. Denis, and the

The female dancer is surely going to put her foot down. In step with women's liberation during the 20th century, modern dance claimed its independence from music (Victoria May in Tim Feldmann's *Ansigtstræk* (*Features*), 2000, New Danish Dance Theatre. Photo: David Amzallag).

true technical inventors – the mothers of modern dance – being Martha Graham and Doris Humphrey. Secondly, the development of modern dance is a movement of liberation from the ballet tradition which is seen to represent the conservation of traditional gender roles or even to suppress or degrade women.

Metaphor and consequences

So far the purpose of my article has been to demonstrate how the relationship between music and dance has been understood by means of comparing it with the male/female relationship – music being male, dance female. At this point it might be useful to look at the very different metaphorical understanding of music in another collaborative art form, namely film. In a book called *Unheard Melodies* (1987) Claudia Gorbman explains how music functions as a signifier of emotion within the classical Hollywood film. Not only does music emphasise specific emotions suggested in the narrative, but in its very capacity of being music, it signifies the notion of emotion. Suggesting a scheme of binary oppositions Gorbman lists some of the oppositional qualities that the moving images and music represent:

Film	Music
Logic	The Irrational
Everyday reality	Dream
Control	Loss of control
Man	Woman
Objectivity	Subjectivity
Work	Leisure
Reason	Emotion
Realism	Romantic Fantasy
The Particular	The Universal
The Prosaic	The Poetic
The Present	Mythic Time
The Literal	The Symbolic

(Gorbman, quoted into a visual scheme of binary oppositions of my creation)[15]

It is clear from the list above, that music is conceived of as being "the woman" in its relation to the moving images (the man). As we have seen earlier, in the context of dance works, music comes to represent 'the spiritual' whereas dance represents 'the body'. However in its relation to film, which signifies all the hard qualities (logic, control, reality, reason etc.) music acquires the role of the woman representing soft qualities (the irrational, dream, emotion etc.) Not surprisingly the notion of music as female in relation to film is also related to the notion of subordination and inaudibility (the purpose of film music is not to be noticed for itself but to perform its role without intervening in the conscious act of perception). Again we are confronted with a parallel to the feminist discourse of the 20th century – the man (film) is more or less directly criticized for his tendency to dominate the woman (music). And as such Gorbman's enterprise in *Unheard Melodies* is to draw attention to the overheard female.

In this comparison between the different understandings of dance and film, it is particularly important that we are talking about relationships that are aesthetic phenomena of another world. Literally speaking music is of course neither male nor female. And the relationship between music and dance is art – something which goes beyond our immediate reality. This may require some emphasis, thus at the turn of the millennium, it seems that the link between choreomusical poetics and feminist politics has had consequences for the development of dance as an art form. More specifically we might speak of a general ambivalence towards music within modern dance works. This ambivalence primarily emerges as a fear of being controlled by the music. Not only is the act of following the music too closely regarded as old-fashioned, but as a consequence of the marriage metaphor it appears as an act of compromise, if not political treachery.

Since the point of my article has been to show how the marriage metaphor or gendered understanding of the relationship between music and dance is an underlying condition of many centuries, I am also suggesting that we cannot escape this metaphorical understanding. However, it is my hope that the deconstruction of the marriage metaphor has something to contribute in the development of future choreomusical poetics. In other words the recognition of the marriage metaphor might provide a commentary on any instinctive fear of 'giving in to the music' or 'letting the dance be dominated by the music'. The important thing is to be aware that the relationship between music and dance is something of another world. And throughout centuries we have sought to understand it by means of a metaphorical transference of the structures we know from the relationship between man and woman. In other words, we continually try to capture the sylph by means of a gendered metaphor.

Notes

1. For Aristotle and his contemporaries, the word "aesthesis" marks out one side of the division between the sensory perception of things and the intellectual apprehension of them. In our time, the term aesthetic experience is used predominantly in the discussion of art, or the experience of art.

2. I am referring to the theories of cognitive semantics developed by George Lakoff and Mark Johnson among others. See eg. *Metaphors we live by,* Chicago, the University of Chicago Press, 1980.

3. E.g. in Guillaume Dumanoir (1664): "Le marriage de la musique avec la dance, contenant la réponse au livre des treize prétendus academistes, touchant ces deux arts" - quoted in J. L. Schwarts and C. L. Schlundt, *French Court Dance and Dance Music: A Guide to Primary Source Writings. 1643-1789,* NY, Pendragon Press, 1987, p. 265.

4. J. G. Noverre, *Letters on Dancing and Ballets,* (tr. Cyril W. Beaumont) New York, Dance Horizons, 1966, p. 144 (first published in 1760).

5. Ibid. pp. 129-130.

6. S. L. Foster, *Choreography and Narrative,* Bloomington, Indiana University Press, 1996, p. 10.

7. In the article "Why philosophy neglects the dance", Francis Sparshott describes the treatment of dance in philosophy in relation to the two schemata of arts derived from Aristotle and Hegel. See R. Copeland and M. Cohen, eds., *What Is Dance? Readings in Theory and Criticism,* Oxford, Oxford University Press, 1983, pp. 94-102.

8. C. Lambert, "Music and Action", 1936, in *Copeland,* op. cit., pp. 208-9.

9. N. Lloyd in *Dance Perspectives,* no. 16, New York, 1963, p. 52.

10. S. K. Langer, *Feeling and Form,* New York, Charles Scribner's Sons, 1953, p. 171.

11. M. Cunningham, "The Creative Experience", 1970, in C. Steinberg, ed., *The Dance Anthology,* New York, New American Library, 1980, p. 52.

12. D. Humphrey, *The Art of Making Dances,* New York, Grove Press Inc., 1977 (first published in 1959), pp. 132 & 165.

13. E. Evans, *Music and the Dance,* London, Herbert Jenkins Limited, 1948, p. 9.

14. S. K. Langer, *Problems of Art,* New York, Charles Scribner's Sons, 1957, p. 86.

15. C. Gorbman, *Unheard Melodies,* London, BFI, 1987, pp. 80-82.

Contributors

DINNA BJØRN (DENMARK)

is Artistic Director of the Finnish National Ballet. Before that she was Artistic Director of the Norwegian National Ballet (1990-2001). She was for many years a dancer at the Royal Danish Ballet. In 1976 she formed Soloists of the Royal Danish Ballet together with Frank Andersen, a Bournonville company which toured all over the world. Bjørn has been a Bournonville consultant at the Royal Danish Ballet, and she has taught Bournonville, staged and reconstructed his ballets in Denmark as well as in other countries.

INGER DAMSHOLT (DENMARK)

is Assistant Professor at the Department of Art History, Dance and Theatre Studies, University of Copenhagen. Having studied with Erik Aschengreen she went on to introduce dance as an A-level discipline in Denmark. Her Ph.D. dissertation is titled *Choreomusical Discourse. The relationship between music and dance*.

MONNA DITHMER (DENMARK)

is a critic and editor of theatre and dance for the Danish newspaper *Politiken,* previously she was a critic for the newspaper *Information*. She lectures on dance and theatre at the University of Copenhagen. For a number of years she was a member of the Danish State Arts Foundation.

IVOR GUEST (GREAT BRITAIN)

is one of Britain's most highly respected ballet historians. Guest has promoted both a popular and scholarly awareness of dance history. His long list of publications includes titles about the history of the Paris Opéra Ballet such as *The Ballet of the Enlightenment, Ballet under Napoleon* and *The Romantic Ballet in Paris* and *The Ballet of the Second Empire,* and biographies such as *Jules Perrot, Fanny Elssler, Fanny Cerrito,* and *Adeline Genée*. He is a founding member of The Society of Dance Research and has been on the editorial board for *The Dancing Times* since 1963. He was given a doctorate by the University of Surrey in 1997, and was appointed a Chevalier of the Ordre des Arts et des Lettres in 1998. He received the Queen Elizabeth II Coronation Award in 1992 and a Lifetime Achievement Award in 2000.

LENA HAMMERGREN (SWEDEN)

is Associate Professor at the Department of Theatre Studies, Stockholm University. Her scholarly production includes her Ph.D. dissertation *Form och Mening i Dansen* as well as articles and essays in anthologies such as *Corporealities* (ed. Susan L. Foster).

NIKOLAJ HÜBBE (DENMARK)

is a principal at the New York City Ballet where he has been dancing since 1992. His repertoire includes Balanchine's *Agon, Apollo, Donizetti Variations, Bourrée Fantasque, The Nutcracker, Rubies, La Sonnambula, Western Symphony* and *Who Cares*. He has danced in ballets by Jerome Robbins, Richard Tanner, Sean Lavery and Peter Martins. Prior to his American career, Hübbe was a principal at the Royal Danish Ballet, where he danced *Romeo and Juliet, Onegin, Giselle, The Nutcracker, Don Quijote, L'Après-midi d'un faune* as well as the Bournonville ballets.

STEPHANIE JORDAN (GREAT BRITAIN)

is Research Professor in Dance at Roehampton University of Surrey where she directs the Centre for Dance Research. A former dancer, musician and dance critic, she now publishes and presents at conferences internationally. Amongst her publications are *Striding Out: Aspects of Contemporary and New Dance in Britain* and *Moving Music: Dialogues with Music in Twentieth-Century Ballet*. She has also co-edited *Parallel Lines: Media Representations of Dance* and *Europe Dancing: Perspectives on Theatre, Dance and Cultural Identity*.

DEBORAH JOWITT (USA)

is a dance critic and historian, who began her career as a dancer and choreographer. She has written a column on dance for The Village Voice since 1967 and published two collections: *Dance Beat* and *The Dance in Mind*. Jowitt is also the author of *Time and the Dancing Image*. While directing the Critics Conference at the American Dance Festival during the 1970s, she met Erik Aschengreen and later, through him, gave guest lectures at the University of Copenhagen. She is a Master teacher in the Dance Department of New York University's Tisch School of the Arts.

JOHN CHRISTIAN JØRGENSEN (DENMARK)

is Associate Professor at the Department of Nordic Philology, University of Copenhagen, where he teaches literature and cultural journalism. His list of publications includes i.a. a doctoral dissertation *Det danske anmelderis historie*, *Kultur i Avisen* and *Dagbladskritikeren*. Jørgensen is a literary editor and critic for the Danish newspaper *Ekstra Bladet*.

EBBE MØRK (DENMARK)

writes for the Danish newspaper *Politiken* where he was also a daily essay editor and a dance critic for many years. He has been chairman of the Bartholin International Ballet Seminar in Copenhagen and a member of the Theatre Council under the Ministry of Culture. He is the author of several books eg. *Bag mange masker*, *Det Kongelige Teater bag kulisserne* and *Marguerite Viby - Det var sjovt at være til*.

OLE NØRLYNG (DENMARK)

is a dance and art critic for the Danish newspaper *Berlingske Tidende*. He teaches music and dance history at the Royal Danish Ballet School and at the University of Copenhagen. He is the author of *Apollons Mange Masker* and co-author of *Balletbogen*, *Billedhuggeren og Balletmesteren*, *Bournonville Tradition og Fornyelse*.

Tabula Gratulatoria

Lisbeth og Jakob Albinus

Marianne Alenius

Cand. jur. Bendt Andersen

Kirsten og Vagn Andersen
Den Kongelige Ballets Venner

Jack Anderson and George Dorris
co-editors Dance Chronicle

Solveig Arnstrup von Bressendorff, BA
Dansens Æstetik og Historie
Københavns Universitet

Jordemoder
Birthe Aschengreen

Dorthe Aschengreen

Lis og Peter Augustinus

Per-Oluf Avsum og Jørn Grønbech

Kirsten Biltoft

Dinna Bjørn

Paul Boos
Teacher and Repetiteur for
The George Balanchine Trust

Lene og Thomas Bredsdorff

Louise Breum Brekke

Karakterdanser Jette Buchwald
Den Kongelige Danske Ballet

Mag.art. Heino Byrgesen
Danmarks Radio

Cand.mag., danseanmelder
Anne Middelboe Christensen

Annette Christiansen

Selma Jeanne Cohen
Dance writer (retired)

Flemming Conrad

Adjunkt Inger Damsholt
Dansens Æstetik og Historie
Københavns Universitet

Torben og Nanna Damsholt

Dansens Æstetik og Historie
Institut for Kunsthistorie,
Dans og Teatervidenskab
Københavns Universitet Amager

Dansescenen

Den Danske Balletklub

Anne-Marie Dessau

Monna Dithmer, mag.art.
Teaterredaktør, Politiken

Marie Ebbesen
Samba & salsa instruktør
Stud.mag. i teatervidenskab

BA Kurt Effersøe og
Bjarne Foldberg

Anne-Marie Elmby

Sorella Englund

Solodanserinde ved Det Kgl. Teater
Vivi Flindt

Susanne Foersom

Monica von Folsach

Trine Frederiksen
Studerende, KUA

Inge From

Læge
Anne Frølund

Mirjam Gelfer- Jørgensen, dr.phil. og
Niels Peder Jørgensen, mag.art.

Museumsinspektør, mag.art.
Lisbeth Grandjean
Teatermuseet i Hofteatret

Marianne Grøndahl

Dr. Ivor Guest

Marianne Hallar

Lena Hammergren, docent
Teatervetenskapliga institutionen,
Stockholms Universitet

Teaterforlægger
Hanne Wilhelm Hansen

Ib Fischer Hansen

Ann-Kristin Hauge
Arkitekt m.a.a./Kgl. Balletdanser

Stud.mag.
Neel Hatt

Socialrådgiver
Birthe Heckscher

Mikala Heckscher

Pianistinde Elvi Henriksen

Majbrit Hjelmsbo
Dansekritiker, Weekendavisen

Karen Hoffmann
Operasuffløse ved Det Kgl. Teater

Bill Holmberg
Koreograf

Graziella Hsu
danser, koreograf og sinolog B.A.
Dansens Æstetik og Historie
Københavns Universitet Amager

Else og Per Hübbe

Nikolaj Hübbe

Charlotte Højme

Vibeke og Niels Haagen

Institut for Nordisk Filologi

Per og Sofie Isbrand

Palle Jacobsen
Solodanser ved Det Kgl. Teater

Stig Jarl
Lektor ved Institut for Teatervidenskab,
KUA

Anni Jensen

Inge Jensen og Lars Holm Johansen

Jes Tange Jessen

Fotograf
John R. Johnsen

Stephanie Jordan
Research Professor in Dance,
Roehampton University of Surrey

Deborah Jowitt, senior dance critic,
"The Village Voice", master teacher
New York University
– Tisch School of the Arts

Cand.mag.
Kirsten Merete Juncher

Dr.phil., seniorforsker
Knud Arne Jürgensen
Dramatisk Bibliotek,
Det Kongelige Bibliotek

Lektor, dr.phil.
John Christian Jørgensen
Institut for Nordisk Filologi

Lise og Niels Kehlet

Direktør Iver Kjær
Det Danske Sprog- og Litteraturselskab

Lisa Kjær
Formand for Hvidovre Hospitals
Kunstforening

Fhv. balletdanser
Anne-Lise Klinge

Eva Kloborg og
Frank Andersen

Det Kongelige Teater

Det Kongelige Teaters
Arkiv & Bibliotek

257

Koreograf Dorte Kreutzfeldt
New Territories

Hanne og Mogens Kristensen

Lars Juhl Kristensen

Redaktør
Michael P. Krog

Mag.art.
Karen Krogh

Professor Kela Kvam
Inst. F. Kunsthistorie, Dans og
Teatervidenskab, KUA

258

Familien Kvorning

Gaye Kynoch

Vibeke Køie

Danselærer
Melinda Young Langeland

Fhv. Balletmester ved Det Kgl. Teater
Niels Bjørn Larsen

Kapelmester
Peter Ernst Lassen

Fhv. minister, MF
Grethe Laustsen

Claus og Marianne Levy

Lektor
Inger Lous

Antoine Lund

Britta Lund

Louise Lund

Solodanser Thomas Lund og
skuespiller Henrik Emmer

Jette Lundbo Levy

Lørdagsklubben

Professor
Inge Marstal, Det Kgl. Danske
Musikkonservatorium

Alexander Meinertz

Birgit Meister og
Hans J. Petersen

Balletpædagog
Vibeke Mertins

Per Morsing

Balletpædagog Jette Muus
Jette Muus' Klassiske Balletskole

Bo Myhrmann

Lise Lander Møldrup

Journalist Ebbe Mørk

Pianist og lektor
Michael Netschajeff
Espergærde Gymnasium,
Censor ved Institut for Dansens
Æstetik og Historie

Lotte Boyer Neukirch
Det Kgl. Teater
Ballettens Læseskole

John Neumeier
Choreographer
Hamburg Ballet

Adjunkt Lotte Nielsen
Nørre Gymnasium

Tine Winther Nissen
Balletadministrator ved Det Kgl.
Teater

Marianne Nordal

The Norwegian National Ballet

Lone Nyhuus
Freelance journalist

Erik Näslund
Fil.dr. Museumsdirektør

Studielektor Maj-Britt Nørgaard

Cand. mag. Ole Nørlyng
Det Kongelige Teater,
Berlingske Tidende

Advokat Vagn Ohlsen
Bestyrelsen for Den Danske Balletklub

Mia Okkels

Cand.mag. Stine Bille Olander

Claus Oldenburg

Fil.dr. Cecilia Olsson
Stockholms Universitet

Hanne Outzen
Formand for Den Danske Balletklub

Ph.d. Vibeke A. Pedersen
Institut for Nordisk Filologi

Lærer Dede Persson
Ballettens Læseskole

Lotte Langkilde Perthen
tidligere ved Den Kongelige Ballet

Souschef Kim Petersen

Dorte Petersson

Balletadministrator Paul Podolski
The Norwegian National Ballet

Museumsinspektør, mag.art
Ida Poulsen
Teatermuseet i Hofteatret

Benedikte Paaske
Dansens Hus

Anne-Lise og Helge Ralov

Psykolog Birte Rasmus-Nielsen

Birthe og Jesper Bruun Rasmussen

Cand.phil. Edel Rasmussen

Studielektor Susanne Ravn
Institut for Idræt og Biomekanik
Syddansk Universitet

Nancy Reynolds
Director of Research
The George Balanchine
Foundation

Karen Margrethe Riis

Elsa Marianne von Rosen

Fredrik Rütter
Aftenposten, Oslo

Fotograf
Martin Mydtskov Rønne

Marcel Marquis de Sade

Mag.art. Alette Scavenius

Margrethe Schanne og
Kjeld Noack
Det Kongelige Teater

Lise Scherfig

Birgit Schmølker

Teaterchef
Louise Seibæk

Marcia B. Siegel
Dance critic, The Boston Phoenix

Kirsten Sindby

Jette Skjoldborg
Danseanmelder,
Århus Stiftstidende

Skolen For Moderne Dans

Kgl. Balletdanserinde og Balletpædagog
Ulla Skow

Cand.mag. Lilo Skaarup
Det Kgl. Teaters Arkiv & Bibliotek

Annelise Snedevig

Jonna Steenberg

Mag.art. Ulla Strømberg

Per Stylvig

Annelise Tarnov

Cand.mag., danselærer Eva Tarp
Danseafd. på Idrætsskolerne i Oure

Terpsichore
Tidsskriftet for moderne dans

O. Friis Theisen

Lærer Dorte Thiele
Det Kgl. Teater

Peter Thygesen
Journalist, Politiken

Kirsten Würtz Trnka

Sten Tulinius
Det Kongelige Bibliotek

Christa Twile

Henning Urup, mag.art
Dansk Dansehistorisk Arkiv

Peter Braams Valore
mag.art. & cand.mag.

Kandidatstipendiat Karen Vedel
Center for Tværæstetiske Studier,
Århus Universitet

Anne Marie Vessel Schlüter
Det Kgl. Teaters Balletskole

Annemari Vingård

Christel Wallin
Dancer, Balletmaster, Director,
Founding Director of
Skolen for Moderne
Dans in Copenhagen

Fotograf Jørgen Watz

Vincent van Webber
Dancer, The Royal Ballet,
Copenhagen

Arlette Weinrich

Cand.mag. et brom. Vibeke Wern
Danseanmelder Berlingske Tidende,
ekstern lektor Dansens Æstetik og
Historie, KUA

Lise og Erik Werner

Nina & Jens W. Werner

Jytte Wiingaard
Teatervidenskab

Merete Wilkenschildt og
Preben Hansen

Jette Wolsing

Mag.art. Lars Wredstrøm

Sofia Zafirakos

Teaterchef Jan Zetterberg,
Dansens Hus

Kathleen Quinlan Zetterberg
Danssolist

Susanne Ørskov
Kgl. Balletdanserinde og Balletpædagog